THE SPIRITUALITY OF AFRICAN PEOPLES

THE SPIRITUALITY OF AFRICAN PEOPLES

The Search for a Common Moral Discourse

Peter J. Paris

Fortress Press // Minneapolis

for Shirley

and to the memory of
E. Bolaji Idowu,
and
Kelly Miller Smith, Sr.

THE SPIRITUALITY OF AFRICAN PEOPLES
The Search for a Common Moral Discourse

Cover graphic: Mimmo Paladino, "Le tane di Napoli," 1983, by permission of Sperone Westwater

Cover design: Ann Elliot Artz Hadland

Author photo: Chuck Robison

Library of Congress Cataloging-in-Publication Data

Paris, Peter J., 1933–
The spirituality of African peoples : the search for a common moral discourse / Peter J. Paris.
p. cm.
Includes bibliographical references and index.
ISBN 0-8006-2854-3 :
1. Afro-Americans—Religion. 2. Africa, Sub-Saharan—Religion. 3. Blacks—Religion. 4. Ethics, Modern—20th century. I. Title.
BR563.N4P38 1995
170'.89'96—dc20 94-32866
CIP

The paper used in this publication meets the minimum requirements of American National Standard for Information Sciences—Permanence of Paper for Printed Library Materials, ANSI Z329.48-1984. ∞™

Manufactured in the United States AF 1–2854

99 98 97 96 95 1 2 3 4 5 6 7 8 9 10

Contents

Preface

As author of this book, I think that it is important for me to identify my relation to its subject matter. I am a naturalized African American citizen who was born and reared in Nova Scotia. My Canadian roots precede the Confederation of Canada by almost a century, extending back to 1782 when, for military reasons, the British persuaded a group of so-called Black Loyalists[1] to accept their offer of freedom by emigrating to Canada. Accordingly, under the leadership of a black Baptist preacher, David George, approximately 3000 blacks (both freed and enslaved) along with approximately 1000 whites, arrived in Nova Scotia aboard British ships from the United States. Fully two-thirds of the black immigrants were household slaves of the white Loyalists, who tended to call them "indentured servants." Promised freedom in the British territory of Canada and with guarantees of personal liberty, shelter, land, and other material assistance, my ancestral forbearers soon discovered that most of those promises would not be honored. As a consequence, their suffering was immense. Many perished during their first Canadian winter through starvation and exposure. Thus it is not difficult to understand why, less than a decade later, most of these emigrés accepted the British offer of repatriation in West Africa, where they hoped to find, at long last, relief from their suffering. Once again under the leadership of David George and the protection of the British flag, an exodus of more than a thousand blacks left Halifax in 1792 destined to be the first group of settlers in what would eventually become the British colony of Sierre Leone.

Greatly understudied by most American historians, David George has a renowned place in the history of African Christianity for having founded the first African American churches in three countries of the world, namely, the United States, Canada, and Sierre Leone.[2] His story has only recently become the subject of a full-scale academic treatise.[3]

Those who remained behind in Nova Scotia following the 1792 exodus were joined following the War of 1812 by a second migration of blacks from the United States inspired by similar promises from their British naval guardians. These succeeded in rooting themselves firmly in the soil of Nova Scotia, thus constituting the ancestral base for the enduring African Canadian population in that place.

As minority peoples living in racially hostile environments, the post-bellum experiences of African Canadians and African Americans were strikingly similar. After centuries of slavery they were viewed by the majority population as social outcasts, unwelcomed as equals into the arenas of socio-political participation. Because of their small numbers, African Canadians have always sought inspiration from and identification with the struggles of African Americans for freedom and dignity. Geographical proximity and common historical roots should have afforded the two groups considerable cause for social interaction. But the generalized poverty of African Canadians and the ignorance of African Americans about their existence long prohibited much sustained interaction.

Emigration to the United States has been highly prized by peoples from all over the world, and Africans in the diaspora have been no exception, especially those from Canada. In every period, small numbers of African Canadians have emigrated to the United States in search for a better life both socially and economically. Ironically, since my ancestors migrated from slavery in the United States to "freedom" in eastern Nova Scotia more than 200 years ago, I view myself as part of a small contemporary cadre of immigrants bent on reversing our ancestral migration-pattern. Yet in our own respective ways most of us strive to continue the struggle of our forbears for freedom and justice, something I personally prize more than anything else I know.

Before coming to the United States, nearly three decades ago, I had the good fortune to live and work in Nigeria during the years 1961–64. As National Travelling Secretary of the Student Christian Movement of Nigeria, an independent, ecumenical organization founded by Nigerians in the 1930s and affiliated with the World Student Christian Federation, I had the privilege to work under the guidance and supervision of a council of Nigeria's educated elite. Three years prior to that date, however, I had been a participant in the first Crossroads Africa Program founded by Dr. James Robinson of New York City: a program that President John F. Kennedy referred to as the model for his Peace Corps.

The late '50s and early '60s were periods unique in African history. The former colonial Gold Coast became the sovereign nation of Ghana in 1957 under the brilliant, audacious leadership of Kwame Nkrumah. Both Nkrumah and Ghana became worldwide symbols of the highly visible

African independence movement that was sweeping the continent during that period. In 1959 Nigeria became the second African nation to gain its independence from colonial rule. What a memorable experience it was for me to be in an African country that was being toasted round the world for its immense political and economic promise.

During those early years of independence, the Student Christian Movement of Nigeria, inspired by a publication called "Christian Responsibility in an Independent Nigeria,"[4] organized several regional and national conferences on themes related to that subject. The function of African traditions in all spheres of the newly independent nation was an overriding concern of students, teachers and clergy alike. It seemed that virtually every Nigerian wanted to participate in the task of historical retrieval and reappropriation as the first step in reconstructing their national purpose. Everyone wanted to help in determining the extent to which their ageless traditions could and should contribute necessary resources for nation-building in the twentieth century. In a very short while, the academic study of traditional African cultures rapidly became the most interesting field of study in African universities, replacing forever one of the dominant disciplines of colonial education, namely, the Greek and Roman classics.

In a real sense, the project of this book had its beginnings at that time. Interestingly, less than a decade later, the spirit that continued to energize the quest for the African past on the continent was transplanted to African peoples throughout the diaspora, where it shaped individual psyches and inspired collective endeavors for radical social change in race relations everywhere. Then and now, religious and moral values pervaded all dimensions of that quest both on the African continent and in the African diaspora. The energizing and unifying power of those values was and is embodied in the thought and practice of African peoples everywhere. That power constitutes the core of African spirituality. The clarification of its character, along with a plausible explanation of its transmission from the continent to the diaspora, is the first step in understanding the theology and ethics of African peoples everywhere and, especially, in the diaspora.

Acknowledgments

I should like to acknowledge the helpfulness I have received from friends, colleagues, and students. Without their encouragement and assistance, the goal I set for myself a decade ago would not have been realized.

Over the years I have been privileged to know a select number of learned and wise African scholars whom I view as friends. I am grateful for our many conversations which have been important sources of blessing and learning for me. These persons are the late E. Bolaji Idowu, Modupe Oduyoye, Mercy Amba Oduyoye, E. A. Adeolu Adegbola, J. Omosade Awolalu, Jacob K. Olupona, Lamin O. Sanneh, Gabriel M. Setiloane, Simon Maimela, Takatso Mofokeng, Elia Mashai Tema. In addition, I have benefited greatly from my former students, David L. Mosoma, Nyambura J. Njoroge, Harvey J. Sindima, and Rene Nkanga Bokembya.

This project began a decade ago when I spent a sabbatical leave at the Institute of Church and Society of the Christian Council of Nigeria. I am grateful to the then Director, Daisy Ngozichukwuka U. Obi and her staff for the excellent hospitality they afforded me during that period. Several visits to South Africa during the past several years have been most helpful and especially the 1993 meeting of South African and African American Theologians in Johannesburg under the sponsorship of the Ecumenical Association of Third World Theologians (ETWOT).

I am most indebted to the following for their enduring friendship, collegiality, and helpfulness: Howard Harrod, Thomas W. Ogletree, Emilie M. Townes, Dwight N. Hopkins, Walter E. Fluker, Robert Michael Franklin, Riggins R. Earl, Jr. Similarly, I am grateful to the Social Ethics Seminar and especially to the following members for reading and commenting on several draft chapters of this work: George W. Pickering, Alan B. Anderson, James A. Capo, Warren R. Copeland, Roger D. Hatch, Lois Gehr Livezey, Lowell W. Livezey, and William A. Simpson whose carefully written reviews and conversations have been immensely helpful.

I am grateful to the Fellows at the Center of Theological Inquiry who read the final chapter of this book and engaged me for several hours in a most helpful conversation. David Hackett also read earlier versions of several chapters and offered helpful comments.

During the past five years I have been pleased to lecture on various themes of this book in the following locations: Acadia University Divinity College, Dalhousie University, York University, Columbia Theological Seminary, Fairfield University, the Lutheran Theological Seminary in Philadelphia, the University of Missouri and Yale University Divinity School. In addition I have presented papers on selected chapters at the American Academy of Religion and the Society of Christian Ethics. The questions and comments from those various audiences were invariably helpful.

I am grateful to the following for the financial assistance they provided in support of this project: the Vanderbilt University Research Council; Princeton Theological Seminary and the Center of Theological Inquiry where I wrote the final draft. A sabbatical leave spent at the W.E.B. DuBois Institute of Harvard University during the spring semester of 1990 provided a most stimulating atmosphere for my research. I am grateful to the then Associate Director, Randall K. Burkett and his staff for all their assistance.

The encouragement and helpfulness I have received from Fortress Press has been a special motivating force. I am grateful to Marshall D. Johnson, Director of Publishing, Fortress Press, and his staff for all that they have done to expedite this project into print. The excellent service Michael West provided in copyediting the text has greatly improved the final product.

At differing points in the life of this project I have been privileged to have had two excellent research assistants. The enthusiasm that Michelle J. Bartel brought to the task was always encouraging, and Willette A. Burgie-Gipson's untiring devotion to every aspect of the project has been a constant source of joy.

Finally, but not least, I am grateful to my spouse, Shirley, for her strong moral support throughout this arduous process.

1

AFRICA

Revolution in Understanding

Moral Challenges to Scholarship

Recent decades have witnessed a virtual revolution in the traditional modes of academic scholarship in the humanities. This radical change was brought about by a variety of conditions that originated a generation ago. At that time the predominantly white-male-controlled universities in the United States (and elsewhere) were pressed to open their doors to admit increasing numbers of African Americans, various other ethnic minorities and white women as students, teachers, and administrators. These nascent changes in admission and hiring policies marked the beginning of a new era in the academic world, ushered in by the cumulative effect of concurrent political and cultural movements fervently opposed to all forms of undemocratic thought and practice.

In the United States, these movements included the civil rights movement, the free speech movement, the feminist movement, the black power movement, the anti-Vietnam War movement, to mention only a few. Virtually all of these coexisting social movements had their counterparts in many other countries of the world. All of them were united, however, in their common mission to make the democratic principle efficacious for all groups of people. That is to say, each of these movements affirmed the proposition that all humans are by nature free agents with equal rights to participate in all decisions affecting their lives. Consequently, they were highly suspicious of every form of "established" thought and practice which had long denied them such basic rights. As a matter of fact, they actually believed that all forms of traditional authority, power, and privilege were antithetical to democratic procedures. Further, they also believed that the long-treasured principles of racial and gender discrimination facilitated the ascendency of a white-male bias in academic thought, which seriously distorted vast areas of human understanding.[1]

The primacy that these movements gave to the moral and political spheres of human relationships was soon extended to all dimensions of the academic enterprise. Guided by a pragmatic principle that all knowledge serves some practical purpose, these new voices in academe were more than a little interested in pursuing varying types of contextual studies. In other words, they were motivated by the desire to produce useful knowledge that would contribute not only to academic discourse but, more importantly, would enhance the quality of life in their respective communities of origin. Indeed, many of them argued that the only authentic validation for the pursuit of knowledge is its helpfulness in solving practical problems, a usefulness which they believed had greater value than the construction of comprehensive theories and universal concepts. As a result, teaching and research in the newly emerging fields of racial, ethnic, and gender studies aimed at conjoining theoretical concerns with practical goals. Such projects laid the foundations for the development of new fields of academic inquiry bent on critical analysis of all assumptions underlying "traditional scholarship" and advocacy for new explanatory theories, hermeneutical principles, and epistemological methods. Needless to say, perhaps, they introduced to the academy new reservoirs of source materials that had been either ignored or neglected by the older scholarship. More often than not, these resources pertained to various dimensions of human experience that were often preserved in personal diaries, oral traditions, folklore, imaginative literature, and other narratives. Yet characteristically these new scholars also invariably gave special attention to the relevant historical and societal contexts since they were convinced that all human experience was both personal and social.

In retrospect, it is clear that the second half of the twentieth century constituted a veritable watershed in academic scholarship. Often, for the first time the voices of racial and ethnic minorities, so-called third-world peoples, and white women were clearly heard challenging the traditional methods of Western scholarship in the humanities, the social sciences, and the professions. Their forceful criticisms centered on basic epistemological questions. Most importantly, they critically analyzed the presuppositions underlying traditional Western scholarship, which hitherto had privileged white-male bias to the detriment of all other groups.

Though strongly resisted by the established custodians of the academic traditions, these new voices of dissent eventually had significant impact on virtually all disciplines of study. A major mark of their scholarship was seen in their common aim to empower the subjects of their respective studies rather than to denigrate them as so much of the older scholarship had done. Needless to say, this renaissance in modern scholarship was especially liberating for the new scholars themselves. While still in its nascent stage at the present time, however, all signs indicate that its impact in the academic world will persist in the future. That is to say, the impact of this new academic challenge across the disciplines has been so significant that Western scholarship is destined, henceforth, to treat all human beings with the same dignity befitting all rational subjects and to view none merely as invisible, inaudible objects of Western curiosity. This, in itself, is a significant ethical advance throughout academe.

Further, as social critics, these newcomers to the academy tended to be deeply involved in and committed to programs of social reform. Their strong opposition to all forms of social domination and oppression and their endeavoring to forge new structures of justice both within and without the academy have had considerable impact throughout the society at large. Thus the feminist philosopher Iris Young rightly concludes that:

> Ideas and experience born in the new left social movements of the 1960's and 1970's continue to inform the thoughts and actions of many individuals and organizations in contemporary American political life: democratic and socialist, environmentalist, Black, Chicano, Puerto Rican, and American Indian movements; movements against U.S. military intervention in the Third World; gay and lesbian liberation; movements of the disabled, the old, tenants, and the poor; and the feminist movement.[2]

On the whole, these new academic voices tended to be disinterested in the traditions of speculative thought as such and, accordingly, they shunned many of the major metaphysical impulses of the Enlightenment project and especially the latter's stress on the autonomy of human reason as the foundation of all reality. Their criticism of rational idealism was based largely on their understanding of the sociology of knowledge, which they claimed repudiated the reality of pure reason and upheld the notion that all reason is both culturally conditioned and purposive.

Thus, in contrast to the idealism inherent in many forms of Enlightenment thought, these new scholars favored academic inquiries into specific problem areas of human life. While not totally abandoning abstract thought, they were interested in studying the ways formal ideas find concrete expression in human societies and, more especially, they were interested in the political significance of such ideas for human freedom and social order. Further, in relation to their respective academic environments, they were deeply concerned about the underlying philosophy of university curricula along with the principles governing institutional policies concerning student admissions and the hiring, promotion, and retention of faculty members. In all of their concerns and interests the democratic principle of inclusion comprised their basic criterion for transforming the academic community. Obviously, they drew heavily on the resources of the American tradition of moral pragmatism.

Undoubtedly, these and similar changes in academe have been fueled over the years by the explosive development of technology in communications and the mass media; these developments have brought the world to the brink of a major paradigm shift not only in the ways knowledge is produced but also in its purpose, function, and dissemination.

In my judgment, this new genre of academic scholar contributed in no small way to the rise of the so-called postmodernist movement and its rejection of the Enlightenment's quest for epistemic wholeness and universality.[3] Thus, it is not surprising that the arguments of many postmodernist scholars have been a significant epistemological resource for this new wave of scholarship.

As indicated above, these new scholars were imbued with a moral mission to refocus the aims of the academic community on the task of enhancing the quality of life for the world's poor and oppressed peoples. Traditionally excluded from membership in the academic community, they themselves brought with them their own agenda deeply rooted in values, interests, and perspectives that challenged the validity of many of the taken-for-granted canons of academic scholarship. They came with a moral interest in the production and dissemination of knowledge, believing that it should contribute to the well-being of all peoples rather than the privileged alone. They believed that none should be excluded from participation in the academic world—or anywhere else—on the basis of race, class, gender, religion, age, physical disability, national origin, or any similar social condition. Clearly these scholars had pragmatic concerns which they believed were, in principle, not new to the academy. Rather, they were convinced that the academy had always served the peculiar interests of a particular class of people, namely, the ruling academic male elites and their patrons.

African Challenges to Colonial Scholarship

For over five centuries the encounter of the Western world with Africa has constituted an enduring moral problem. Yet until recently moral philosophers, including religious ethicists, have shown little interest in the subject. That the matter has any visibility whatsoever in contemporary academic study is due, in large part, to a series of historical events that occurred immediately following the end of World War II, events that marked the beginning of a new age in global history.

Early in that post-war period, many significant changes in international politics were already underway signalling the impending death of European imperialism around the world and the gradual, yet inevitable, transition of colonial territories into independent sovereign nations. The founding of the United Nations with its charter for world peace provided additional evidence of the dawn of a new epoch in international relations. The independence of India from British domination occurred in 1947 and the founding of the State of Israel in 1948. Similarly, the independence of the former Gold Coast (now Ghana) in 1957 inaugurated events that would eventually change the map of Africa from a continent of European colonies to a land of newly emerging modern states.

Clearly these and similar movements inspired the rapid expansion of the democratic spirit around the world and especially in Africa. In a relatively short period of time, the world witnessed the rise of countless new voices in its many and varied public realms, voices that now claimed their moral and political right to be self-determining citizens in independent nations.

In their zeal for constructive participation in helping their respective societies recover from centuries of oppression, African scholars knew that much revisionist scholarship was needed to combat and eradicate the legacy of colonial scholarship that had dominated the continent for many generations. To meet that need, they soon found themselves engaged in critically appreciative analyses of traditional African cultures for the purpose of clarifying old realities and advancing new understandings. Implicit in all such inquiries was the desire to realize the practical goal of helping their people enhance the quality of their lives by reinforcing and rebuilding pride and honor both in themselves and in their respective nations. All of this implied profound criticisms of the presuppositions of colonial scholarship which had consistently ignored, distorted and undermined the integrity of African cultures. While persisting in their war against the abusive aspects of colonial scholarship, most contemporary African scholars continued their quest for relevant and valid indigenous criteria for the improvement of self-understanding and societal conditions in a post-colonial Africa.

In their quest for scholarly authenticity independent of the colonial inheritance, African religious scholars have been in the vanguard of a veritable renaissance in African studies. They have given primary attention to both historical and anthropological studies of traditional African cultures.[4] Their chief aims have been to make the hitherto silent African voice audible in the world of academic scholarship and to mine new empirical data by the rigorous study of their pre-colonial past. Admittedly, many of the post-colonial African pioneer scholars were also theologians, not historians or anthropologists. Yet most of them took great care to avoid undue prejudice by adhering to all the canons of critical scholarship.

For many centuries Europeans had defined Africans as a subhuman species. In his essay, "A Genealogy of Modern Racism," the philosopher Cornel West writes, "The notion that black people are human beings is a relatively new discovery in the modern West."[5] Clearly, by the middle of the nineteenth century the vast majority of European scholars believed unquestionably in the biologistic Aryan doctrine of racial superiority in which Caucasoid peoples were viewed as genetically superior to both Africans and all other peoples of color. Consequently, they believed that European cultural productions were similarly superior, especially in the sphere of religious beliefs and moral values. Yet, despite a wide range of anthropological studies bent on proving the validity of this theory of racial difference, modern scholars have not yet agreed upon a scientific definition of race per se. Nevertheless, commitment to the doctrine of Aryan superiority dominated virtually all European relationships with Africans up to the middle of the twentieth century. As a result, countless negative stereotypes about African peoples pervaded the Western mind and greatly distorted understanding. In his study of the doctrine, Olisanwuche Esedebe writes that it was affirmed by such notables as "the Englishman Thomas Carlyle, the Edinburgh anatomist Robert Knox, the French sociologist Arthur De Bobineau and the American naval officer Commander A.H. Foote."[6] These figures comprise some of the most influential supporters of the genetic doctrine. St. Clair Drake quotes

Thomas Jefferson, the principal author of the Declaration of Independence, with evidence of his sympathetic support for the notion:

> This unfortunate difference of colour, and perhaps of faculty, is a powerful obstacle to the emancipation of these people. . . . I advance it therefore as a suspicion only, that the blacks, whether originally a distinct race, or made distinct by time and circumstances, are inferior to the whites in the endowments both of body and mind.[7]

The basic features of the doctrine are clearly described by two contemporary scholars, Michael Omi and Howard Winant:

> Whites were considered the superior race; white skin was the norm while other skin colors were exotic mutations which had to be explained. Race was equated with distinct hereditary characteristics. Differences in intelligence, temperament and sexuality (among other traits) were deemed to be racial in character. Racial intermixture was seen as a sin against nature which would lead to the creation of "biological throwbacks." These were some of the assumptions in social Darwinist, Spencerist and eugenicist thinking about race and race relations.[8]

In rejecting the validity of the doctrine, Omi and Winant (and most other contemporary social scientists) rightly claim that race is a *sociohistorical* concept with no biologistic basis.[9] That this doctrine has formed the foundation of virtually all relationships between whites and blacks throughout their five centuries of encounter is vividly manifested in such practices as:

(1) the treatment of Africans as livestock by buying and selling them as slaves
(2) the imposition of colonial rule over Africa's traditional political authorities and, concomitantly, the confiscation of the continent's natural resources for the imperial governments of Europe
(3) the practice of racial discrimination and segregation in all social relationships with Africans both on the continent and throughout the diaspora, and
(4) the justification of all the above by colonial scholarship.

Africans with the closest personal association with Europeans, however, were most vulnerable to the insidious impact of this doctrine of racial superiority on their psyches. Especially on the continent, but throughout the diaspora as well, Western educational institutions, operating through the aegis of Christian missions, provided the primary means for indoctrinating African children in Western values and perspectives. For example, under the conditions of colonialism all students educated by Europeans were exposed to textbooks, teachers, and counselors who espoused denigrating views about Africans. In a nutshell, this comprised the essentials of what has come to be regarded as the Eurocentric perspective in colonial education. After years of such authoritative teaching and learning the desired result was often realized in the training of educated African youth. More often than not, the latter tended to despise their traditional cultures and often celebrated their own alienation from them by forming exclusive cultural enclaves that were often facilitated by the conditions of "study abroad" and a desk in the colonial administration. This included such entitlements as a residence in a specially designed housing area, household servants, car allowance, educational vouchers for children, hardship allowances, and periodic visits to the colonial "homeland."[10] Clearly, these people were groomed to assume the attitudes and lifestyles of their colonial rulers with education as the gateway to such cultural alienation.

As a principal tool for alienating Africans from their indigenous cultures, the goal of colonial education was to effect a profound loss of self-esteem and self-identity among a new African elite. The process by which that loss occurred is graphically evidenced in Alioune Diop's tragic remembrance of his history classes in which he and his peers were taught to recite references to their Gallic ancestors as having blond hair.[11] Thus, in accordance with France's colonial philosophy in Africa, it was hoped that the thoroughly assimilated African would embody the psyche of a native French person with no noticeable trace of his or her African culture remaining. In his discussion of the political implications of this doctrine in justifying colonialism and its impact on the African struggle for independence, Ndabaningi Sithole said of the Portuguese policy of *assimilado,* "The African is taught, under the *assimilado* system, to think of himself as a Portuguese in Portugal, not as an African. The Portuguese policy aims at killing the African in the African and at replacing him with a Portuguese."[12] Similarly, Ki-Zerbo describes the nature of this racist perspective most aptly:

> Racism is a scourge that is capable of taking on a multiplicity of forms, from the most discreetly concealed to the most bloodthirsty, as in the case of the slave trade and the Second World War. Like a living fossil, it bides its time, buried in the subconscious of hundreds of millions of people, until it re-awakens in the shape of pseudo-scientific doctrines and claims; for

> example, that everything remarkable about Africa must be of foreign origin, because Africans themselves have never invented anything. This attitude was carried to such lengths that the main issue raised in connection with the masterpieces of Ife sculpture was that of finding out what foreign peoples had managed to travel as far as that region in order to produce such works of art.[13]

In their resistance to such a systematic program of alienation, dehumanization, and domination, a generation of African scholars in alliance with a small cadre of European intellectuals devoted their professional lives to the academic repudiation of colonial philosophy in its entirety.[14] Their work and that of all others engaged in opposing Eurocentric colonial philosophy were clearly revolutionary.

In spite of the colonial educational system in Africa and elsewhere, the majority of Africans did not acquiesce in the doctrine of racial superiority. This fact alone evidences the failure of colonial education in fully realizing its intended objective. In fact, countless Africans constantly resisted the doctrine in every possible way, not least through the generation of new, subversive knowledge. This endeavor eventually culminated in a relatively small cadre of African scholars who, under the leadership of Cheikh Anta Diop, gained worldwide visibility in the 1960s for their careful academic investigations. Diop, a professor at the University of Senegal and a specialist in linguistics, history, and Egyptology, soon gained recognition as the foremost African scholar to sustain a major challenge to the dominant perspectives that had long governed the field of Egyptology. He argued persuasively that since all ancient Egyptians fitted modern-day European and American definitions of the so-called Negro race, they should be viewed as Africans rather than as part of the Hellenistic mediterranean world. Interestingly, few white scholars have conceded the debate. To that project, however, Diop devoted his entire professional career and today he has come to be revered by all African Egyptologists (whom, incidentally, St. Clair Drake preferred to call "African vindicationists") both on the continent and in the diaspora as their single most important academic predecessor.[15] *The Journal of African Civilizations,* founded in 1978 by African Caribbean and African American scholars is the main source for the continued promotion of his academic program, which aimed at proving that ancient Egypt was a product of African blacks: a thesis that most prominent European scholars long thought absurd. In the United States, Professor Molefe Asante[16] of Temple University is the most prominent bearer of that scholarly tradition.

The new African scholarship, however, has not been limited to those engaged in the so-called Egyptology debate. On the contrary, many contemporary African scholars are deeply involved in local and regional studies in sub-Saharan Africa with little or no interest in the racial debate concerning ancient Egypt as such. Their major contribution to African studies lies in the revised perspectives and new empirical evidence they have contributed to anthropology, history, and ethnography on the one hand, and to aesthetics, literature, art, music, and religion, on the other hand. Undoubtedly, the single most important development in this respect has been the eight-volume work of the UNESCO International Scientific Committee for the Drafting of a General History of Africa, which took nearly twenty-five years to complete and is published in a large number of the languages represented in the United Nations, including many African languages. Of primary importancc is the fact that the team of international scholars for the project was two-thirds African and one-third non-African. In the Preface of the first volume, Amadou-Mahtar M'Bow, former Director-General of UNESCO writes the following:

> An increasing number of historians have endeavoured to tackle the study of Africa with a more rigorous, objective and open-minded outlook by using—with all due precautions—actual African sources. In exercising their right to take the historical initiative, Africans themselves have felt a deep-seated need to re-establish the historical authenticity of their societies on solid foundations. . . . In this context, the importance of the eight-volume *General History of Africa,* which UNESCO is publishing, speaks for itself.[17]

In addition to historical studies, this scholarship has influenced the theoretical perspectives of many disciplines in African studies, including economics, political science, religion, sociology, anthropology, agriculture, to mention only a few.

Thus, both implicitly and explicitly, African resistance to the Aryan doctrine and its manifold political, social, and academic consequences is a dominant factor in all contemporary African scholarship undertaken by African people. I contend that similar forms of resistance have occurred whenever Africans have encountered European domination. Under the conditions of colonialism, however, much of the resistance was necessarily equivocal and indirect due to the colonial administration's absolute opposition to all forms of public criticism. Nevertheless, many brave resisters suffered imprisonment, torture, and death in their endeavoring to liberate their peoples from the ravages of colonial hegemony. The heroic stories of virtually every African fighter for independence evidence the truth of this statement. Clearly the new-found freedom of academic inquiry and expression became legitimate only after the dawn of political independence.

Though the African spirit of resistance must have been inspired by many factors, none superseded the natural longing of an oppressed people to be free from the domination and control of their captors. Surely there can be nothing more repugnant than strangers usurping the territory of others and declaring themselves the rightful owners of its wealth and rulers of its peoples. That repugnance is greatly increased when the confiscators seize the moral high ground and self-righteously argue that they alone serve the good of the indigenous peoples. Clearly all resisters, whether direct or indirect, share a rightful place of honor in the history of African independence. Many of the giants in that struggle have already gained immortality in the hearts and minds of their people, and generations yet unborn will sing their praises.

African historiography has made many remarkable contributions to worldwide historical studies not only in its effective disparagement of racist colonial scholarship but in its demonstration of the validity of oral traditions as a historical source.[18] When subjected to critical controls, these latter are now viewed as equal to linguistics and archeology as historical sources, a viewpoint that was thoroughly condemned by all colonial scholars.

African American Challenges to Racist Scholarship

The history of African Americans begins with the trans-Atlantic slave trade, which lasted for more than three and one-half centuries. Through its cruel design millions of Africans were extracted from their homeland as chattel to furnish a labor market. No person of African descent in America has escaped the enduring stigma of that period. Every freed slave was continually vulnerable to the ubiquitous threat of being forced back into slavery by the arbitrary whims of unscrupulous persons. Yet even the abolition of slavery in the United States was not a sufficient cause for the admission of African peoples into full citizenship. In fact, Abraham Lincoln's Emancipation Proclamation and the post-bellum constitutional amendments were soon followed by what Rayford Logan called "the nadir" in race relations. The all-too-brief period of Reconstruction gave way to the disfranchisement of blacks throughout the former Confederacy; and, following the 1896 Supreme Court ruling in *Plessy v. Ferguson,* racial segregation and discrimination were legally practiced throughout the nation's schools and public accommodations. As with colonialism in Africa, slavery and its sequel of racial apartheid were America's institutional expressions of the previously mentioned Aryan doctrine of racial superiority. In other words, structural racism has been the paramount social reality African peoples have endured for hundreds of years both on the African continent and in the African diaspora. Patrick Manning claims that, for reasons that are far from clear, this racist ordering of society became virtually a worldwide phenomenon following the abolition of slavery:

> The case for modern racism as the heritage of slavery relies on the amazing temporal coincidence of the restrictions imposed on black people on all shores of the Atlantic at the end of the nineteenth century. Black Americans gained political rights from the national government in the 1860s, and lost them to state and local governments beginning in the 1870s; black office holders fell rapidly from power. Soon followed the Jim Crow laws of the 1890s, segregating housing, schooling, and all public facilities. In the British West Indies, well-placed black teachers and administrators found themselves removed from power in the 1880s. In British West Africa Samuel Ajayi Crowther, Anglican Bishop of the Niger since 1875, was humiliated and stripped of his powers by young English clergymen in 1890. Black civil servants and merchants in Sierra Leone, the Gold Coast, and Lagos found themselves on the defensive. Racial segregation in housing was now implemented ostensibly for reasons of health; the French administration segregated Dakar in 1914 after an outbreak of plague. Still in the 1890s, the black leaders of Luanda now found their press restricted and their access to good positions in the Portuguese administration limited. In South Africa the segregation of the labor force began as the diamond and gold mines expanded.[19]

It would be an understatement to claim that all African peoples are united by a common collective memory of racial oppression based on the doctrine of racial superiority. Yet, although this shared experience has taken many different forms over the centuries, African peoples have been persistent in their resistance to oppression and resilient in their endurance of it. Although countless numbers either perished or were permanently maimed by its crippling effects, few lost their souls through acquiescence. Like many survival strategies, acquiescence served more than one purpose. On the one hand, it caused slave masters to think of their human livestock as content with their condition while, on the other hand, it meant something quite different to the slaves themselves. In fact, evidence abounds to support the claim that the vast majority of slaves maintained their spiritual integrity by many and varied creative acts of indirect resistance.[20]

As in Africa, the post-bellum educational system became the principal teacher of racial inequality. Effective resistance to its impact was well-nigh impossible in predominantly white schools. The description by America's greatest African American scholar, W.E.B. DuBois, of his own experience is representative of that of most educated African Americans, similarly trained both then and now. At his 1888 graduation from Fisk University, DuBois delivered a commencement address on Bismark, his favorite historical leader. He later commented on that occasion in one of his autobiographies by saying, "I was blithely European and imperialist in outlook; democratic as democracy was conceived in America."[21] In time, DuBois' critical thought would lead him to a radically different outlook. He came to see in the soul of African Americans a dualism that he named "double-consciousness," an ambiguous concept that has been widely affirmed by all generations of African American scholars throughout the twentieth century. DuBois described the concept in the following way:

> It is a peculiar sensation, this double-consciousness, this sense of always looking past one's self through the eyes of others, of measuring one's soul by the tape of a world that looks on in amused contempt and pity. One ever feels his twoness—an American, a Negro; two souls, two thoughts, two unreconciled strivings; two warring ideals in one dark body, whose dogged strength alone keeps it from being torn asunder.[22]

Similar to the founders of *Africaine Presence* and their relevant predecessors, DuBois and a host of contemporaries and successors similarly dedicated their professional lives to the goal of repudiating and eradicating every trace of systemic racism in America and around the world.

I contend that the history of African American scholarship is replete with persistent efforts to disprove the Aryan doctrine of racial superiority. To that end generations of scholars have sought to describe the major contributions African peoples have made to human civilization. They have believed and strongly advocated that such cumulative data would be sufficient to negate the doctrine and restore the dignity of African peoples. Evidence of such efforts dominate the works of the first generation of post-bellum African American scholars. Accordingly, in the last decade of the nineteenth century and the early part of the twentieth century scholars such as Alexander Crummel, Arthur A. Schomburg, Casely

Hayford, Carter G. Woodson, W.E.B. DuBois, Edward Blyden, and others became the progenitors of the black history movement in the United States. In 1895 Crummel founded the American Negro Academy, and twenty years later Woodson established the Association for the Study of Negro Life and History. St. Clair Drake writes that the aim of the latter was "to challenge, correct, and supplement what was erroneously claimed to be the truth about Negroes, and to do it from a black perspective, using both detached scholarship and polemics."[23] In the following year, 1916, the Association established a periodical forum, *The Journal of Negro History,* and soon afterwards it inaugurated the annual celebratory event that is presently called Black History Month. This nascent black-history movement greatly influenced the thought of all African American scholars of the day. Yet it had a special effect on Alain Locke (the first African American Rhodes Scholar) in the inspiration it provided for his ground-breaking book, *The New Negro,*[24] which made him a leading spirit in the newly emerging Harlem Renaissance.

During the first half of the twentieth century the established methodologies in various disciplines often hindered African American scholars from vigorously pursuing their goal of vindicating African peoples by setting the record straight. Yet in doing so they remained adamant in their resolve to honor the canons of good scholarship and to avoid the risk of becoming polemicists. Nevertheless, they inevitably found themselves inquiring into subject matter and defending criteria of relevance that many of their Caucasian colleagues had difficulty in supporting. More often than not, however, such lack of support was deeply rooted in the presupposition that there was no academic value to be gained from the study of African American thought and practice. Still, from within the confines of their segregated colleges and universities, African American scholars continued their study and research with all the rigor and academic integrity they could muster. Thus, under the conditions of great duress, the combined endeavors of these academic pioneers issued in a massive literary record of the "spiritual strivings" of an oppressed people.[25]

St. Clair Drake claims that those African American scholars who were self-conscious about wanting to present an African American perspective often did so by adopting a number of stylistic innovations to maintain compliance with the canons of objective scholarship. For example, he mentions Dubois' idiosyncratic method in his *Black Reconstruction* of appending a passionately rhetorical commentary at the end of each carefully researched chapter.[26] Another technique, which Drake admits he himself had employed, was the practice of subtitling a work "an essay," which permitted a mixture of "fact" and opinion.

The birth of independent African nations along with the death of racial discrimination and segregation in the United States occasioned on both continents new academic initiatives in the humanities and social sciences. Scholars of color here, there, and everywhere quickly discerned the pressing need for revisionist scholarship in order to correct the many errors, intentional omissions, and deliberate distortions of an earlier era. As I have already indicated, their efforts were not wholly novel since important predecessors[27] had made significant contributions to similar projects in the past, even though the earlier works had little impact at that time on the mainstream of their respective disciplines.

Concomitant with the renaissance in African studies by African scholars in the 1960s, a new consciousness among African American scholars arose. Like their African allies, these latter were bent on expressing their independence from the methodological constraints of the former era by vigorously discounting all claims of generic neutrality in academic scholarship and, as a corrective, employing an African American perspective as their major hermeneutical principle. In other words, they argued for the unity of thought and experience by claiming that all attempts to divorce the two inevitably led to the distortion of both. Their contention that theory and practice are united implied rigorous opposition to many of the universal claims of traditional academic scholarship.

The widespread interest among African American religious scholars in bringing their own perspectives to bear on their research subjects can be clearly illustrated by reference to the works of a major African American theologian, James H. Cone, whose constructive thought has greatly influenced a generation of scholars including this present author. In 1969 Cone published a small book[28] that marked the beginning of a new era in African American theological thought. That book was destined to have a profound impact not only on African American religious scholars but on the theological thought of so-called third-world peoples everywhere. Cone was soon acknowledged as the indisputable progenitor of the Black Theology Movement. Yet, it is important to note that Cone's work received an ongoing appreciative though critical response in the writings of J. Deotis Roberts,[29] whose project emphasized the dialectical relationship between liberation and reconciliation both in the African American experience and in an authentic Christian theology. In that work, Roberts, more than Cone, tried hard to bring black theology into continuity with the black church tradition.

Both Cone's academic competence and rightful rage were united in his zealous attempt to persuade the academic community to respect black theology and its challenge. Clearly showing the influence of European existentialism on his own methodology, this first book also exhibited the unmistakable influence of two giants in Protestant neo-orthodoxy, namely, Paul Tillich and Karl Barth. Cone's understanding of the interdependence of historical experience and theological reflection reveals Tillich's influence, while his assumption of the centrality of biblical authority in theological thought bears the unmistakable impact of Karl Barth.[30] Further, and in my judgment most importantly, Cone was able to affirm those methodological features of Tillich and Barth because each represented a basic perspective long affirmed by the African Methodist Episcopal Church in which he had been nurtured all of his life.

Soon after the publication of Cone's first book, the Society for the Study of Black Religion[31] was formed to provide an academic forum for discussion and debate among colleagues concerned with promoting the basic tenets of Black Theology. In that context two principal criticisms of Cone's work emerged, centering on his neglect of two important factors: African American historical source material for his black theology, and the relation of African American Christianity to traditional African religions. Respectively, Gayraud S. Wilmore and Charles H. Long were the major proponents of those criticisms. Soon Wilmore published a book on the black churches[32] that became an important historical source for black theology. As a result of this criticism Cone's third book[33] constituted an analysis of the spirituals and the blues as historical sources for his theology. Cone soon also participated in a number of consultations with African scholars concerning African theologies and their relation to Black Theology.

In subsequent years various African American religious ethicists,[34] along with church historians and others have focused their scholarly attention on various dimensions of the African American historical experience in search of the basic elements for characterizing the perspective(s) of African Americans. Only a few[35] of these, however, have given serious attention to contemporary African religious thought and practice. Yet all are agreed on the importance of such relatedness. As evidence of such interest, the Society for the Study of Black Religion held its 1974 annual meeting in Ghana,[36] consulting there with a number of African theologians, and in 1976 the society consulted with Carribean theologians at the University of the West Indies in Kingston, Jamaica.[37]

In the last decade and a half African American women have made their own distinctive contribution to scholarship by initiating a new theological movement. Called Womanist Theology,[38] this movement is closely allied with Black Theology. Yet it is distinguished from the latter in at least two decisive ways: (1) by its critical attention to and constructive analysis of the communal experience and religious perspective of African American women and (2) by its interest in making a distinctive theoretical contribution to the general field of women's studies by mining the experience of African American women in literature, history, religion, and folk traditions. Academic movements corresponding with those of black and womanist theologies have occurred throughout the humanities and the social sciences.

As demonstrated above, both African and African American scholarship have been consistent in their respective challenges to the traditional modes of academic scholarship. Those challenges may be classified in accordance with two closely related though differing styles. First, in the traditional style various dimensions of African life (whether on the African continent or in the African diaspora) are subjected to the traditional methods of mainstream scholarship for the following reasons: (1) to demonstrate the many and varied commonalities between African and Caucasoid peoples by analyzing the nature of social and environmental forces and their determinative effects on the life-chances of human beings; (2) to make visible the many and varied cultural contributions African peoples have made to human civilization. Prior to World War II this style of scholarship predominated among Africans both on the continent and in the diaspora.[39] Looked at from the vantage point of the late twentieth century, this type of scholarship made no major methodological contribution to academe. Rather, it merely used the established methodologies for introducing new subject matter into the academic community.

Second, since mid-century, the vindicationist[40] style has tended to be the predominant form of African and African American scholarship. This style aims at overturning the findings of all colonialist and racist scholarship by bringing an African and African American perspective to bear on its subject matter. The most distinguishing characteristic of this style is its search for an independent form of knowledge emanating from the African and African American historical experience.[41] Further and most importantly, this new breed of scholars has been adamant in its claim that the history of Africa is the common heritage of all African peoples.

It is an interesting fact that some African American scholars can rightly be placed in both categories. W.E.B. DuBois is one such person. Many of his books easily fit into the first schema, while his 1915 book, *The Negro,* and his 1941 revised, updated edition of it under the title *Black Folk Then and Now* are clear evidence of identification with the African vindicationists. A similar case can be made for the works of St. Clair Drake and many others.

While African American scholars celebrate the above-mentioned UNESCO General History of Africa Project, we have had very little similar support in our efforts to reconstitute our African American past. We concur with our kinfolk in Africa in believing that historical retrieval and reinterpretation are essential steps for preserving and enhancing our dignity, self-respect, and social development.

African and African American Challenges to Social Ethics

The many and varied ways by which Africans and African Americans responded to exploitation and oppression reveal theological understandings and moral virtues that are deeply embedded in the sacred traditions of Africa. The time is right to identify and critically appropriate this great treasure for religious and ethical reflection. In spite of the immense diversity of the latter, however, I am convinced that many commonalities exist among the various African cosmologies. In fact, a vast amount of anthropological and ethnographical evidence supports my claim that basic systemic elements, themes, and concepts are recurrent in African traditional thought and practice throughout the continent.[42] Further, there has recently emerged a steady growth of similar evidence supportive of the claim that more African culture was transmitted through the diaspora than was formerly thought to be the case.

It should be noted, however, that I make no attempt to argue for the uniqueness of either African or African American worldviews. Rather, in this respect, I concur with Winthrop S. Hudson and others who claim that there is no need to trace every so-called "primitism" among African Americans back to Africa. Accordingly, I find Hudson's concurrence with Kenneth Stampp's position apt:

> "There is no need," Kenneth Stampp has noted, "to trace back to Africa the slave's fear of beginning to plant a crop on Friday, his dread of witches,

> ghosts, and hobgoblins, his confidence in good-luck charms, his alarm at evil omens, his belief in dreams, and his reluctance to visit burying grounds after dark. These superstitions were all firmly rooted in Anglo-Saxon folklore. Beliefs associated with good and evil spirits, demon possession, visions, trances, frenzies, second sight, out-of-body travel, and noisy and ecstatic physical behavior were commonplace in Europe and in America."[43]

Nevertheless, in spite of the many similarities of beliefs and practices between the two groups, African American religious experience has differed markedly from that of Euro-Americans. Hudson also agrees on this point, as the following statement clearly indicates:

> To find parallels elsewhere is not to contend that blacks did not develop their own style of religious life in America out of their own experience, utilizing available elements which met their own needs and reshaping them in the process. Black religion has not been identical with white religion.[44]

Unlike Hudson and others, however, my purpose is to concentrate on the peculiar worldview of blacks in order to clarify their common basis for religious and moral discourse. Consequently, my task is to explicate the common features implicit in the traditional worldviews of African peoples as foundational for an African and African American moral philosophy. Accordingly, I will make plausible arguments concerning the continuities of African experience on the continent and in the North American diaspora. In my judgment, it is unfortunate that a whole generation of scholars—including E. Franklin Frazier, Winthrop Hudson and many others—should have concluded that since the sociological and historical evidence of so-called African survivals appears to be weak, the African factor in the African American experience is of little or no importance. Hudson's conclusion is representative of that school of thought, and I quote it at length because of its dominant and long-standing impact on historical studies:

> In America blacks forged something new, the product of their own experience in a new land. An overemphasis on African survivals obscures their accomplishment. It also distorts the story of the black churches. By focusing attention on that which is largely unknowable, it diverts attention from a rich heritage of faith and courage, knowledge of which *can* be recovered. At bottom it is a question of which generation of forebears one wishes to honor: the forebears of a distant, shadowy past who can be known only obscurely, ambiguously, and with much uncertainty, or those known ancestors (named and identified) who, with great heroism and remarkable

> creativity, fashioned out of the Christian faith a strategy of survival and mutual care, first, amid the inhumanity of a slave society and then during the post-emancipation years of white oppression. One can express only one's own sense of wistfulness. In the quest for a distant past, it would be sad for the remarkable achievements of known ancestors to be left unhonored and unsung.[45]

Although I fully appreciate Hudson's goodwill in not wanting to commit an injustice by undervaluing the accomplishments of African Americans, his myopic vision and that of his contemporaries has been in serious need of correction for a long time. His fear that any scholarly concentration on African survivals would obscure the many great accomplishments of African Americans is wholly unconvincing. As a matter of fact, his position leads to a diminution of African American accomplishments in its failure to liberate them from captivity to a Eurocentric perspective. Such a position obfuscates the African factor in the African American experience. Thus I contend that the African American experience cannot be fully understood apart from its ongoing connectedness with the religious and moral ethos of its African homeland. To limit the continuity of the latter to an objective data base procurable by sociological and historical methods alone is insufficient reason for dismissing its reality or underestimating its importance. Without minimizing the difficulties involved, emphasizing the continuities between African and African American traditions strengthens rather than weakens their creative accomplishments. Thus, I seek the African factor in the African American experience without which there remains only a variant of Eurocentricity, a problem that Frantz Fanon clearly explicated nearly three decades ago in his ground-breaking work, *Black Skin, White Masks.*[46]

It should not be surprising to discover, however, that the search for African roots is likely to evoke greater interest among present-day Africans in the diaspora than among those on the continent. Yet the work of the former must depend on the findings of African scholars on the continent because the latter are more likely to possess the requisite linguistic skills and experiential background for competent primary research in African cultural studies. Access to their research is the first methodological requirement in the search for African roots. More specifically, the quest for such continuities must rely not only on the findings of African studies in traditional African religions but also in the African appropriation of Christianity and Islam. The task of relating those findings to the cultures of Africans in the diaspora must, in turn, rely on the knowledge and experience of scholars in the diaspora. In other words, a continuing reciprocal relationship between the two is of paramount importance.

A basic presupposition underlying this volume is that historical experience shapes the nature of theology and ethics. Since religion and morality are respectively the subject matter of theology and ethics, a plurality of the one (that is, either religion or morality) implies a plurality of the other (that is, either theology and ethics). As with all living phenomena, both religion and morality continually change while preserving their basic identities. Thus theology and ethics must exhibit similar variability.

While there are certainly different schools of thought within both theology and ethics that manifest various internal differences within the fields, I claim that both disciplines are arts and not sciences in any modern sense of the term. The aim of each is to set forth some general rules and principles that can be practical guideposts for the enhancement of thought and action in specific contexts. Such a position as this precludes absolute truth claims from either. Yet some measure of truth attends every theological and ethical position insofar as it is an adequate reflection of the cultural thought of the people, is not contradictory, and is compatible with their sacred traditions. Thus, no theological or ethical position is wholly perverted. Yet, as I have argued elsewhere,[47] the important question of criteria for the adjudication of conflicting theological or moral positions can only be determined in the context of an open forum wherein all the relevant diversity is actively engaged.

Although universal commitment to any one theological or ethical position is unlikely ever to occur, I assume that the maintenance of the necessary conditions for the preservation of such an open inquiry is itself both a theological and ethical commitment. In fact, the contemporary scholarly academy itself, operating under the principle of freedom, may well be viewed as a significant model for theological and ethical inquiry. The hallmark of the academy's existence is freedom of speech, the *sine qua non* for every democratic situation. Thus, as with democracy itself, process is more important than outcome because the quality of the latter can never be guaranteed. Nor can its ultimate goal ever be completely realized.

Yet freedom requires the exercise of law[48] for the prevention of anarchy. Hence, there is always some measure of tension between the two since the purpose of the law is to restrict as well as to protect the exercise of freedom.

In this book I will argue that the traditions of African peoples both on the continent and in the diaspora are diverse in cultural form yet united in their underlying spirituality. The former is evidenced mainly by the differences of language and other cultural mores. The latter is seen in the broad consensus among African peoples that the three forms of life, namely, nature, history, and spirit are ontologically united and hence interdependent. This viewpoint is deeply rooted in the many African mythologies which form the basis for all African culture, including the theology and ethics of its peoples.

The "spirituality" of a people refers to the animating and integrative power that constitutes the principal frame of meaning for individual and collective experiences. Metaphorically, the spirituality of a people is synonymous with the soul of a people: the integrating center of their power and meaning. In contrast with that of some peoples, however, African spirituality is never disembodied but always integrally connected with the dynamic movement of life. On the one hand, the goal of that movement is the struggle for survival while, on the other hand, it is the union of those forces of life that have the power either to threaten and destroy life, on the one hand, or to preserve and enhance it, on the other hand.

Unity in diversity is another metaphor for African spirituality. When a musician plays variations on a melody, we all recognize the melody as the unifying thread among the variations. In fact, the latter actually implies an underlying unity. So also with African peoples. The linguistic and cultural diversity both on the continent and in the diaspora implies a factor that is common to all. That so-called African factor is the reality I seek to explicate both in its theological and ethical forms.

Second, I will argue that the realities of cultural diversity and the unity of African spirituality both separate and unite African and African American religious and moral traditions. This is seen most graphically in the spirit of tolerance that exists among African peoples with respect to difference. As the Ghanaian theologian Mercy Amba Oduyoye writes, "A benign tolerance of the religious views of others is firmly rooted in Africa: it is part of African hospitality. Nevertheless, strangers who want to be accepted and to be taken into confidence are expected to learn the ways of the natives."[49]

Contrary to the opinions of many, however, I claim that the pluralism of gods, spirits, and so-called tribal groups in Africa not only constitutes a basic condition for their societal life but, most importantly, has constantly nurtured the spirit of tolerance that exists among African peoples. More often than not, observers of African cultures have overlooked this fact and, hence, have failed to understand the nature of African hospitality. In fact, Europeans long viewed the goodwill of Africans toward strangers as evidence of their "child-like" nature and, hence, justification for their enslavement.

It is important to state, however, that I do not wish to romanticize traditional African cultures. For certain, they did not always live together in a state of idyllic harmony and peace in the past, nor do they do so in the present. But, contrary to most early European reports, Africans were not continuously engaged in internecine warfare either. Regardless of the actual relationships among differing groups, African peoples had many cultural resources at their disposal which they could and often did draw upon constructively for the establishment and maintenance of peaceful relationships with their neighbors.

In fact, it may be surprising to many to discover that African traditional societies were not strangers to the basic tenets of democratic governance, even though it would be foolish to suggest that any of them practiced democracy in ways similar to that of the modern Western world. Nevertheless, in many of their large kingdoms, village palavers and the election of local chiefs, including that of reigning monarchs, involved the participation of the whole people often through a representative system. These and many similar procedures constituted important checks and balances against the rise of despots.

Third, I will argue that a dynamic principle of unity permeates the diversity of African cultural traditions both on the continent and in the African diaspora. This principle was discerned long ago by numerous pioneer Pan-Africanists who eagerly advocated the need for all African peoples to affirm their common identity and unite in a common cause, namely, advocacy for political freedom and the necessary material resources with which to exercise it.

I concur with the attitude of that new breed of African scholars whom Ki-Zerbo describes in the following way:

> The *General History* sheds light both on the historical unity of Africa and also its relations with the other continents, particularly the Americas and the Caribbean. For a long time, the creative manifestations of the descendants of Africans in the Americas were lumped together by some historians as a heterogeneous collection of *Africanisms.* Needless to say, this is not the attitude of the authors of the *History,* in which the resistance of the slaves shipped to America, the constant and massive participation of the descendants of Africans in the struggles for the initial independence

> of America and in the national liberation movements, are rightly perceived for what they were: vigorous assertions of identity, which helped forged the universal concept of mankind. Although the phenomenon may vary in different places, it is now quite clear that ways of feeling, thinking, dreaming and acting in certain nations of the western hemisphere have been marked by their African heritage. The cultural heritage of Africa is visible everywhere, from the southern United States to northern Brazil, across the Caribbean and on the Pacific seaboard. In certain places it even underpins the cultural identity of some of the most important elements of the population.[50]

In keeping with my claim that the so-called new breed of scholars who entered the academy a generation ago had a pragmatic understanding of knowledge, readers will discover in this book ample evidence to support a similar judgment concerning the type of knowledge African traditional seers were expected to have, namely, sufficient practical knowledge with which to guide their people in every sphere of life.

Thus I will clarify the nature of theological and ethical perspectives that are grounded in and reflective of the spirituality of African peoples. Perhaps the best way to characterize this inquiry is to view it as a commonsense discourse about moral and religious commonalities and continuities among and between diverse African cultures on the continent and in the African diaspora. Admittedly, I have limited the latter largely to African peoples in North America. Yet I hypothesize that similar developments pertain throughout the diaspora.

Along with Mechal Sobel[51] and others,[52] I contend that Africans brought their worldviews with them into the diaspora and, as a result of their interaction with their new environments, their African worldviews were gradually altered into a new-African consciousness. As a result of the influence of traditional African cosmological thought on each, important continuities of moral thought and practice exist between African Christians in the diaspora and those on the continent. Further, both the African and African American appropriation of Christianity evidence a complex amalgam of religious and moral values drawn from both the African and Western cultural contexts. Both arguments (that is, that African Christians on the continent and in the diaspora are similarly influenced by traditional African cosmology on the one hand, and by Western theological and cultural thought on the other hand) are necessary steps in demonstrating the thesis that among African peoples on the continent and in the diaspora good moral character constitutes the nature of the moral life and is rooted in and derived from God the Creator and Preserver of all that is. Further, the form of the moral life is determined by the community's traditional understanding of good moral character as it is embodied in specific persons whom the community reveres as exemplars of moral virtue.

In keeping with the understanding of how the moral life is formed, it must be emphasized that the standard of moral virtue among African peoples is thoroughly historical and always embodied in exemplary persons. Since the African continent exhibits a large number of tribal cultures, the moral life of African peoples varies greatly in particulars yet is united at the level of basic principles, the moral coherence of which emerges from the common features in their cosmological understandings.

Happily, this book is being written while a renaissance is occurring among African peoples everywhere. In their strivings for renewed understandings of their African past both on the continent and in the diaspora, this renaissance is destined to release many and varied creative forces which for centuries have been greatly hindered by the power of racism. I hope that my findings will contribute to that outcome by helping to energize the spirit of unity among African peoples and by nurturing all concerned in their constructive efforts to preserve and enhance the dignity and freedom of African peoples everywhere.

Based on the assumption that the moral understandings of African peoples cannot be understood apart from their common cosmological understandings, four major chapters of this book will center on the following integrally related and overlapping dimensions of African cosmological and societal thought:

(1) the realm of spirit (inclusive of the Supreme Deity, the subdivinities, the ancestral spirits), which is the source and preserver of all life
(2) the realm of tribal or ethnic community which, in equilibrium with the realm of spirit, constitutes the paramount goal of human life
(3) the realm of family, which in equilibrium with the realms of tribe and spirit, constitutes the principal guiding force for personal development, and
(4) the individual person who strives to integrate the three realms in his or her soul.

Much attention will be given to a constructive analysis of how those understandings fared under the conditions of North American slavery and the eventual formation of a syncretized cosmology comprising an amalgam of Christian and African elements: a cosmology that shaped the African expressions of Christianity both on the continent and in the African diaspora. Finally, this constructive analysis will issue in the building blocks for an African and African American religious social ethic.

2

GOD

The Source and Ground of All Life

African Understandings of God

Undoubtedly, many will argue that the immense diversity of cultures there prohibits any generalizations whatsoever about Africa. Yet in my judgment respect for the rich diversity of African cultures need not lead to such a conclusion. Rather, as certain generalizations can be made about Americans or Europeans without implying widespread uniformity among them all, similar generalizations can be made about African religious and moral understandings without violating either the integrity or the particularity of tribal groups. Calling some things European or American or Asian is analogous to calling other things African. Since we do the one with impunity, why not the latter? In brief, I seek to identify broad structural components comprising the moral and religious thought of African peoples while recognizing the vast differences of content in each particular cultural context. Thus, my aim is to demonstrate how that structural factor which originated on the continent of Africa has survived in many modified forms throughout the African diaspora. While not identifying the principal causative factor(s) for its survival, I strongly repudiate any and all racial biologisms as explanatory principles.

Scholars have always agreed that religion permeates every dimension of African life. In spite of their many and varied religious systems the ubiquity of religious consciousness among African peoples constitutes their single most important common characteristic. Thus, John S. Mbiti's claim that secularity has no reality in the African experience is affirmed by all scholars of African religion. None, perhaps, has expressed this point better than he:

> Wherever the African is, there is his religion: he carries it to the fields where he is sowing seeds or harvesting a new crop; he takes it with him to the beer party or to attend a funeral ceremony; and if he is educated, he takes religion with him to the examination room at school or in the university; if he is a politician he takes it to the house of parliament. Although many African languages do not have a word for religion as such, it nevertheless accompanies the individual from long before his birth to long after his physical death.[1]

Contrary to the opinions of most of their predecessors, contemporary scholars of African religion generally agree that all peoples throughout the continent believe in a self-existent supreme deity who, as J. Omosade Awolalu claims,

> is believed to be responsible for the creation and maintenance of heaven and earth, men and women, and who also has brought into being divinities and spirits who are believed to be his functionaries in the theocratic world as well as intermediaries between mankind and the self-existent Being.[2]

Contemporary African scholars are also in general agreement that this supreme deity constitutes the primary cohesive power in every African cosmology: the power that unites the realms of nature, history and spirit. In large part, my thought on this matter relies heavily on Mbiti's classification scheme for depicting African cosmological thought:

> (1) God as the ultimate explanation of the genesis and sustenance of both man and all things.
> (2) Spirits being made up of superhuman beings and the spirits of men who died a long time ago.
> (3) Man including human beings who are alive and those about to be born.
> (4) Animals and plants, or the remainder of biological life.
> (5) Phenomena and objects without biological life.[3]

The notion of a supreme deity presiding over a realm of lesser divinities, ancestral spirits, and the whole universe as creator and preserver constitutes a clear rejection of the Western idea of African polytheism: belief in and loyalty to many autonomous divinities.[4] On the contrary, all divinities within the African pantheon are thought to be derivative from and dependent on the one supreme being, so much so that many scholars choose to refer to them as subdivinities who function in ways similar to the heavenly angels in Jewish and Christian cosmologies. As with these latter, African mythologies are replete with the viewpoint that the numerous divinities, along with all other existent reality nature and in history, were created by the supreme deity and, have no independent powers of their own.

In his discussion of the "unicity" of God for the Igbos, Metuh even claims that the people cannot imagine many deities:

> The phrase "Two Gods" is a contradiction in terms. Some writers perhaps do not appreciate how jarring it could be to the ear of an Igbo to refer to the deities or the Arusi, nature spirits, as gods. Understandably, the claim of God's unicity becomes very perplexing when one considers the large numbers of these Arusi, and that some of them have certain divine attributes and are worshipped. But this presents no difficulty to the Igbo . . . . The belief in one God and many deities is not contradictory but complementary. In fact, the unicity of God is enhanced rather than compromised by belief in deities who are not gods, nor are they equal to God. They differ from God not only in their power and excellence, but by their very nature.[5]

Thus, in contrast with the predominant views of many Christian theologians and missionaries, many contemporary African scholars describe a distinct monotheism at the heart of African traditional religions. More importantly, they argue that traditional African understandings of God share much in common with Christian understandings of the deity. In fact, many African scholars continue to urge Christian theologians to reassess their assumptions about the uniqueness of the Christian deity and to acknowledge that God's revelation has not been limited to the Jews alone but has been extended similarly to many other peoples as well. One major implication of this viewpoint is nowhere stated more poignantly than in Mbiti's claim: "The God described in the Bible is none other than the God who is already known in the framework of traditional African religiosity."[6] An important impact of such a belief is to turn the entire Christian missionary enterprise on its head since the latter's primary purpose was to bring the true God to the Africans as well as to all others who were thought to worship false gods. Mbiti and others strongly oppose the arrogance implied in that mission:

> The missionaries who introduced the gospel to Africa in the past 200 years did not bring God to our continent. Instead, God brought them. They proclaimed the name of Jesus Christ. But they used the names of the God who was and is already known by African peoples—such as Mungu, Mulungu, Katonda, Ngai, Olodumare, Asis, Ruwa, Ruhanga, Jok, Modimo, Unkulunkulu and thousands more. These were not empty names. They were names of one and the same God, the creator of the world, the father of our Lord Jesus Christ.[7]

Gabriel Setiloane claims that the essence of African theology is contained in words that the Reverend Z.R. Mahabane declared at the 1926 Le Zoute Conference of the International Missionary Council. Said Mahabane, "The black man still believes that Christianity comes from God (Modimo) so he clings to it although his mind is in a state of revolt against Western Christianity."[8] Setiloane's insertion of the word *Modimo* after *God* indicates that Mahabane was referring to Modimo as understood by his forebears as well as himself. Thus, Setiloane concludes,

> For that is the contention of African Theology, namely: That when the missionary preached about God, and they accepted his teaching (Christianity) the Africans nevertheless continued to conceive of God as MODIMO, that is, in their African terms. It is accepted by us all now that the Christian message to Africa through the Western missionaries did not find a *Tabula Rasa* . . . . It is this awareness of God and religious disposition that made the evangelization of Africa possible and provided a basis for it.[9]

African henotheism has always assumed that every so-called tribe or ethnic group has its own pantheon of divinities, each of which is relevantly related to the specific needs of the community. Further, Africans have also assumed that in each tribal pantheon a plurality of divinities comprises a hierarchy with the supreme deity at the apex, omnipotent and enshrouded in mystery, followed by numerous subdivinities and ancestral spirits in rank order. Further, they have also believed that the supreme deity is both willful and just. Though God is remote from humans, Africans have no doubt that "everyone knows of God's existence almost by instinct, and even children know Him."[10] In fact, the remoteness of this "High God" is analogous to that of a tribal king or a familial patriarch. That is to say, the deity's remoteness is the primary sign of authority and power. Yet it is readily assumed by everyone that the deity's protective care is steadfast.

It may surprise many to learn that Evan Zuesse and others have argued that the remoteness of the supreme deity in traditional African thought symbolizes divine benevolence because human beings do not have the capacity to withstand any direct encounter with the deity. Africans sometimes refer to the sun as analogous to God. Humans delight in having the sun at a great distance from them because, were it otherwise, they would be destroyed rather than empowered by it. Thus the deity's remoteness does not evidence any lack of concern for humanity. It rather connotes the reverse. By maintaining distance from nature and humanity the deity manifests divine care. Thus Africans are grateful for God's remoteness and pray regularly for God's continued protective care through the mediation of the subdivinities and ancestral spirits. The following is an apt summation of this interesting viewpoint, a viewpoint, we might add, that is not unique to Africans:

> God is concerned above all to cooperate in maintaining a world in which crops will grow and health will abound. But because of this, God is not the usual center of worship. Indeed, it is an expression of his continuing benevolence that he has withdrawn his overwhelming power and presence *behind* the intermediary beings he has appointed to govern the modulated realm of specific beings. God does not involve himself too directly in the world that he sustains, for too particular and intense an involvement might destroy the fabric of the divine order he sustains. It is a peculiarity seldom mentioned by students of African religions that we often encounter prayers to God *to keep away* from the petitions and to permit the intermediaries and "refractions" of the spirit that maintain the differentiated realms of the universe to exist. Throughout east, central and southern Africa it is believed that illness, madness and even death come from God's nearness. God is present above all in the catastrophic thunderstorm and the lightning that kills, in the earthquake that levels houses and the epidemics that depopulate regions. It is at such times that one petitions God directly and not through intermediaries, but these petitions are above all appeals to God that he return his alien remoteness to a distance, that he have mercy and restore the network of the divine order as it had been.[11]

It is important to note another characteristic feature pertaining to the African understanding of God. Since African names all have meanings that communicate important information about the thing or person named, each society has many names for God because no one name is adequate for describing all of God's manifold attributes.[12] Thus an African will characteristically call upon God by different names depending on the particular divine function that claims one's attention at a particular time. Emefie Metuh describes some of the numerous theophoric names the Igbo peoples give to their children: names that indicate that the child comes from God and represents one of God's attributes.[13] All of these practices long baffled Europeans.

In concluding this section, we need to make one thing abundantly clear, namely, that more often than not, African metaphors for the supreme deity are neither male nor female. On this subject, Omoyajowo offers the following overview:

> The African concept of God is not altogether masculine. In many parts of Africa, God is conceived as male, but in some other parts, he is conceived

> as female; the Ndebele and Shona ethnic groups of former Rhodesia have a triad made up of God the Father, God the Mother, and God the Son. The Nuba of the Sudan regard God as "Great Mother" and speak of him in feminine pronouns. The Ovabo of South West Africa say that "the mother of pots is a hole in the ground, and the mother of people is God." Although called the queen of Lovedu in South Africa, the mysterious "She" is not primarily a ruler but a rain-maker; she is regarded as a changer of seasons and the guarantor of their cyclic regularity.[14]

Similarly, Geoffrey Parrinder provides evidence to show that some African peoples view God as possessing two natures, the one male and the other female. He illustrates this with reference to Mawu among the Benin people:

> Mawu has a partner called Lisa, and they may be spoken of as twins. One myth says that these twins were born from a primordial mother, Nana Buluku, who created the world and then retired.[15]

Further and more specifically, Parrinder writes,

> Mawu is moon, beloved of men while Lisa the sun is fierce and harsh. Mawu is older, woman and mother, gentle and refreshing. During the day men suffer under the sun's heat, but in the cool moonlight they tell stories and dance. Coolness is a sign of wisdom and age, so Mawu is the wisdom of the world and Lisa is strength. Sometimes Nyame, God of the Ashanti, is personified as the moon and represented by the queen mother, whereas another personification of the truly great Nyame, Nyankopon, is in the sun and the king.[16]

Finally, the following is a description of a most prominent goddess worshipped by the Ibo people of Nigeria as the ruler of the earth:

> One of the most important earth goddesses in Africa is Ala of the Ibo people of eastern Nigeria. Ala is ruler of men, source of morality, and protector of the harvest. As a mother she gives fertility to the crops, and also to human beings. As queen of the underworld she receives the dead into her pocket or womb. The cult of Ala is shown vividly in sculptures which show the attitude of the people to divinity and to life in general. Shrines to Ala are found all over Ibo country, but in the southern regions of Owerri special houses, called Mbari, are erected.[17]

Thus it appears that African understandings of the supreme deity are much less sexist than those of many other religions including Christianity, Judaism, and Islam. Yet it is difficult to get a precise estimate of the extent of female imagery pertaining to the supreme deity in Africa because many African languages do not have gender-specific pronouns. Nevertheless, various subdivinities are male, female, or androgynous. Female imagery with respect to the supreme deity and the reality of female subdivinities and their priestesses enhances the status of women in the sphere of religion in spite of the fact that women are not allowed even to observe many religious rituals. Yet, in their own sphere, goddesses are fully autonomous. That is to say, in their spheres of operation, they are answerable to no male authority. Thus African cosmological thought not only demonstrates the limits of male authority but also provides considerable resources for the exercise of female authority.

Also, it should be noted that both men and women are included among the ancestral spirits even though Awalalu claims that the male ancestors are more important.[18] Parrinder reports that in Dinka mythology "Garang and Abuk are the first ancestors. Abuk is patron of women and their produce, the gardens and the grain."[19] He also displays a mask of the Baga tribe of Guinea representing "the goddess of maternity, protector of mothers worshipped by the Simo society."[20] Further still, Parrinder reports a myth among the Gikuyu people of Kenya wherein the goddess Moombi is depicted as the mother of the female clan system.[21] Finally, much of African sculpture characteristically depicts female ancestors.

African American Theological Syncretism

One of the most important marks of continuity between Africans on the continent and those in the diaspora is their common belief in a transcendent divine power primordially related to them as the creator and preserver of all that is. Thus, when Raboteau concludes, "In the United States the gods of Africa died,"[22] he is referring to the demise of the specific content of African cosmological thought, namely, its sacred symbols, ritual practices, particular divinities and ancestral spirits. In spite of the loss of that specific substance, however, we claim that the "deep structures of African spirituality"[23] survived throughout the African diaspora even though they assumed many different expressive forms.

As was implied above, there is no evidence that either the slaves or their African forebears ever believed in the modern Western distinction between sacred and profane. Rather, both presupposed a sacred cosmos. That is to say, in traditional African thought all reality (human and natural, animate and inanimate) was thought to be derived from a common, primeval, divine source on which its continuing existence depended. Hence they viewed everything as sacred in some respect and saw nothing as totally profane. The theological and moral implications of this belief are manifold, some of which Holloway makes abundantly clear in the following statement:

> Religion was (and remains) a vital part of the lives of most Africans. For some it encompassed their entire existence. It substantiated and explained their place in the universe; their culture, and their relationship to nature and humankind; it also dictated their roles in the community and society at large. Religion among most African ethnic groups was not simply a faith or worship system; it was a way of life, a system of social control, a provider of medicine, and an organizing mechanism.[24]

Undoubtedly, African societies on the continent have produced extremely complex cosmologies in their many and varied attempts to explain and relate the three realms of reality: spirit, history, and nature. Traditional understandings of those relationships are deeply rooted in mythologies and cosmologies which, in turn, greatly influenced the cognitive understandings and emotional expressions of the people. More importantly, the impact of modernity has not dissipated the power of these understandings. Even among the most sophisticated contemporary urban dwellers in Africa, these traditional worldviews are revealed in such familial and communal rituals as naming ceremonies, rites of passage, marriage betrothals, funeral traditions, and reverence for elders, to mention only a few. It is important to note that all of these deeply meaningful rituals take place within the context of family life.

As have all peoples who are uprooted from their cultures and transplanted to an alien environment, African slaves brought their worldviews with them into the diaspora. Though different in many respects, they all shared one primary feature, namely, their belief in a sacred cosmos created and preserved by a supreme deity. In fact, everything they thought and did reflected the sacred nature of the cosmos. In other words, their cultural creations—their songs, music, dances, stories, art—transcended any secular-sacred dichotomy. In fact, they were considered relevant for the whole of life: work, play, and worship. Levine writes accordingly: "For the slaves, then, songs of God and the mythic heroes of their religion were not confined to a specific time or place, but were appropriate to almost every situation."[25] This orientation enabled African peoples on the continent and in the diaspora to live in the presence of their gods and to view all things as ordered or disordered by the latter's will. In Africa (as will be discussed more fully below) the tribe and the family were thought to constitute the principal links between the historical world of humans and the transhistorical realm of the divinities and ancestral spirits. Mbiti calls these links an ontological relationship because the latter depicts the nature of reality itself, apart from which there would be nothing at all.[26] Similarly, Levine concludes: "For the most part when they looked upon the cosmos they saw Man, Nature and God as a unity; distinct but inseparable aspects of a sacred whole."[27] Yet Africans on the continent and in slavery knew that human beings are capable of persistent irreverent acts that could cut them off from the sacred community and, as a consequence, wreak havoc on them, their family and the entire tribal community. Witches and sorcerers were thought to share such a destiny.

Due to the circumstances of their departure from Africa, Africans had no choice but to leave their cultural artifacts on the continent. Yet they did not arrive on these shores as a *tabula rasa.* Rather, different groups brought their respective cosmological understandings with them and gradually shaped a new world of spiritual and moral meaning by appropriating and interpreting various elements in their new environment in accord with their African cosmologies.[28] Thus the condition of slavery did not cut them off from their ultimate source of meaning, God, who was the reservoir for all their religious and moral strivings. Hence, in spite of the massive pathological impact of three and one half centuries of inherited chattel slavery, the acculturation of the Africans to their new environment did not result in a total loss of their religious and moral understandings. On the contrary, Africans in the diaspora were able to preserve the structural dimensions of their spirituality: belief in a spirit-filled cosmos and acceptance of a moral obligation to build a community in harmony with all the various powers in the cosmos. The preservation of their spirituality under the conditions of slavery was an astounding accomplishment, due principally to their creative genius in making the Euro-American cultural forms and practices serve as vehicles for the transmission of African cultural elements.[29] This feat involved no small amount of imaginative skill and creative ingenuity. We concur with Levine that by utilizing all their capacities, "important elements of their shared African heritage remained alive not just as quaint cultural vestiges but as vitally creative elements of slave culture."[30] In his discussion of the religion of the Sea Island slaves Holloway makes a similar argument in support of this syncretistic process:

> The Gullahs converted Christianity to their African world view, using the new religion to justify combating objective forces, to collectively perpetuate community-culture, and as an ideology of freedom. Thus it was less a case of Christianity instilling a sense of resignation because of beliefs in future rewards than of an African philosophical tradition being asserted in the slave quarters.[31]

The conversion of African slaves to Christianity was made easier by the structural similarities between Christian and African cosmologies. In other words, African conversion to Christianity, whether on the continent or in the diaspora, did not mean the wholesale exchange of their indigenous religion for a new one but, as Kwasi Wiredu says, "an amalgamation of the two, made more possible by the common elements in their respect cosmologies, not least of which being their common belief in spirits."[32] Blassingame presents a good summary of that amalgamation process:

> In America Jehovah replaced the Creator, and Jesus, the Holy Ghost, and the Saints replaced the lesser gods. The Africans preserved many of their sacred ceremonies, songs, dances, feasts, festivals, funeral dirges, amulets, prayers, images, and priests. After a few generations the slaves forgot the African deities represented by the Judeo-Christian gods. Still, it was a long time before some blacks completely forgot their gods . . . . Whatever the name of the deity they worshipped in many facets of their religious services the slaves retained many African elements.[33]

For our purposes it is not necessary to demonstrate the full extent of the continuities between the two cultural contexts. It is sufficient only that we show how the slaves inevitably brought their cosmological structures with them and creatively preserved them through processes of adaptation and syncretism. Accordingly, Blassingame writes:

> The similarities between many European and African cultural elements enabled the slave to continue to engage in many traditional activities or to create a synthesis of European and African cultures. In the process of acculturation the slaves made European forms serve African functions. An example of this is religion. Most Africans believed in a Creator, or all-powerful God whom one addressed directly through prayers, sacrifices, rituals, songs and dances. At the same time, they had a panoply of lesser gods each of whom governed one aspect of life. Publicly supported priests, sacred festivals, funeral rites, dirges and wakes, dances and festivals expressing joy and thanksgiving, sacred objects and images, and charms and amulets for protection against evil spirits were the usual elements found in traditional religions. Funerals were especially important to Africans, and

> often were expensive, drawn-out affairs involving a long period of mourning and the burial of personal objects with the deceased. All the friends and relatives of the deceased visited the family for a month after his death, delivered their condolences, and periodically arranged great feasts with much singing, dancing, and drinking to prevent the family from brooding over their loss. The merriment was also indicative of the African belief that upon dying one went "home."[34]

One cannot overemphasize the similarity between African and Christian theism and, as Blassingame has argued, the ease with which Africans both on the continent and in the diaspora could incorporate the Judeo-Christian deity into their African cosmological framework. In our judgment, this was the principal reason not only for the so-called success of the Christian missionary movement in Africa but also its eventual expansion among the African slaves in North America. Genovese argues similarly: "When Africans took over the Christian God they simultaneously extended, rather than transcended, their own particular practice."[35] That is to say, Africans added Christianity to their cosmological framework, as Jacob Olupona describes:

> In the African context what this means is that the old world views are not entirely destroyed as whole systems and replaced by other complete world views. It is better to say that elements from the world views that "make sense" are added while those which have proven inadequate are deleted. The process occurs in all cultures, for world views themselves are dynamic organisms. Conversion, then, represents both a continuity and discontinuity with the old traditions.[36]

Margaret Washington Creel advances a similar argument in describing the way the Gullahs converted Christianity to their African worldview. Thus, she writes:

> I argue that traditional African spiritual belief and cosmology, particularly that of the BaKongo and other Bantu peoples, found a significant niche within Gullah Christian practices and helped stage their folk religion. The strength and flexibility of some African spiritual customs, such as the use of sacred medicines, ancestor reverence, and beliefs about immortality facilitated merger into an African-Christian synthesis among the Gullahs.[37]

Similarly, in speaking about the Bantu people who predominated the slave population of the southern states, Holloway argues that the retention of African culture was enabled by the conditions of isolation:

> Once the Bantu reached America they were able to retain much of their cultural identity. Enforced isolation of these Africans by plantation owners allowed them to retain their religion, philosophy, culture, folklore, folkways, folk beliefs, folk tales, storytelling, naming practices, home economics, arts, kinship, and music. These Africanisms were shared and adopted by the various African ethnic groups of the field slave community, and they gradually developed into African-American cooking (soul food), music (jazz, blues, spirituals, gospels), language, religion, philosophy, customs, and arts.[38]

It seems reasonable to suppose that the only way Africans could make Christianity their own whether on the continent or in the diaspora was to Africanize it in much the same way as Europeans before them had westernized Christianity. Only then could they give their devotion to it. Thus, since religion must always be expressed in some cultural form, Africans who desired to be Christians could do nothing other than Africanize Christianity whenever they were free to do so. We must hasten to add, however, that this does not imply the absence of the reverse, that is, the Christianization of African religions. It is our argument that neither was total but, rather, both underwent syncretistic processes that gradually resulted in an amalgamated whole.

When Christian missionaries went from the Western world to Africa as well as to other "foreign mission fields," they found it necessary to translate the Christian message into indigenous languages. Unwittingly they advanced the first step in the process of enculturating Christianity into the respective indigenous context. Ironically, this enculturation process did not originate in the post-colonial period of the twentieth century as so many have presupposed, but, rather, it began at the very beginning of the missionary enterprise.[39] It remained for Africans, however, to follow the logic of that process to its completion, which has been their primary aim in this post-colonial period.

Interestingly, in many concealed ways, the slaves' gradual appropriation of Christianity involved a similar process of translating the latter into their African cosmological framework. Yet, due to the limitation of language and the severe proscriptions against the exhibition of any African cultural practices, this Africanization process was largely confined to the internal life of the human spirit which, during the early period of slavery was shared communally only in clandestine ways. Eventually, however, this internal process found external expression through the creative use of the oral tradition: music, songs, sermons, prayers, testimonies, and folklore. This constructive enterprise evidences the peculiar propensity of Africans, especially in religion, to retain inner values in spite of changes in their external conditions,[40] a point also strongly supported by Blassingame, who concludes: "West African peoples have been adept at borrowing cultural elements from their conquerors and victims and fusing them with their own."[41]

Thus, as with language and other cultural expressions, African slaves turned many Euro-American cultural forms into receptors and conveyors of African religious and moral meanings.[42] Evidence of this process is regularly being brought to light in the contemporary period by scholars in several different disciplines.[43] Their respective findings have enabled us to see more clearly how the African cultural past continued to be efficacious in the consciousness of the slaves. Those who have studied the form and content of such distinctive African American cultural expressions as music, song, folklore, witchcraft, conjuring, or magic, have clearly demonstrated significant continuity between African cultures both on the continent and in the diaspora.[44] In our judgment, the clearest mark of continuity among Africans everywhere is their mutual belief in and communal devotion to a supreme transcendent being primordially related to them as creator and preserver.

It is beyond the scope of this essay to give a detailed description of the process by which Africans in the diaspora made Christianity their own. Suffice it to say that the religious spirit that the slaves nurtured and promoted in various secret assemblies was undoubtedly subversive if, for no other reason, than the fact that the slaves were engaged in constructing a means of helping themselves by coopting the religion of the slaveowners. As a consequence, those secret meetings became the locus for the development of an alternative understanding of the Christian gospel which the slaves celebrated and proclaimed in many and varied ways:

> Not being allowed to hold meetings in the plantation, the slaves assemble in the swamps, out of reach of the patrols. They have an understanding among themselves as to the time and place of getting together. This is often done by the first one arriving breaking boughs from the trees, and bending them in the direction of the selected spot. Arrangements are then made for conducting the exercises. They first ask each other how they feel, the state of their minds, etc. The male members then select a certain space in separate groups, for their division of the meeting. Preaching in order, by the brethren; then praying and singing all round, until they generally feel quite happy . . . . The slave forgets all his sufferings except to remind others of the trials during the past week, exclaiming, "Thank God, I shall not live here always." Then they pass from one to another, shaking hands, and bidding each other farewell, promising, should they meet no more on

> earth, to strive and meet in heaven, where all is joy, happiness and liberty. As they separate, they sing a parting hymn of praise . . . . Most of the songs used in worship are composed by the slaves themselves and describe their own sufferings.[45]

W.E.B. DuBois called the slave songs "Sorrow Songs" because they focused on the condition of suffering. Their plaintive tones often betrayed their liberating message and their jubilant expectations of the afterlife always concealed their implied criticism of slavery. These songs, more accurately called "spirituals," have been bequeathed to the world as the slaves' legacy of spiritual strife and triumph. They tell the story of suffering and hope, of endurance and transcendence, of history and eternity. Most importantly, they nurtured every generation in the belief that because of their alliance with God, they, the weak ones, have the capacity to conquer the strong and the powerful. Levine illustrates this point by referring to the content of an old spiritual:

> *Ef salvation wuz a thing money could buy*
> *Den de rich would live an' de po'would die.*
> *But ah'm so glad God fix it so,*
> *Dat de rich mus' die jes'as well as de po'!*[46]

The sentiment contained in this spiritual pervaded the consciousness of slaves and evidences their capacity for religious transcendence and social criticism. Both nurtured hope which saved them from a cynical, fatalistic view of history.

Written by "unknown bards" of long ago, the spirituals contain the substance of slave Christianity in distinction from slave owning Christianity. The former proclaimed a supreme deity who is no respecter of persons but, rather, the parent of all humanity who wills that all should live in community as one family honoring and respecting the dignity of all. In constructing such a theology for themselves, the slaves were engaged in a radical praxis because their Christian anthropology contradicted that of slave owning Christianity. Yet, viewed from an African perspective, one would expect the slaves to think of God as creator and protector primarily serving their communal needs and preserving their well-being.

From the earliest times up to the present day, Africans in the diaspora were convinced that the substance of slave Christianity was, for them, the authentic gospel of Jesus Christ: a gospel that was both corrupted and rejected by the personal and societal practices of slaveowners. Then and now, they viewed this authentic gospel as centering on the parenthood of God and the kinship of all peoples under God.[47] Since kinship among Christians implies the equality of persons in community, the kinship of all peoples under God implies God's opposition to those who threaten or destroy the equality of God's people. This Christian vision was born in slavery, protected in the so-called invisible churches that emerged in the secret meetings of the slaves, and later was institutionalized in the independent church movement among freed slaves. Elsewhere, we have called this authentic gospel the "Black Christian Tradition."[48]

Even though the slaves were forbidden to learn how to read and write, and in spite of the biblical indoctrination they sometimes received from their slave-holders, they gradually perceived an alternative gospel from that which they received from their owners. The new gospel that they enthusiastically embraced portrayed God as the liberator of all oppressed peoples and opposed to all who are bent on maintaining oppressive social systems. Such a God could be easily conjoined with the character of the God known and served by their forbears. Henceforth, this God has constituted the ultimate grounding for their understanding of human nature and the organizing principle for all their nonracist associational life. Further, their belief that God wills that the good of all peoples should be realized in community is both commensurate with and expansive of the African traditional understanding of God. That is to say, their Christian God serves the well-being of the race (the tribal group) in particular and of all peoples universally.

African and African American Moral Syncretism

The moral significance of traditional African understandings of God is similar to that of Christianity, Judaism, and Islam. All value in general and moral value in particular is thought to be grounded in and derived from the supreme deity. In Christianity the normative sources of morality are the Bible, tradition, reason, and experience. In traditional African religion the normative sources of morality are mythology, proverbs, folktales, the oral tradition as mediated through the elders, the ritual practices of priests or priestesses, and reason in both its pragmatic and aesthetic functions.

As in the pre-Enlightenment West, traditional African religious thought and practice served to produce a people who were profoundly passive in the presence of legitimate authority. Virtually nothing in their cultural context encouraged criticism of or dissent from those who exercised legitimate authority over them. These included all tribal leaders, priests, and elders (both male and female).[49] This state of affairs was reinforced by the belief that wrongdoing rarely issued from the top of any legitimate hierarchical order but, rather, arose from some lower echelon. Accordingly, moral virtue was constituted by respect for and obedience to religious, political, and familial authority, each of which was viewed as ordained by the supreme deity, the creator and preserver of all things.[50] Yet, in spite of all of this, they were adept at devising various checks and balances against despotism as well as designing very complex procedures for determining all matters of succession in governance.

Yet these same people could become ferocious whenever required to confront illegitimate authorities. Justification for such violent reprisals was grounded in the most basic instinct of human nature, namely, the will to survive. Since illegitimate authority necessarily violates the life it dominates, it is repulsive universally. In the African context, such illegitimate authority was sufficient cause for an otherwise hospitable people to wage war. Once committed to such an enterprise one could be sure that the enemy was viewed as wholly evil and the avenger as thoroughly good. The vocation of the latter was to seek the complete eradication of the former. Though African slaves had similar sentiments, they were held in check for the most part through many and various indirect daily acts of resistance. From time to time, the overt expression of such sentiments was seen in slave revolts and insurrections.

The African understanding of the supreme deity as creator and preserver of all that is implies divine order and harmony both in and among the realms of spirit, nature, and history. In the realm of spirit that hierarchical relationship among the supreme deity, the subdivinities, and the ancestral spirits is the paramount exemplar of order and harmony, and African peoples seek to emulate it in their familial and tribal communities.[51] Clearly this view of authority and its implied obligations of respect, loyalty, and obedience have produced many societal constraints against dissent which, in turn, have greatly influenced the way African peoples have responded to adversity.

On the one hand, their strong belief in predestination encouraged a propensity for intercultural absorption and adaptation, especially under the conditions of oppression. Yet, on the other hand, that same belief contributed to the formation of a peculiarly patient and hospitable people with a strong sense of communal solidarity and family devotion.

Accordingly, African slaves in the Americas and elsewhere responded to their situation in much the same way as African slaves did on the continent. Whenever conquered peoples are removed from their geographical environment and all hope of return has vanished, the ability to adapt themselves to the new cultural context is a necessary survival skill. Many elements in their traditional worldview nurtured development of that capacity.

Since the highest good in African societies is the preservation of order and harmony within the community, on the one hand, and between the community and its spiritual protectors (the divinities and ancestors), on the other hand, much time and energy was spent observing and participating in juridical practices. This enabled virtually everyone in the community to develop some measure of skill in reasoned debate because all human activity was justifiable only in so far as it contributed to the preservation of order and harmony within the community and between it and the realm of divinities and ancestors. Moreover, these latter beings were never viewed apart from the community since, as spiritual protectors of the community, they controlled its life and destiny.

As in every hierarchical order internal relationships are characterized by a chain of command based on an ethic of reciprocity. Those of higher rank are obligated to protect their subordinates and the duty of the latter is to acknowledge their dependency by always seeking the good will and blessing of the former. Unquestioned obedience guaranteed both. Such a pattern of reciprocity permeates all African societies on the continent, and significant continuities persist among the African diaspora to the present day.

Contrary to the opinions of many outsiders, Africans do not experience the supreme deity as capricious but as one who serves the well-being of all as their creator and preserver. Yet the consistent character of the supreme deity does not apply *en masse* to the subordinate divinities. Although not capricious, they, like humans, possess certain weaknesses of character. That is to say, they cannot always be relied upon to do the good. Awolalu gives an apt description of their "ambidextrous" character:

> Surprisingly enough, the divinities are sometimes believed to have weaknesses in terms of moral order of things. They can be used to inflict sickness, death, or other misfortunes on the innocent. They are thus ambidextrous—they can be both good and bad simultaneously.[52]

In spite of their ambiguous moral nature, however, the divinities can be relied upon to respond reciprocally to their devotees. Because of their vulnerability to the influence of the latter, however, they may from time to time lend assistance to those whose supplications emerge from a spirit of ill-will. That is to say, they can be co-opted to serve contrary purposes. Yet it would be a serious error to confuse these so-called ambidextrous divinities with Christian dualist thought about good and evil. In fact, African cosmological thought admits no notion of absolute evil. The traditional Western interpretation of the Yoruba "trickster" deity, Esu, as synonymous with Satan was erroneous.[53]

Thus humans need to learn precisely their duties and obligations to both the divinities and the ancestors and the importance of exercising them with utmost diligence and faithfulness. In return for such devotion the divinities and the ancestors can be relied upon, for the most part, to reciprocate in appropriate ways. That is to say, they have the power to bestow blessings and if they fail to do so, the fault lies with their devotees. Both unintentional and willful neglect by humans in performing such duties can have devastating effects not only on individuals but on the whole community. Since mercy and compassion are not characteristic qualities of either the divinities or the ancestors, the effects of wrongdoing can be neutralized, however, through ritual practices carried out under the direction of professional priests or priestesses. The wrath of the spirits and divinities can be appeased through proper sacrifices.

African and African American Survival Theologies

The African view of God is covenantal. That is to say, God is viewed as reciprocally related to the tribal community, sustaining and preserving the latter in return for steadfast obedience and faithful devotion. Hence, once the African slaves had discovered that the biblical God had taken initiative in forming a covenantal relationship with a band of slaves in Egypt and had promised to lead them to freedom in return for their obedience and faithfulness, they knew that that God was not the possession of slaveholders but, rather, the latter's opponents. That discovery made possible their easy acceptance of the Christian worldview because it meshed so well with their traditional African understandings of a tribal deity. Further, African American Christianity enabled the slaves to deepen their experience of racial unity by giving them the basic elements for the constitution of a new myth of origin wherein the major biblical personages were transformed and began functioning much as African ancestors had inspired them to greater devotion. Further still, their clandestine ritualistic gatherings and liturgical practices of worship became the locus for syncretising African and Christian worldviews into a dynamic unified whole. Thus, in the midst of their suffering, Africans discovered that they had not left God on the continent with their material cultural artifacts, but had discovered their God anew in this alien land inhabited by such a cruel people. In continuity with their African experience, this God constituted the ultimate grounding for their understanding of human nature and the organizing principle for their associational life. Their Christian belief that God wills that the good of all peoples should be realized in community (that is, in harmony with others) is both commensurate with and expansive of the African traditional understanding of God. As African religionists before them had believed, these African Christians in the diaspora had come to believe that God serves the well-being of the race (that is, the tribal group) in particular and of all peoples disposed towards entering into a similar covenantal relationship.

Like that of their African forebears, the basic theology of Africans in the diaspora reflected the survival orientation of the community, on the one hand, and the community's longing for relief from oppression, on the other hand. With respect to the latter, it is important to point out that whenever they were faced with suffering of any kind, traditional African peoples became preoccupied with the quest for relief: a two-directional search that centered on God as the agent of relief and on themselves and others as the cause of their misfortune.

In traditional African religions, evil is thought to have its origin in human wrongdoing, which in turn causes some form of imbalance to occur between the human community and the realm of spirit. Some form of suffering inevitably results from such a circumstance. Consequently, in the face of the suffering (diseases, accidents, drought, natural disaster, death), priests and all concerned expend much energy investigating the circumstances in search for the human causative factor. Often the cause is attributed to witchcraft, which also must entail the most careful investigation, lest the prospective exorcism be ineffective.

Africans in the North American diaspora held similar views about evil. Slavery being for them the paramount evil, some attributed the cause to their having acquired a bad destiny before birth. Accordingly, they made every effort to comply with the purpose of the deity in so far as they were able to discern it. A goodly number of them viewed that purpose as consonant with the Christian evangelization of Africa, often referred to as the "redemption of Africa." The most prominent proponent of this view was the eighteenth-century African American poet

Phyllis Wheatley, who expressed herself accordingly in these lines of an early poem:

> Twas mercy brought me from my *Pagan* land,
> Taught my benighted soul to understand
> That there's a God, that there's a *Saviour* too . . . .[54]

While Martin Delaney, Alexander Crummell, Bishop Henry McNeil Turner, and many other nineteenth-century African American Christian nationalists believed that African Americans should assume primary responsibility for Africa's redemption religiously, politically, and socially, they did not ascribe to the belief that the condition of slavery was predestined by God. Rather, along with the vast majority of African Americans, they placed the full and complete blame for slavery on the moral depravity of slave-owners. Along with all African Americans they also believed that the owners would not escape damnation in the afterlife for their wrongdoing. Most importantly, however, African Americans' unequivocal designation of humans as the cause of their misery is wholly commensurate with the traditional African view of evil. Since the latter upsets cosmic equilibrium, the realm of spirit must be engaged in order to restore the balance. This is as good a reason as any for explaining the importance of the spirit realm in the African struggle for survival and social change. Consequently, both on the continent and in the diaspora, religion has maintained a central place in the struggle for social justice.

Interestingly, unlike much of the Protestant theology taught the slaves by the slaveholders' preachers, the slaves lent little importance to the doctrine of original sin. In the words of Genovese, "sin meant wrongdoing—injustice to others and violation of accepted moral codes."[55] In commenting on Genovese's viewpoint, Sobel elaborates:

> Africans did not have a sense of original sin. Their understanding of misfortune was that it was indeed a punishment, but its cause was the breaking of a taboo or negligence in regard to proper ritual conduct, seen as an offense to elders, spirits, the living dead, or the live rulers of the society; or the use of sorcery by an enemy. Conduct and not thought, was to be judged, and immorality came to be anything that hindered the development of the community. Long after the slave period, black Christians continued thinking in these terms, still understanding sin as the breaking of the new Christian taboos or that which hindered the development of the new Christian community.[56]

Not only did this view of wrongdoing fit their traditional African understanding, which had no sense of "original fault" affecting the whole of creation, Africans in the diaspora responded to their oppression by making the quest for freedom their paramount goal. Hence, their eschatological focus on heaven fit their traditional cosmological view of the realm of spirit from which all humans came and to which all hoped to return. Yet the African's vision of the realm of spirit did not differ appreciably from the realities of the tribal community. Rather, life in the spirit world was a virtual reflection of life in the flesh. It was not only composed of good and bad people, but also people maintained their same socio-economic status. Yet it should be noted that Africans do not share the notion of an afterlife. Rather, life is eternal in the sense that it is cyclical. One merely passes from one form of life to another form and, under the best of circumstances, returns to historical life time and again.

Clearly Africans on the continent viewed the realm of spirit partly as the abode of their ancestors, the place where all the generations of the family are reunited. Yet, as indicated above, reunion was figurative because in the African experience death was not viewed as separation from the living but merely a transition of the soul from the body to the realm of spirit. Accordingly, the so-called departed one is never separated from the family but always present and treated with great reverence by the daily offering of libations. In order to maintain this understanding, Mbiti prefers to refer to the ancestors as the "living-dead."[57]

This background enabled Africans in the diaspora not to view heaven merely as a distant reality far removed from historical experience. Rather, the Christian slaves maintained certain aspects of their foreparents' understanding of a sacred cosmos wherein the three realms of reality (namely, nature, history, and spirit) are united. For certain, that harmony occurred in the realm of spirit. Thus the slave Christianity viewed heaven as the locus of harmony manifested in the experience of freedom: the community of peace and justice (that is, goodwill) and the fruit of their lifelong hopes and dreams. In the experience of joyful worship they sought to give full expression to this vision, and it became the moral norm for their communal life. Since authentic worship reflects the life of the people and their pressing needs, African peoples have always viewed the political struggle for freedom as mirrored in their worship.

Since survival is a necessary condition for social change, survival theology logically precedes liberation theology. Relative to biblical symbolism, the theology of the African American diaspora has centered more on the theology of the "wilderness"[58] than on that of the "promised land." Although the latter was always the source of African American political inspiration, its constant betrayal by their oppressors resulted in a destiny of dependency and deprivation instead of the desired freedom and equality. Consequently, the promised land has been viewed largely in eschatological terms while the pragmatic experience of coping with suffering and effecting some measure of incremental benefits preoccupied every dimension of African American life for several centuries.

The practical meaning of life in the midst of the actual experience of suffering and the existential threat of death is the subject matter of survival theology. How does one believe in a protective God in the midst of seemingly interminable misery? This is the problem of theodicy; the problem of Hagar who was betrayed by Abraham and Sarah and exiled from their household;[59] the problem of the disillusioned Hebrews in the wilderness; the problem of Job; the problem of the Babylonian captivity; the problem of the psalmist, who feels forsaken by God; the problem of the passion and crucifixion of Jesus. Africans in the diaspora have identified closely with all of these biblical narratives and have reflected for centuries on their meanings for them.

Survival theology implies neither contentment with adversity nor justification of oppression. Rather, the maintenance, preservation, and enhancement of meaningful life in community is its primary concern. The covenantal relationship between African peoples and God has empowered them to endure the pain of injustice while not affirming it. It has motivated them to do battle in one form or other against the perpetuation of injustice. In both cases, they have felt themselves imbued with the spirit of triumph because their God was allied with them.

Like their African forebears, Africans in the diaspora have continued being a religious people believing that they live and move in a sacred cosmos closely related to God as their protector and provider. Consequently, they had no difficulty in appropriating similar Christian metaphors for God, such as comforter, protector, shepherd, friend, father, mother, and the like. In short, belief in an ever-present divine power capable of delivering them from any measure of trouble has been characteristic of their faith from the most ancient times up to the present.

Thus, like that of their African predecessors, the basic theology of Africans in the diaspora reflected primarily the survival orientation of their racial community. As stated above, since survival is a necessary condition for social change, survival theology is logically prior to liberation theology. They are related to each other as pre-political is related to the political, or as the present child is related to the future adult. The former necessarily precedes the latter.

The first step therefore in laying the foundation for a common moral discourse among African peoples is to recognize the high degree of Christian and African syncretism that exists both on the continent and in the diaspora and its implications for ethical thought and the moral life.

3

COMMUNITY

The Goal of the Moral Life

African and African American Understandings of Ancestral Life

All African peoples agree that the tribal or ethnic community is the paramount social reality apart from which humanity cannot exist. Similarly, all agree that the community is a sacred phenomenon created by the supreme God, protected by the divinities, and governed by the ancestral spirits. Thus full participation in the community is a fundamental requirement of all humans. It comprises the nature of religious devotion. John Mbiti says it well:

> To be human is to belong to the whole community, and to do so involves participating in the beliefs, ceremonies, rituals and festivals of that community. A person cannot detach himself from the religion of his group, for to do so is to be severed from his roots, his foundation, his context of security, his kinships and the entire group of those who make him aware of his own existence. To be without one of these corporate elements is to be out of the whole picture. Therefore, to be without religion amounts to a self-excommunication from the entire life of society, and African peoples do not know how to exist without religion.[1]

In African societies the ancestors comprise the principal link between the ethnic community and the realm of spirit. Their interaction with and appeasement by the living are necessary for the preservation of peace and harmony. As Mbiti argues, the various realms of reality within the African cosmological order are created by the supreme deity, ranked hierarchically, and designed to function harmoniously with one another. Thus the drive for harmony is ontologically established. Most importantly, he argues that the realm of spirit is integrally related to both the historical and the natural realms of existence. For example, the integral relation of the realm of spirit with that of history is seen most vividly in the African conception of life, which, incidently, differs markedly from Western understandings. In the African worldview there is no death in the sense of radical separation from either the family or the tribal community. Rather, Africans believe that life is eternal and that its motion is not linear but cyclical. In fact, they are convinced that the temporal movement of human life is a continuous cyclical process from the realm of spirit to that history. Thus, they expect a so-called *good* death to follow a *good* life. The latter is manifested in a person who has reached old age and has many prosperous children and whose time has arrived to join the realm of ancestral spirits. Thus, to speak of such a process as death is a misnomer. Rather, departure from physical life marks a transition of the human spirit from the state of mortality to that of ancestral immortality. Henceforth the ancestor is thought to live on in the realm of the spirit world in a state of existence that Mbiti calls the "living dead,"[2] a term he prefers over *ancestor* because of the tendency of Westerners to associate the latter with the state of death. The term *living dead* conveys both continuity with and transition from temporal life.

Interestingly, the ancestral spirits are thought to continue life in much the same way as they lived it in history. That is to say, they retain their moral character, social status, and familial consciousness. Margaret Creel concludes:

> Ancestors retained their normal human passions and appetites, which had to be gratified in death as in life. Ancestors felt hunger and thirst. They became angry or happy depending on the behavior of their living "children." The living dead were vindictive if neglected but propitious if shown respect. Just as filial loyalty prevents one from allowing a parent to go hungry, "so must food be offered to the ancestors."[3]

Though reciprocal in nature, it appears that the primary mission of ancestors is to serve as intermediaries between their families and the various divinities. That function is described well by Awolalu:

> The ancestors are also there for God's use. They, acting as agents of God, also take part in the maintenance and control of the universe. They act as intermediaries between man and God, and between man and divinities. They still have interest in the day-to-day running of the affairs of the family to which they belonged while there were still alive. They are regarded as the guardians of morality. They can come down to help or hinder, to cause adversity or happiness. . . .[4]

Families are expected to be grateful for the protection of their ancestors and to reciprocate by performing certain rituals in order to maintain harmonious relations between them. Those rituals include the provision of a splendid funeral (a celebratory homecoming event that ushers the person safely and honorably into the ancestral abode), followed by periodic public memorials usually beginning sometime within the first year (often called "the second funeral"),[5] and, depending on the family's economic situation, subsequent memorial celebrations as often thereafter as possible.[6] The ancestral relationship continues for as long as there are persons alive who knew the person in the flesh. When historical memory ends, and no one can remember them by name, they may be said to have fully died. Henceforth each of these becomes what I call an "objectified spirit" which Africans refer to as an "it." These latter can pose great danger to humans because their activities are no longer guided by family devotion and responsibility. Thus the loss of communal relationship causes these objectified spirits to act capriciously.[7] In fact, Africans usually view the forests as the abode of such objectified spirits and, hence, a place greatly feared. For example, the Nigerian scholar 'Zulu Sofola describes this central dimension of the forest in her description of Nobel Laureate Wole Soyinka's play, *A Dance of the Forests,* written to celebrate Nigerian independence in 1960. Instead of a play depicting the joys of the human spirit, Soyinka attends to the threatening realm of bad spirits hovering about in the forest surrounding the village:

> Wole Soyinka envisioned the birth of independence as taking place in the chaotic dungeon of the forest. To him the forest was a place of utter disorder and chaos, the direct opposite of a place of human abode, a place where the spirits of those who died prematurely lingered until the time of their appointed death released them and they could settle in the spirit world. It was the abode of those denied burial because of some abominable act, a place where spirits lingered, burdened with fear and guilt, while they wandered about destroying human life and vegetation and polluting the earth. It was likewise a place where mothers who died before an illegitimate childbirth were buried, and the forest was filled with the dreadful cries of the unborn children whose destinies were unfulfilled.
>
> The playwright saw the country as sick with corruption, injustice, bitterness, confusion of purpose and objectives, a loss of direction, and in the clutch of a demonic presence that would destroy the new life as soon as it was born. Independence was seen as a very significant movement of transition, but the past and the present were so grim that one feared for the newly born.
>
> The forest in this play, therefore, is not the abode of ancestors who interact with and are appeased by the living. Setting the birth of Nigerian

> independence in this type of forest, foretold the crises which were to follow, and which confirmed Soyinka's farsightedness.[8]

Sofola's discussion provides insight into the African understanding of evil as spirits disconnected from the web of communal relationships and treating all that is encountered as mere prey. Since such evil forces are not easily pacified, one should take care to avoid meeting them. Variations of such demonic forces have been ubiquitous throughout the African diaspora. African American folklore is replete with stories of mean-spirited haunts, spooks, ghosts, and spirits bent on making life uncomfortable for those whom they encounter.

This discussion of ancestral spirits also implies a peculiar understanding of time, the understanding of which is necessary to grasp how the realms of spirit and history are related to each other. In his apt analysis Mbiti divides the subject into what he calls "potential time and actual time."[9]

> According to traditional concepts, time is a two-dimensional phenomenon, with a long past, a present and virtually no future. The linear concept of time in western thought, with an indefinite past, present and infinite future, is practically foreign to African thinking. The future is virtually absent because events which lie in it have not taken place, they have not been realized and cannot therefore, constitute time. If, however, future events are certain to occur, or if they fall within the inevitable rhythm of nature, they at best constitute only *potential time,* not *actual time.* What is taking place now no doubt unfolds the future, but once an event has taken place, it is no longer in the future but in the present and the past. *Actual time* is therefore what is present and what is past. It moves "backward" rather than "forward"; and people set their minds not on future things, but chiefly on what has taken place.[10]

Mbiti uses two Swahili words for time, namely, *sasa* to describe potential time and *zamini* for actual time:

> In African thought, the Sasa "swallows" up what in western or linear concept of time would be considered the future. Events (which compose time) in the Sasa dimension must be either about to occur, or in the process of realization, or recently experienced. Sasa is the most meaningful period for the individual, because he has a personal recollection of the events or phenomena of this period. Sasa is really an experiential extension of the Now-moment. . . . The older a person is, the longer is his Sasa period. Sasa is the time region in which people are conscious of their existence, and within which they project themselves both into existence, and within which they project themselves both into the short future and mainly into

> the past (Zamini). Sasa is in itself a complete or full time dimension, with its own short future, a dynamic present, and an experienced past. We might call it the Micro-Time (Little Time).
>
> Zamini is not limited to what in English is called the past. It also has its own "past," "present" and "future" but on a wider scale. We might call it the Macro-Time (Big Time). Zamini overlaps with Sasa and the two are not separable. Sasa feeds or disappears into Zamini. But before events become incorporated into the Zamini, they have to become realized or actualized within the Sasa dimension. When this has taken place, then the events "move" backwards from the Sasa into the Zamini. So Zamini becomes the period beyond which nothing can go. Zamini is the graveyard of time, the period of termination, the dimension in which everything finds its halting place. It is the final storehouse for all phenomena and events, the ocean of time in which everything becomes absorbed into a reality that is neither after nor before. . . . Sasa generally binds individuals and their immediate environment together. It is the period of conscious living. On the other hand, Zamini is the period of the myth, giving a sense of foundation or security to the Sasa period; and binding together all created things, so that all things are embraced within the Macro-Time.[11]

The above has been quoted at length in order to facilitate a full comprehension of what it means to speak of the gradual movement of the living dead into the distant past and their foundational relationship in the ongoing life of the people. In fact, the living dead are the spiritual protectors of the family and the larger community. The relationship between the two is reciprocal. That is to say, each is dependent on the other. The living dead need the family to keep alive their memory and ensure their immortality. Hence the importance of marriage and procreation,[12] which have long been considered necessary for every African from ancient times up to the present day. Without progeny individuals can have no immortality in the realm of spirit because there would be no one to preserve their memory by sustaining a communal relationship with them after they should have made the transition from the realm of history to that of spirit. In short, progeny is a prerequisite for becoming an ancestor: the existence of the latter depends on the family.

Further, since Africans believe not only in the immortality of souls but also in their rebirth, the living dead are dependent on the family for their reincarnation in subsequent generations. Thus procreation evidences the reciprocal relationship between the living dead and the family. No greater misfortune can befall an African person than the inability to procreate.

Such a circumstance severs the person from the realm of spirit and terminates his or her place in the ongoing process of life.

Apart from their relationship with the living dead, families would be deprived of any direct access to the spiritual realm since neither the objectified spirits nor the divinities have the capacity to establish personal relationships. The mutual exchange of responsibilities and duties between the living dead and their families is reflective of the moral ethos in general. Harmony is the paramount goal within and among all the possible relationships within the cosmological order, and herein lies its ethical significance. As the source and justification of all moral obligations, the cosmological order implies the loyalty and obedience of each subordinate in the relationship. In fact, the preservation of the social order depends on it. Negligence at any level can result in devastating consequences not only for the agent but also for his or her family as well as the larger tribal community. Any such negligence, willful or otherwise, upsets the equilibrium in the cosmos, which in turn produces catastrophic results. Fear of such consequences serves as a strong warrant against all such willful neglect. Reciprocity of obligations and duties faithfully practiced by each and every member of the tribe is thought to guarantee harmony and prosperity for the whole community.

It is important to note, at this point, that much of the scholarly literature contains very little concerning the African understanding of female ancestors. Although all scholars readily admit that the spirits of women are present in the ancestral realm, very little attention is given to them either in scholarly inquiry or, for the most part, in the daily devotion of the people. One explanation for this may well lie in the fact that the realm of spirit mirrors the realm of history. Thus, as the male predominates in the latter, so also the male spirits are thought to predominate in the ancestral realm.

Yet, it appears to me that many women who had become ancestors a long time ago have now become goddesses. These are of paramount importance especially in the lives of women, since they offer the latter special protection and encouragement. None is more important in this respect than the Yoruba goddess, Oya, whose several functions include that of being the spiritual guardian of market women.[13]

Without a doubt, societal stability is a necessary condition for the preservation of ancestral memory. The rituals of story-telling, ceremonial celebrations, ritual performances, sacrificial offerings, daily devotion, and the like, all presuppose the presence of social order even as they contribute to its preservation and enhancement.

Alas, under the conditions of slavery, Africans were subjected to an alien social order in which they were bought and sold as property and deprived of the most rudimentary conditions of civilization such as the preservation of family life and the maintenance of traditional customs. The impulse of slave-owners to obliterate every trace of the African heritage in their captives clearly contributed to their dehumanizing intent. Yet, in spite of such severe proscriptions, the African slaves maintained their cosmic understandings of family life. In their eventual appropriation of Christianity, their theology was gradually expressed through the oral medium of the so-called spirituals. Even a casual examination of those lyrics reveals the image of the family permeating the slave's worldview. References to father, mother, brothers, sisters, uncles, aunts, as well as of the extended family of preachers, deacons, and fellow-sinners are commonplace throughout the spirituals.[14] Nowhere, however, do the songs refer explicitly to Europeans or Americans who, by definition, have no place in the African's frame of reference. By giving their family members such a prominent place in their sacred songs, the slaves were expressing the basic structure of African communal life through ancestral devotion. Similarly, as with all captive peoples uprooted from their respective homelands, African slaves gradually adopted many relevant ancestors of their captors which, in this situation, turned out to be various biblical personages who eventually function for them as surrogate ancestral protectors. Thus, the inclusion of Moses, Joshua, Daniel, Mary, Jonah, or Paul in their spirituals was tantamount to granting them membership in the African realm of spirit. Further, all slaves expected reunion with their families in heaven, and to that end they often sent messages to them through the spirits of the dying and gave careful attention to the care of their graves. In many and varied ways, their belief in ancestral spirits was kept alive, and most believed that their souls would return to Africa after death, where they would be reunited with their ancestors.

As social cohesion and social order increased among freed African American peoples, their leaders exemplified the moral norms and traditions of the community that had been preserved through slavery in modified form. In continuity with their native Africa, the well-being of the community was the foremost moral value among the slaves. Those whose lives exemplified that goal received the community's highest praise.

They were destined to be immortalized in the community's oral and literary traditions as well as in a variety of public rituals. In time, they came to be viewed as ancestors, and the evidence of their spiritual efficacy was seen in the continuing effectiveness of their practical wisdom.

African and African American Understandings of Leadership

In traditional African societies, each tribal community (that is, language group) had its own myths of origins, which depicted the supreme deity as creator of the community and all of its societal structures. For example, in monarchical societies the sovereign was thought to rule in accordance with God's favor. Thus selection of the ruler was the single most important matter in the community's life. As God's paramount priest the monarch represented the authoritative moral, political, and religious center of the tribal community. Thus Thompson says of Yoruba rulers:

> Yoruba kings provide the highest link between the people, the ancestors, and the gods. Their relation to the Creator is given in the praise poem Oba alashe ekeji orisha, "The King, as master of ashe, becomes the second of the gods."[15]

African monarchs were the official guardians of the ancestral charters. Their authority placed them "at the ritual apex of their people's socio-moral order,"[16] and accordingly they were separated from ordinary humanity. Yet, apart from some of the Egyptian pharaohs, African kings do not seem to have claimed divinity for themselves. Traditionally, however, they were supposed to live their lives in private, never to be seen doing the mundane things of life except by their closest servants. Their sacred symbols of office commanded the reverence and respect of all concerned. Their chief duties were to perform certain regular rituals so as to bind the ancestors closely to the community, to protect all who exercise priestly functions at the altars of specific divinities, and to maintain harmony between the society and its natural environment. Basil Davidson says that the duties of the monarch are "to perform the daily rites for which he was uniquely qualified by office: to provide for and direct the activities of other cults; and to sustain and control his own spiritual potency."[17]

In traditional African societies, it was necessary for the king to be a person of exemplary moral integrity because a direct correlation existed between his character and the community's well-being. He was permitted no moral blemish lest it diminish the efficacy of his mediating powers. Thus:

> Ideally, the king should be strong and comely, generous of mind, bold in warfare, cunning in council and devout in everyday life. He should epitomize a people at one with its moral order, at peace with itself, at every point in harmony with the ancestors "who brought us into our land and gave us life." From this it followed that he should never go on reigning when his powers had failed, or when. . . . he "became tyrannical and departed from the rules of justice." . . . Then he had to go, no matter how prestigious he might be.[18]

It is important to note that the significance of the office of kingship transcended the incumbent himself. Clearly the latter was entitled to rule only as long as his capacities lasted. Widespread disease and famine implied a loss of the ruler's spiritual potency, which in turn led to the community's displeasure with him and provided sufficient grounds for his removal from office. Similarly, long-term sickness or senility was also grounds for removal, as was any tendency towards tyranny. In all of these circumstances, the removal of a king from office was a very delicate matter and had to be undertaken in the most careful manner either by inducing the ruler to commit suicide or by ceremonial assassination. Traditional societies could not imagine deposed kings living among the people with diminished status.

The process of choosing a successor from the field of royal candidates involved the most painstaking, deliberative process. In many ways the proceedings were surprisingly democratic in that the consent of the masses through their representatives was determinative. Although heredity was often an important factor, rarely did the office pass directly from father to son. Rather, the pool of candidates was usually provided by royal families. Thus, the difficulties of selection become apparent. Royal families are usually quite recognizable for generations both by their names and their communal status. For example, among the Yorubas the prefix *Ade* in a person's name signals his or her membership in a royal family.

Once duly enthroned, however, the king enjoyed the unquestioned loyalty and obedience of all his subjects. Yet Africans have never been naive about the power of royalty. They have always been adept at devising numerous checks and balances against the growth of despotism, which, in spite of its cause, constituted the greatest potential threat to the well-being of the community. Some have argued that one of the reasons for the rise of secret societies in traditional African culture was the task of surveillance and protection against the possible rise of despotism.[19] Clearly, the study of kingship[20] is one of the most fascinating subjects in the history of African politics.

W.E.B. DuBois was probably the first African American scholar to discern that the origins of African American religious leadership are deeply embedded in traditional African culture.[21] Among freed African Americans, the spirit of African kingship was transmitted to the clergy, whom the community viewed as their primary leaders embued with charismatic powers. Traditionally the latter always exercised enormous authority and influence, although their powers were always considerably more limited in scope than those of African kings. Yet from the earliest times up to the present day African American clergy have been acknowledged as the titular heads of their local communities and have enjoyed the highest respect and loyalty of their people, who care for their material needs and often bestow lavish gifts on them and their families. Since the churches have been the primary institutions owned and controlled by African Americans, and since their pre-eminence among community organizations has rarely been challenged, these leaders have been the gateway to the community. Traditionally, they have been for their people the authoritative interpreters both of God and social reality. Often blessed with charismatic personalities[22] and enviable oratorical skills, their exemplary abilities have long been models of community leadership.

Although the churches often put various control mechanisms in place to guard against despotism, they have not always been effective. Longevity of office has often nullified their efficacy. Also, like all authorities, the clergy have sometimes been vulnerable to corruption. More often than not, the latter has been evidenced by their seeming alliance with the white power structure in return for certain material gains either for themselves or their churches.

Nevertheless, African American clergy often enjoy a regal lifestyle not unlike that of traditional African kings. That is to say, because of their office, they enjoy immense social status often in the face of very limited material benefits. Clearly, nothing affecting the well-being of their community is outside their purview. They have long been viewed as intermediaries not only between their people and God but also between their people and the white community. Maintaining harmony with both has been their principal aim. Thus their styles of leadership have tended to be more priestly than prophetic, not unlike that of African kings.

Whenever a person is elected to the episcopacy in the tradition of African American Methodism, for example, that person's family gains a status within the denomination analogous to that of royal families in traditional Africa. With few exceptions, similar analogies can be seen in the magnificent way congregations treat virtually all African American clergy and their families.

African and African American Understandings of Slavery

African complicity with both the Atlantic and the Asiatic slave trade constitutes a startling moral dilemma for contemporary Africans everywhere. Their moral sensitivity is greatly violated by the knowledge that so-called African middlemen[23] eagerly controlled the supply of the slave trade from the sixteenth to the twentieth century. Not only did slavery rob the continent of millions of its peoples and subject them to indescribable suffering but it also had a profound effect on the infrastructures of African societies themselves. Suffice it to say that the entire continent continues to live in the aftermath of its devastating impact.[24]

For several centuries neither Africans nor Christians viewed slave trading or slave holding as immoral. The African worldview, being essentially tribal, contained no "universal" conception of humanity either on the African continent or elsewhere. In this respect, they did not differ from either Western or Eastern peoples of the world. It is important to note, however, the important argument Patrick Manning makes that during the early period of the slave trade Africans did not have either a pan-African or racial identity. "Africans, while they could recognize racial and cultural groupings as well as anyone else, did not have a consciousness of themselves as a unitary group in the eighteenth century."[25] Thus it would be quite unrealistic to read back into history ideas of African identity that are deeply rooted in twentieth-century consciousness. Manning also argues that Africans were unaware of the impact of the slave trade on their continent and could not resist what appeared to be considerable economic gain from their participation in the trade.[26]

Clearly, traditional African moral codes contained no principled warrants against the treatment of human beings as economic commodities so long as the captives were not wantonly taken from within their own tribal community. Virtually all African societies sentenced individuals to slavery for certain egregious offenses. These and similar wrongful acts implied the need for moral cleansing which eventually gave rise to an enormous number of spiritual rites and ritual practices among the slaves themselves.

Also, Africans had long practiced domestic slavery where the captive became attached to the family and gradually was assimilated into it at the lowest rank. Usually, by the second or third generation such persons had become fully integrated into the family. In this respect the African treatment of domestic slaves was quite different from that of either the Europeans or the Americans. Yet it was impossible for the Africans at that time to have had any accurate knowledge of how the slaves would be treated across the seas.

Unfortunately, little is known about either the moral thinking of the so-called African middlemen or their treatment of the slaves in Africa while awaiting their trans-Atlantic transport. It is reasonable to assume, however, that their African captors imagined the conditions of slavery in foreign lands to be similar to their own, even though we have no reason to suppose that they felt either empathy towards them or concern of any kind for their welfare. In short, we can rightly assume that Africans did not feel morally connected to anyone whose destiny appeared to be that of slavery.

Thus African slaves did not arrive on these shores as full-blown abolitionists. In fact, with some few marginal exceptions, Europeans did not take on the spirit of abolitionism until the turn of the nineteenth century. Contrary to the vast majority of historical studies on the matter, in which Europeans are viewed as the progenitors of abolitionism, the works of Patrick Manning and others have provided the much-needed corrective to that biased account. They argue that the abolitionist movement was begun by the slave revolts of 1760 in Jamaica and 1791 in St. Domingue, Haiti, alongside the various democratic movements in England, the United States, and France.[27] Thus the resistance of African slaves marked the beginning of their transformation into a new people embued with a desire for freedom and dignity, the bedrock of the new world they were bent on creating.

Interestingly, with respect to the issue of slavery, there was virtually no difference between slave holding Christianity and traditional African religions. Slave traders saw no contradiction between being Christian and being engaged in the sale of human cargo. Although Christians espoused a universal doctrine that all humans were created by God, their theology did not imply the equality of all humanity. On the contrary, their refusal to acknowledge the full humanity of African peoples implied the absence of any moral issue with respect to slavery. Consequently, slave traders saw no contradiction between being Christian, on the one hand, and the buying and selling of human slaves, on the other hand. Such apparent innocence was clearly manifested in many Christian slave traders naming slave ships and slave warehouses after Jesus Christ.[28] None of this comprised a moral dilemma for them. As a matter of fact, some of our most beloved Christian hymns were composed by captains of slave ships during meditative moments on the high seas. It was only after Christians recognized the full humanity of African peoples that the seeds of abolitionism began to appear. It is curious, however, that Christianity seems not to have espoused abolitionist thought during earlier periods of the Christian era.

Nevertheless, the major difference between Christian and traditional African thought lies in this issue. The former was able to find resources within its own theology to oppose that which it had once supported. I contend that traditional African thought also contained resources which could have been utilized in support of abolitionism yet were not. Since Africans believe that the primary goal of the moral life is the preservation and enhancement of the community, a viable argument against slavery would have been the demonstration that it did not contribute to the good of the community but, instead, wrought social havoc and moral destruction on all concerned. Admittedly, such an argument would have implied some type of interdependency among tribal groups, a difficult argument to make in a context where tribal self-sufficiency was the normative mode of thinking. Suffice it to say, however, that traditional African thought was capable of developing such an argument had it been desirous of doing so. That Africans chose not to do so is also morally significant.

Nonetheless, the view that the slaves held of their slaveholders was thoroughly African. For example, as indicated above, Africans made no distinction between tribal culture and tribal religion. It was natural for them to view the one as a reflection of the other. Thus different tribal communities and their respective styles of life were thought to imply differences in the substance of their cosmologies as well as the forms of their religious devotion. Since strangers and/or enemies always represented alien ways of life, Africans believed that all such peoples had their own protective divinities. Consequently, it was virtually self-evident to African slaves that the life and religion of slaveholders (whether in Africa or elsewhere) should constitute an integrated whole. That is to say, the slaves viewed the lifestyle of their slaveholders (their trade in chattel slavery and their Christian devotion) as one consistent, systemic whole. Contrary to the opinions of many, I concluded that the first generation of African slaves in the diaspora perceived no conflict between their slaveholders' solemn devotion in Christian worship and their maintenance of chattel slavery. In their eyes, the one clearly implied the other.

Later generations of slaves, ex-slaves, and some whites discerned a resource within the New Testament that enabled them to declare a contradiction between the biblical understanding of humanity and the institution of slavery. This enabled them to reconstruct the traditional Christian understanding of humanity and, in doing so, to plant the seed for an alternative form of theological thought which became the basis for the abolitionist spirit. This new form of Christianity was rapidly embraced by the slaves, and it soon became foundational for their understanding of God and God's relation to them.

Both traditional African religion and slave holding Christianity had led them to see the cause of their enslavement as internal to themselves, that is, either as divine punishment for wrongdoing or as the destiny they received before birth. Both explanations implied fatalism, which in turn contributed to a general accommodationism as the pragmatic means for survival. In this newly discovered theological understanding of their condition, they were now able to locate the primary cause of their bondage not in themselves but in the actions of their captors. More importantly, they could now use the religion of their captors as a weapon against them. Henceforth African peoples in the diaspora and later on the continent came to a new understanding of Christianity as integrally related to their enduring struggle for freedom and dignity.

Although the slaves appropriated the formal features of their slaveholders' Christianity with respect to ritual practices, language, and symbols, they invested each of them with new meanings. Consequently, they became adept at double entendre, evidenced most clearly throughout the spirituals. For example, Howard Thurman vividly describes the way in which the slaves used heaven not only as an eschatological symbol but also as a concealed normative principle of social criticism:

> The slave had often heard his master's minister talk about heaven, the final abode of the righteous. Naturally the master regarded himself as fitting into that category. On the other hand the slave knew that *he* too was going to heaven. He reasoned, "There must be two separate heavens—no, this could not be true, because there is only one God. God cannot be divided in this way. I have it! I am having my hell now—when I die I shall have my heaven. The master is having his heaven now; when he dies he will have his hell."

The next day, chopping cotton beneath the torrid skies, the slave said to his mate—

I got shoes,
You got shoes,
All God's children got shoes,
When we get to Heaven
We're goin' to put on our shoes
An'shout allover God's Heaven.
Heaven! Heaven!

Then looking up to the big house where the master lived, he said:

But everybody talking 'bout Heaven
Ain't going there.[29]

As with many of the spirituals, this one is also a song of protest cleverly concealed in its format of double entendre. One needs to keep in mind that slave holding Christianity did, in fact, posit segregation in heaven. Hence the refrain, "Shout all over God's Heaven" subtly acknowledges no segregation there whatsoever. Other renditions of the song substitute the verb *walk* for *shout* in order to make the point all the more clear. Similarly, in addition to "I got shoes," other verses are: "I got a robe" and "I got a crown." Such images contrast immensely with the condition of slaves who characteristically had no such possessions. In fact, the context implies that these are the possessions of royalty. Thus, the slave argued accordingly: if God is sovereign and all human beings are God's children, that it should follow that all humans are heirs of sovereignty and, hence, should rightly wear shoes, robes, and crowns. Again it is easy to see the subtlety of the protest that was hidden from the slave holder though abundantly clear to the slaves.

One must not underestimate how dangerous it was to oppose slavery in any overt way. Slaves were whipped, tortured, severely maimed, and often killed for insubordination of any kind. Thus, long after they had committed themselves to their alternative form of Christianity, slaves had no public space in which to exercise a prophetic ministry by challenging slave holding Christianity. Any such attack on Christianity as it was practiced would have subjected them to the counterjudgment of being anti-Christian which, in the eyes of their owners would have confirmed their belief that the slaves were beyond the pale of morality altogether. Such a fear clearly prompted later abolitionists to exercise great care in their rhetorical utterances. Most notably, Frederick Douglass wrote an appendix to his explosive essay, "Slaveholding Religion and the Christianity of Christ," in which he denounced slaveholding religion with all the rhetorical power he could muster. But, since he assumed that normative religious and moral value inhered in the concept "Christian," he wanted to make it perfectly clear that his description of the slave master's religion as an exercise in hypocrisy and deception should in no way be confused with what he called "authentic Christianity." This distinction enabled him, however, to condemn slaveholding Christianity while affirming the Christian ideal, the actualization of which he failed to see among the slave holders:

> What I have said respecting and against religion, I mean strictly to apply to the slaveholding religion of this land, and with no possible reference to Christianity proper; for, between the Christianity of this land, and the Christianity of Christ, I recognize the widest possible difference—so wide, that to receive the one as good, pure, and holy, is of necessity to reject the other as bad, corrupt, and wicked. To be the friend of the one, is of necessity to be the enemy of the other. I love the pure, peaceable, and impartial Christianity of Christ: I therefore hate the corrupt, slaveholding, women-whippping, cradle-plundering, partial and hypocritical Christianity of this land. Indeed, I can see no reason, but the most deceitful one, for calling the religion of this land Christianity, the boldest of all frauds, and the grossest of all libels. . . .
>
> The slave auctioneer's bell and the church-going bell chime in with each other, and the bitter cries of the heart-broken slave are drowned in the religious shouts of his pious master. Revivals of religion and revivals in the slave-trade go hand in hand together. The slave prison and the church stand near each other. The clanking of fetters and the rattling of chains in the prison, and the pious psalm and solemn prayer in the church, may be heard at the same time. The dealers in the bodies and souls of men erect their stand in the presence of the pulpit, and they mutually help each other. The dealer gives his blood-stained gold to support the pulpit, and the pulpit, in return, covers his infernal business with the garb of Christianity. Here we have religion and robbery the allies of each other—devils dressed in angels' robes, and hell presenting the semblance of paradise.[30]

I have quoted the above at length because it represents one of the most profound condemnations of slave holding Christianity emanating from the nineteenth century. In my judgment, Douglass' argument is a splendid example of late-nineteenth-century Western logic in which an ideal is posited, namely, the religion of Christ, in order to demonstrate its contradictory relation to the actual practice of slave holding religion. Such an argument would have been alien to the logic implicit in the traditional cosmological thought of Douglass' African forbears. Thus, on the question of slavery, black abolitionists like Frederick Douglass stood in opposition to the shared perspectives of slave holding Christianity and traditional African religious thought. Yet on the question of African humanity Africans in the diaspora, whether slave or free, had more in common with the traditional African cosmologies than they did with slave holding Christianity because the latter denied their humanity in total while the former never denigrated the people as a species.

Finally, the African American slave experience produced a dilemma for its survivors, namely, that of forgetting and remembering. Nobel laureate Toni Morrison has described slavery as "an unspeakable horror." This was her way of explaining why the first generation of ex-slaves wanted to forget their past altogether. In fact, everyone, including the former slaveholders, felt the same way. Since the ex-slaves could see at first no redemptive reason for remembering such an evil era, there were at least two good reasons for a deliberate lack of remembrance. First, the memory itself was so painful that it tended to immobilize rather than energize the people in their search for a new life outside the house of bondage. Second, in light of a general lack of public sympathy for the condition of the ex-slaves and little sense of guilt on the part of former slaveholders, public acts of remembrance might inadvertently enable the white population to retain their memory of slavery and, more importantly, the attitudes of depravity and inferiority that they had long associated with every form of slave culture. While both reasons pertained in different ways to the internal psychological needs of the ex-slaves, the second also reflects the latter's conviction that they should do everything in their power to help their former slaveholders overcome their racial prejudices while doing nothing that might in any way be construed as contributing to the reverse. Accordingly they felt that anything that might remind whites of the conditions of slavery would not be a constructive means to their desired goal. Thus the first generation of ex-slaves did not seek to institutionalize their memory of slavery but, instead, to focus their attention on the various celebrative events commemorating their emancipation.[31] African peoples have always tended to be disinterested in remembering sorrow and pain unless it pointed to some good and the only good relative to slavery was its end.

Hence, in the aftermath of emancipation, most churches no longer thought it spiritually desirable or prudently wise to sing the spirituals for at least two reasons. First, the sorrow and suffering that they reflected seemed to be counterproductive to the demands of the present situation wherein their message of hope was thought to have been actualized. Moreover, in light of their newly acquired freedom, the spirituals no longer reflected their social condition and, consequently, they had become inadequate means for both spiritual expression and divine grace.

Since the style of African worship on the continent and in the diaspora had always been that of approaching the divine through the medium of existential needs and concerns expressed in cultural forms, the ex-slaves now found themselves in a situation that called for styles of worship reflecting their new social condition. Thus throughout the Reconstruction period they were primarily concerned with the issue of "racial uplift," with what would release them from the abyss of social degradation caused by centuries of bondage. Remembering degradation seemed a most unlikely method for achieving the desired "uplift."

Unfortunately, the enthusiasm of the ex-slaves in America for constructing a new life in freedom was crushed by the fall of Reconstruction, an event that many viewed as descent into a new slavery and, in light of that betrayal, the symbols and rhythms of many of the former slave songs once again seemed relevant for collective worship and personal devotion.[32] This, of course, was a sad commentary on the sociopolitical situation that the ex-slaves were destined to experience. With the passing of time, however, Africans in the diaspora saw the importance of historical memory and began the process of institutionalizing academic research and writing relative to their history and making it publicly available not only to future generations of blacks but to whites as well.[33] But the primary aim was never that of highlighting the evil of slavery as an end in itself but only as a means for demonstrating how the African American race survived and progressed in spite of centuries of oppression. This venture caused blacks to depart to some extent from their customary style of keeping the internal life of their community concealed from whites, a necessary survival mechanism in a hostile environment.

African and African American Views of Pluralism and Unity

Unlike Christianity and Islam, traditional African religions exhibited an enviable spirit of toleration towards different worldviews, philosophies, and religions. In large part this was due to their belief in henotheism (that is, acknowledging a pluralism of gods). Thus traditional African religions did not claim possession of universal and absolute truth and, hence, they had no warrant to prosyletize other peoples. Also, in contrast with Christianity and Islam, traditional African religions did not constitute themselves into large regional centers of authority and power. Rather, their organizational forms were decentralized and their traditions were preserved via the dynamic medium of orality rather than the more static medium of writing. All of this may contribute to the seeming preference of Africans in the diaspora for the free-church tradition whose congregational form of governance and oral extemporaneity were commensurate with the cultural traditions of Africa.

Thus the tolerance implicit in traditional African religions enabled their adaptation to new ideas. There has been no need for the birth of an "enlightenment" age and its concomitant corpus of "secular" knowledge. This does not imply, however, the absence of conflict between traditional African societies and the demands of modernity.

None of the above, however, is intended to deny the reality of African imperialism which was exercised for centuries over many tribal groups. As with all such conditions of conquest, however, traditional African religions provided spiritual reinforcement for their particular peoples, whether they were the conquerors or the conquered. Yet it is important to note also that the warrant for African imperialism neither issued from nor was contradicted by their theological understandings. Nevertheless, whenever conquest did occur, full legitimation was not achieved until the conquerors had persuaded the conquered by the interweaving of their respective cosmogonies. Basil Davidson has illustrated this vividly in his description of two separate myths of origins that are found among the Yoruba people and which depict the unmistakable amalgamation of two ancestral groups:

> In the Beginning there was Olodumare, God the archetypal Spirit. Having decided to create the world, Olodumare engendered Orishanla and sent him down to do the work. This he rapidly completed with the aid of other "archangels." Orishanla then brought mankind out of the sky. They settled at Ife: and from Ife they spread across the Earth and made it fruitful.
>
> But that is only half the story. In another large facet of Yoruba belief, it is not Orishanla who created the world at the bidding of Olodumare, but Oduduwa. Coming from somewhere far away in the east—from Arabia according to a later tradition doubtless inspired by Islam—Oduduwa then brought the Yoruba into their land, ruled them from Ife, and begat the men and women who were to rule or provide rulers for other Yoruba communities. "His eldest daughter, it is said, was the mother of the Olowu of Owu; another was the mother of the Alaketu of Ketu. One son became the Oba of Benin, another the Alake of Ake, another the Onisabe of Sabe, another the Alafin of Oyo."[34]

According to the Oduduwa tradition, Orishanla did receive the initial commission from God. But through an accident he forfeited it to Oduduwa, who thus became the creator of the earth. In this way the incoming Oduduwa tradition became woven with the one found among the population whom the newcomers discovered. Similarly, the priests of the Orishanla tradition offer a compensatory claim. They argue that even though Oduduwa supplanted Orishanla in creating the earth, he was not able to make it function well, so Olodumare had to send Orishanla to correct the mistakes and reestablish order.

Although these mythological events happened centuries ago, the spiritual clash between the two peoples was so intense that it has been kept vigorously alive down to the present day.[35] Similar examples abound throughout the African continent. These myths not only legitimate the people's right to exist but they constitute the grounds for political order, sacred rituals, and moral virtues.

Although diversity was generally tolerated on the continent, Africa produced no moral warrants against African imperialism *per se.* Rather, like much of the rest of the world, African societies lived by the rule that *might* determined *right.* Thus, in the event that a group could not protect itself from an encroaching enemy, it had a limited number of choices, among which were the following: (1) to ally with others whose situation is similar; (2) to pay tribute to a more powerful group for protection; (3) to make a stand against the enemy and risk being overrun. Thus peaceful means of effecting and preserving unity among diverse tribal societies always constituted a major political problem.

Captive peoples, far removed from their homeland, inevitably long for the security of family and the larger community. African slaves in the diaspora were no exception. As long as they retained specific memories of their former life in Africa, nostalgia was a common experience for them. The loss of such memory, however, destroyed the retrospective longing. Hence, the eventual loss of their native languages, beliefs, and customs constituted the loss of tribal specificity, which was tantamount to the loss of primary identity. For Africans such a loss constituted the most devastating aspect of slavery because it effected an irrevocable break with their homeland.

As a substitute for the loss of tribal specificity, Africans in the diaspora gradually developed a more generalized identity based on the name of the African continent. As a matter of fact, the term *Africa* is virtually a European construct used to designate a continental land mass inhabited by a particular race of people with whom they had engaged in a massive trade of goods and humans for many centuries. Although many Africans in the diaspora eventually believed most of the contemporary pejorative attitudes about Africans as uncivilized, idolatrous, savage-like, cannibalistic, they nevertheless reinterpreted the term for themselves and gave it transcendent meaning by elevating it to the symbolic order of discourse. By doing so they expressed their imaginative consciousness so well that the results may well be considered one of their most creative achievements. This symbolization of Africa by Africans in the diaspora enabled them to take possession of their own reality and in so doing, they succeeded in thwarting what Charles Long calls their oppressor's "linguistic conquest."[36]

There can be no literal definitions of symbols because the latter transcend their literal forms. That is to say, symbols point to realms of meaning beyond themselves. Accordingly, the symbol Africa integrated the more than 2000 tribal communities on the continent into a transcendent unity. As a peculiar construct of the African diaspora the term virtually became a sacred symbol for all succeeding generations of Africans in the diaspora. Charles Long aptly describes how this symbol functioned religiously for African slaves:

> So even if they had no conscious memory of Africa, the image of Africa played an enormous part in the religion of the blacks. The image of Africa, as image related to historical beginnings, has been one of the primordial religious images of great significance. It constitutes the religious revalorization of the land, a place where the natural and ordinary gestures of the blacks were and could be authenticated. In this connection, one can trace almost every nationalistic movement among the blacks and find Africa to be the dominating and guiding image. Even among religious groups not strongly nationalistic, the image of Africa or Ethiopia still has relevance. This is present in such diverse figures as Richard Allen, who organized the African Methodist Episcopal Church in the late eighteenth century, through Martin Delaney in the late nineteenth century, and then again in Marcus Garvey's "Back to Africa Movement" of the immediate post-World War I period, and finally in the taking up of this issue again among black leaders of the present time.[37]

Thus the basic struggle against the dehumanization process of slavery took place in the consciousness of the African slaves. In the midst of their suffering they forged new structures of religious meaning, social identity, cultural expression, and moral value. Their creative consciousness was typified in their loyalty and devotion to Africa as a transcendent symbol. This achievement marked a veritable watershed in their moral struggle against racial oppression: a struggle fueled by the human impulse to preserve and enhance its own humanity. The symbol Africa represented the continuity of a people with their past, the specific content of which was rapidly disappearing from their consciousness. Yet the symbol implied *community,* the paramount moral and religious value among African peoples. Thus African Methodists and African Baptists and others used the prefix *African* to denote transformative and foundational meaning and power. Holloway claims that from the eighteenth century through the first third of the nineteenth century, free blacks used the prefix regularly for their religious and educational institutions to provide "a sense of cultural integrity and a link to their African heritage." Holloway provides a number of concrete examples of this practice:

> The first black religious organization established in Savannah in 1787 was the First African Baptist Church. The second oldest black denomination in North America, founded in 1787, was the African Methodist Episcopal. In 1806 blacks constructed the first African Meeting House in Boston. This pattern is also seen in such names as African Free School, African Clarkson Society, African Dorcas Society, Children of Africa, and Sons of Africa. The first mutual beneficial societies that had direct roots in African secret societies called themselves African as late as 1841. One such society was the New York African Society for Mutual Relief.[38]

Clearly, for a long while "Africa" was viewed positively by blacks and negatively by their white oppressors. Holloway carefully points out, however, that the black leadership class ceased identifying themselves as Africans from the 1830s through to the end of the century so as not to encourage the colonizationists bent on sending them back to Africa.[39] Nevertheless, prior to that period and later, identification with Africa enabled the slaves to maintain their dignity and worth as a people. It would be an understatement to say that in the context of slavery, the maintenance and promotion of this sense of self-worth could only be carried out in clandestine ways.

Yet, as we have argued above, the structural elements of African tribal identity became viable vehicles for new cultural content in the diaspora. As we have seen, the symbol Africa became the bearer of their idealized vision of community. Gradually, the diversity of tribal pantheons and the plurality of divinities within each of them were replaced by their reinterpreted version of the triune Christian God. Further, after they had forgotten the names of their traditional ancestors, biblical ancestors were adopted as their own.

Thus the form and function of the African pantheon continue in African American Christianity with Christian substance replacing the African content. In both contexts the supreme deity defined moral standards and virtues and communicated them to the people through divine intermediaries.

As we have seen above, this change of identity from traditional African religionists to African American Christians was a complex process that took place very gradually and was completed at a considerable price, namely, the loss of tribal specificity due to the cruel proscriptions of slavery. Contrary to the thinking of many African Americans, however, the concept of race was neither, then nor now, an adequate principle of unity for all African peoples everywhere.

Slaveholders identified their African slaves by the category of race, which they described both stereotypically and pejoratively. The slaves also employed the category of race in describing their own collective identity though they embued it with positive value. In their minds they were proud to be Africans and they worked hard to instill a sense of dignity and worth in themselves. From that standpoint, Africans who rejected such a valorization of the race rejected themselves, and self-hatred became the primary evidence of their pathological condition.[40]

Thus two contrary understandings of African peoples waged battle against each other: the one negative and the other positive. The former emanated from slaveholders, the latter from the slaves themselves. It would be an understatement to say that the maintenance and preservation of the latter viewpoint could only take place within the concealed confines of the African race.

Wholly repulsed by racism, African Americans made the term *race* into a prophetic principle of social change. That is to say, whenever they used the term *race, African, Negro, Colored,* they were reconstituting themselves into a new tribal unity in which they sought to preserve their dignity and self-respect, even though the majority population treated them as pariahs. While racism was identical with the principle of division and oppression, African Americans united themselves under the principle of "race" and in many and varied indirect ways they established the groundwork for continuous opposition to racism.

The strength of social cohesion depends on the degree to which the people truly desire and need a separate collective identity. Ambiguity on this point renders the identity precarious and the unity ethereal. The strength of the community's unity depends on the power of myths, customs, and rituals that are expressive of their collective self-understanding and capable of inspiring their loyalty to the community's primary cause.

As the specificity of tribal diversity was replaced by the principle of racial unity, so the diversity of tribal pantheons and the plurality of divinities within each of them were gradually replaced by the African appropriation of the Christian God and the biblical ancestors. As discussed above, the constructive appropriation of Christian theology by African slaves implied a radical change of perspective from that of their slaveholders.

It must be noted further that during the first century and one-half of slavery Africans rejected Christianity because they considered it to be the religion of their slaveholders and hence oppositional to their well-being. This line of thought was deeply rooted in the African understanding that a people's religion is synonymous with their way of life. Thus, insofar as Christianity was thought to be expressive of the slaveholder's way of life, slaves could never embrace it as their own.

We must make it clear, however, that the African's rejection of all forms of racism implied their affirmation of the humanity of their oppressors. This stemmed from their view of the supreme deity as creator of one human species. Yet in every period some Africans in the diaspora maintained their view of a parochial (tribal) deity. This has been evidenced in various nationalist movements that have regularly emerged in every generation. Further evidence of this phenomenon can be seen in the African traditions of conjure, voodoo, witchcraft, and sorcery, which have a continuing presence throughout the diaspora.

Thus as the old tribal memory of African slaves grew dimmer and dimmer with each succeeding generation, the structure of their traditional consciousness did not perish. Rather, it was filled with new substance, carefully selected from their new environment and reinterpreted in order to give meaning to their lives. We call this process a renewed "African ethos," which exhibited structural elements from the continent and substantive materials from the American experience. This African ethos expressed itself primarily in music, song, folklore, styles of leadership, liturgical devotion, and a variety of rituals. In each of these we encounter continuities and discontinuities with traditional African thought and practice. Clearly, the cultural continuities were tribally nonspecific and the discontinuities evidence the African ingenuity in constructing a new identity that linked African and Euro-American elements into a new cultural amalgam. The complexity of that task varied from place to place. In the Caribbean, Brazil, and elsewhere in Latin America the circumstances of migration and the concentration of more homogenized populations enabled greater continuity of specific tribal cultures than occurred in North America. In the latter, deliberate attention was given to the diversification of slave populations and severe proscriptions were continually in force against African cultural practices. Nevertheless, in spite of it all, Africans constructed new systems of cultural value, religious meaning, and moral significance that constituted an amalgam of Euro-American forms and African meanings.

4

FAMILY

The Locus of Moral Development

The African Family: Typical Features of Moral Significance

Although there are many variations in African family life, certain features pertain to all of them. The most prevalent of these is the family's primacy in the spheres of social reality and personal identity. Unlike the so-called nuclear family in Western societies, the African family is a large, closely knit community of blood relatives that is constitutive of the life and destiny of each of its members. In short, kinship constitutes the paramount social reality for all African peoples. John Mbiti expresses it well:

> Kinship is reckoned through blood and betrothal (engagement and marriage). It is kinship which controls social relationships between people in a given community: it governs marital customs and regulations, it determines the behaviour of one individual towards another. Indeed, this sense of kinship binds together the entire life of the "tribe," and is even extended to cover animals, plants and non-living objects through the "totemic" system. Almost all the concepts connected with human relationship can be understood and interpreted through the kinship system. This it is which largely governs the behaviour, thinking and whole life of the individual in the society of which he is a member.[1]

In fact, some contend that kinship constitutes the whole of African tribal community, since all the people are believed to be descended from a common ancestor who long ago lived in their territory, married, produced children, and lives now in the spirit world. Also, in traditional

African villages almost everyone was blood related. Then and now all elderly men and women, including uncles and aunts, were called father and mother; while those closer to one's own age were called brothers and sisters. Once kinship relationships were established, all concerned were duty-bound to accept the corresponding behaviors as prescribed by tradition. Thus the village functioned as one large family, a pattern that continues to the present day not only in villages but also among friends and associates in urban centers. As a consequence, African cities appear to be much less impersonal than their Western counterparts. In polygynous families, children had many mothers, grandparents, aunts, uncles, cousins, and older siblings—all actively engaged in their daily nurture and training. Thus it is not an exaggeration to say that older family members exercised authority over all younger members and assumed responsibility for their well-being in every possible way. Sociologists Diane Kayongo-Male and Philista Onyango aptly describe the importance of kinship and the nature of familial reciprocity implied by such kinship relations:

> The most significant feature of African family life is probably the *importance of the larger kin group* beyond the nuclear family. Inheritance was commonly the communal variety wherein the entire kin group owns the land. In many parts of the continent bridewealth is still paid to the family of the bride, with the resulting marriage linking two families rather than simply the bride and the groom. Conflicts between husband and wife were mediated by relatives instead of being sorted out privately by the couple.
>
> Members of the extended family still have a lot of say about the marriages of younger relatives. These family members are also linked in strong reciprocal aid relationships which entail complex rights and responsibilities. Households in urban areas have extended kin members in residence for years. The relatives may or may not be contributing financially or in terms of helping in the division of family labour, yet they are allowed to remain. Children may go to live with distant relatives for schooling or special training courses. Relatives may also have much influence over the decisions of the couple.[2]

Anyone who has lived with a contemporary African family for any period of time can easily discern the adequacy of the above description of the most typical features of the African family. Clearly, it is not natural for Africans to distance any of their blood relatives from the center of their family. Consequently, when traveling in Europe or America, they are invariably startled whenever they are asked the question whether they brought their family with them. On such occasions they must quickly make the necessary mental adjustment to a different structure of meaning. It is also well-known that many African students studying abroad continue to assume their reciprocal responsibilities by sharing portions of their meager incomes with family members back home. Not to do so could jeopardize their status in the family.

The African family is therefore the natural extension of blood lines held together by the ordinary functions of family life, in which each member shares responsibilities and obligations. The communal nature of the African family affects all relationships within that sphere. Time and again I have been startled by hearing Nigerians, Ghanaians, Kenyans, Malawians, South Africans, and others use the expression *our wife* when referring to the spouse of a brother, uncle, or cousin. Since the term *wife* connotes an exclusively private relationship in our Western context, the phrase *my wife* or *his wife* is typically used, while the possessive plural adjective *our* is never employed. Thus, whenever we encounter Africans using the phrase *our wife,* we should hasten to remind ourselves that along with incest, conjugal relations between in-laws have always been taboo throughout Africa excepting in the cases of so-called levirate marriages.[3] Thus, like the expression *our brother* or *our sister,* the phrase *our wife* is not intended to convey any sexual connotations whatsoever. The phrase merely connotes familial belonging, which is the primary social reality for all members. Thus *our wife* is as appropriate as *our sister, our brother, our mother,* etc. It signifies that the relationship has been thoroughly incorporated into the family membership. Similarly, a family member may well refer to his niece or nephew as "my" daughter or "my" son.

Throughout Africa, procreation has always been viewed as the primary purpose of marriage. From time immemorial childless marriages have been regarded as misfortunes because children are the necessary agents for maintaining the link between the ancestors and the living family. As Kayongo-Male and Onyango indicate, "The children would eventually be in charge of remembering the dead through maintenance of family shrines or in other ways."[4] Since Africans view children as God's gifts to the family, their absence implies God's punishment for some kind of wrongdoing that requires appropriate expiation under the direction of professional priests, priestesses, diviners, or others. A childless marriage constitutes a major moral and spiritual problem for all concerned. Traditionally the family would have assumed that the woman was barren; hence the man would have been pressed to take a second wife. Under such circumstances all viewed polygyny as fully justified. Similarly,

Africans have also appealed to the same cultural values to justify levirate marriage as substitutes for male impotency or infertility. With respect to polygyny, however, it is important to note that in his book written for African Christian youth, John S. Mbiti typifies the position of African clergy in arguing that while he, personally, views monogamy to be the preferred marital state over polygyny, he is not prepared to condemn the latter because it is a timeless institution that provides a necessary corrective for a crucial problem. Since the institution can be abused, however, he advocates the following conditions for its appropriate use:

> We face the fact that a number of men who, at one point are members of Churches that forbid polygamy, do nevertheless go ahead and marry a second or third wife. . . . If the man marries another wife for the sole reason that his first wife is medically proven to be barren and she agrees to his marrying another wife, then the marriage should be given the blessing of the Church and the wedding performed in the Church. It is out of a genuine, understandable, and good cause that he gets married, otherwise, under African situations of life and attitudes, the monogamous marriage in which his wife is barren, is bound to be a failure and a miserable relationship. Of course, a childless marriage could work and be a happy one, but children in African marriages are an absolute necessity and a couple without them is simply miserable.[5]

Under the conditions Mbiti describes, one can rightly ask about the extent to which the barren wife has any real freedom of choice in the matter. Although Christian missionaries clearly played havoc with the African family by condemning polygyny outright and directing polygynous converts to forsake their marriages as a condition for baptism, the apologists for polygyny seem always to be African men. Further, in their defense of the institution virtually no attention is given to the implied condemnation of the barren woman. Further still, the voices of African women on this subject are largely silent. Only a few have begun speaking out against the subject and some with vehemence.[6]

Another feature of the African family is the general disdain Africans have for the public display of physical affection between men and women. Kayongo-Male and Onyango assert:

> This is one of the more resilient features of African family life. Whether in front of friends, relatives or children, husband and wife are not supposed to express their affection for each other. In a way, affection is expressed through respect and caring for each other's needs in subtle ways. However, holding hands or kissing in public are frowned upon.[7]

It is a curious fact that although African social life is characterized by much joviality in the form of dance, music, and song, personal feelings for one another are rarely expressed apart from appropriate communal contexts. Embracing one another physically even after a long absence is not typically "African," and those who do so reveal their own adaptation to Western customs. In traditional African societies, deference to all authority including that of parents implied physical acts of kneeling and bowing before them, never embracing or kissing them. It is important to note, however, that gestures of kneeling, bowing, or even prostrating one's body on the ground, do not demean the doer. The gesture honors the other as one's superior and, in doing so, one gains self-respect. None has described the dignity of the act so well as David Livingstone, whom DuBois quotes at length on the subject of "true African dignity":

> When Ilifian men or women salute each other, be it with a plain and easy curtsey (which is here the simplest form adopted), or kneeling down, or throwing oneself upon the ground, or kissing the dust with one's forehead, no matter which, there is yet a deliberateness, a majesty, a dignity, a devoted earnestness in the manner of its doing, which brings to light with every gesture, with every fold of clothing, the deep significance and essential import of every single action. Everyone may, without too greatly straining his attention, notice the very striking precision and weight with which the upper and lower native classes observe these niceties of intercourse.[8]

Contrary to the opinions of many, Africans did not learn the gesture of kneeling and bowing from their colonial masters but, rather, from deep within the heart of their own traditions from which they learned to respect those who exercised authority over them with appropriate acts of bodily submission in much the same way as Europeans greet royalty. Even among peers Africans display very little physical contact. More often than not, they are likely to express their personal feelings for the other by providing a communal celebration in his/her honor. Thus, hosting a communal reception whenever the occasion merits enhances the lives of all rather than the two alone. All who have visited Africa can testify to the splendid hospitality extended to them as honorees at such communal celebrations.

Not only do Africans define themselves in terms of their family. More specifically, they do so in accordance with their place in the family which, like all social reality in Africa, is hierarchically ordered from the oldest living member to the youngest. As Mbiti clearly states, the familial hierarchy is merely an extension of the cosmological order that begins with God and extends through the tribal authorities down to the youngest member of the family:

> In human relationships there is emphasis on the concept of hierarchy based partly on age and partly on status. In practice this amounts to a ladder ranging from God to the youngest child. God is the creator and hence the parent of mankind, and holds the highest position so that He is the final point of reference and appeal. Beneath Him are the divinities and spirits, which are more powerful than man and some of which were founders and forefathers of different societies. Next come the living-dead, the more important ones being those who were full human beings by virtue of going through the initiation rites, getting married and raising children. Among human beings the hierarchy includes kings, rulers, rainmakers, priests, diviners, medicine-men, elders in each household, parents, older brothers and sisters, and finally the youngest members of the community. Authority is recognized as increasing from the youngest child to the highest Being. As for the individual, the highest authority is the community of which he is a corporate member.[9]

Since patriarchal rule in the family is the norm throughout Africa, the eldest son in each generation has a place of primacy among all his siblings. In a similar way age differentiates authority among daughters as well. Yet, since inheritance occurs through the male lines of descent, however, women in patriarchal societies inherit indirectly through their sons who, incidently, are their insurance for material security, especially in widowhood. This constitutes one of the most important explanations for the strong desire of women to bear sons even in matrilineal[10] societies where the inheritance of daughters comes through their maternal uncles.[11]

As observed earlier, kingship represented the authoritative moral, political, and religious center of the traditional African tribal community. As the primary link between the tribal community and the world of spirit, the king served as royal priest by maintaining ritual faithfulness at the altars of the tribal ancestors and divinities. In short, the king functioned as patriarch and priest of all the people. Through his faithful acts of intercession, he sought both their material well-being and their protection from evil forces.

In African traditional societies, the role of the father in the family was analogous to that of the king. Like the latter, the former also bore similar responsibilities for the family's well-being economically, socially and spiritually. As the King was the intermediary between the tribal community and the realm of spirit, so the father was the chief mediator between the family and its ancestral spirits. Clearly the status of patriarchal primacy befell the oldest male member of the family, who alone had the authority to approach the ancestral spirits directly. Thus the father of the household was the eldest male member whose authority was passed on to his eldest son, who in turn could not exercise that authority until his own father had become an ancestor.

The African familial patriarch is the supreme judge over all matters pertaining to the family's well-being even though much delegation of authority inevitably occurs, chiefly through the division of domestic labor. While called upon to settle domestic disputes, the patriarch was often expected to assist in judging more serious conflicts in the larger community. In recent years patriarchal rule has come under attack by progressive African women scholars who view the institution as the major impediment to all matters concerning gender equality.

As with the tribe itself, the roots of the African family lie in the paramount ancestor who is believed to take an active interest in the family's well-being. Obviously, the ancestor has enormous powers since he[12] is no longer limited by the conditions of mortality. Idowu aptly describes the function of the familial ancestor:

> The ancestor is believed to take an active interest in the family or community and his power over it is now considerably increased as he is no longer restricted by earthly conditions. Matters affecting the family or the community are thus referred to him for sanction or judgment. Therefore, he is naturally brought into the picture as a superintending spirit who gives approval to any proposals or actions which make for the well-being of the community, and shows displeasure at anything which may tend to disrupt it. Thus, in a sense, but only in that sense, he is concerned with the effective discharge of moral obligations.[13]

Hence families have always made offerings of food and libations to the so-called living dead because they are regarded as an integral part of the family and function as the latter's spiritual rulers and protectors. "The food and libation so offered are tokens of the fellowship, communion, remembrance, respect and hospitality, being extended to those who are the immediate pillars or roots of the family. The living-dead solidify and mystically bind together the whole family."[14] Accordingly, it is a moving experience to be at an African wedding and to observe the great reverence with which the blessings of the ancestors are requested through the libations and petitions extended to them.

Africans take great care in teaching their genealogies to their children in order to instill in them a profound sense of familial belonging and a deep pride in their heritage, both of which aid in inculcating in them the sacred obligation to extend the family line. In addition to the living members of the family and their ancestors, the African family also includes those who are not yet born, those whom Mbiti says "are still in the loins of the living." Thus, in preparation for the unborn to become born, parents participate fully in the marriage arrangements of their children in order to extend the family and to enable the unborn to see the light of day. Obviously, such widespread understandings of marriage and procreation imply strong opposition to artificial birth-control methods and deliberate abortions.

African marriages are family affairs and as such the parents play an integral role in all the negotiations related to them. In traditional societies the man and woman had very little to say about the matter. In modern times they participate more fully yet they leave much of the process in the hands of their parents not only because of their great respect for the wisdom of age and experience but also because they acknowledge that African marriages are much more than the union of two persons. Rather, marriage is the union of two families who are contractually bound for the indefinite future through the dowry or "bridewealth" paid by the groom's family to the bride's family. Undoubtedly, the act of marrying is one of the most sacred activities in life, as Mbiti says:

> For African peoples, marriage is the focus of existence. It is the point where all the members of a given community meet: the departed, the living and those yet to be born. All the dimensions of time meet here, and the whole drama of history is repeated, renewed and revitalized . . . . marriage is a duty, a requirement from the corporate society, and a rhythm of life in which everyone must participate. Otherwise, he who does not participate in it is a curse to the community, he is a rebel and a law-breaker, he is not only abnormal but "under-human." Failure to get married under normal circumstances means that the person concerned has rejected society and society rejects him in return.[15]

Marriage is integrally tied up with the whole cosmological scheme. As we have seen, the living dead continue life in the spiritual realm as long as they have descendents who remember them and pour out libations to them. When that memory terminates it can be rightly said that the ancestor has fully died. Similarly, those who have no children are potentially dead. As Mbiti says, "A person who, therefore, has no descendents in effect quenches the fire of life, and becomes forever dead since his line of physical continuation is blocked if he does not get married and bear children."[16]

In its procreative functions marriage is the gateway to the life cycle, which is marked by the events of birth, naming, puberty, marriage, and transition to the world of ancestral spirit. Thus, the life cycle binds together the spiritual and the historical realms of life. Appropriate ceremonies and rituals are performed at each turning point along the way in order to preserve harmony throughout the cosmological order.

As already indicated, hierarchical patterns characterize all African relationships from the realm of the spirits through the royal court to all social institutions, including the family. In each sphere harmony of relationships constitutes the nature of the good that is desired by all. Harmony within hierarchy is achieved only by each actor knowing his or her status, functions, and responsibilities in the scheme of things and, above all, taking care to avoid insubordination. Unquestioned loyalty and obedience to legitimate authority are taken-for-granted moral virtues. Yet at every level, from kingship to sibling rivalry, many checks and balances are designed to ensure justice and prevent injustice for all concerned. As with all hierarchical orders, however, the effectiveness of appeals are minimal because the biases implicit in appellate procedures tend to favor those in authority. Perhaps the major deterrent to injustice is the knowledge that one's wrong acts can anger the spirits and thereby bring disaster not only to oneself but to the entire community.

The hierarchical structure of the African family is based on age and authority is distributed accordingly. That is to say, the eldest living member of the family is the highest authority. According to Mbiti's understanding of time, that person has the longest *sasa;* hence he or she is closest to the ancestors, having known them while they were still alive. African children are taught from their earliest days to respect all their elders and to give the highest honor to the eldest of all. Unlike in the Western world, one feels no diminution of status in Africa by virtue of growing old. On the contrary, one's status increases with age. Since there is no such thing as the nuclear family divorced from the extended family, parents feel no shame or embarrassment in being cared for by their children nor do the children view such a circumstance as an unwarranted imposition. Rather, it is their duty and responsibility, which they affirm as part of being a member of the family. Even among children it is the duty of the older ones to assume responsibility for the younger ones and for neither to be found wanting in carrying out their respective duties and obligations toward each other. Since there is no equality apart from age groups, each person is brought up significantly related to his or her age group. Only in that context does the individual experience equality. But the inequality of hierarchy does not imply injustice as long as trust exists among those who interact with one another and as long as all share a common dedication to the paramount value of maintaining harmony within the community.

The various duties and responsibilities of family life imply a definite agenda for moral development, which begins at an early age. As a result, by the time children are seven or eight years old their socialization is well under way as they are trained in specific responsibilities and duties pertaining to family life. This training reaches a climax during the rites of puberty, and the training continues for the rest of their lives through the symbiotic activities of the home, school, age group, and various other associations.

The ethical systems of Africans tend to be covenantal. That is to say, all relations between persons as well as those with the spiritual realm are covenantal in nature. In fact, the relationships are reciprocal in that each party is bound to the other by bilateral obligations. Idowu describes covenant in the following way:

> In the ethical system of the Yoruba, covenant plays an important role. In fact, the whole of person-to-person, and divinity-to-person, relations have their basis largely in covenants. The covenant between person and person is usually a parity covenant in that it is "reciprocal—that is, both parties bind themselves to each other by bilateral obligations . . . . It is believed that to be trusted by a friend, to be bosom friends, to eat together, or to be received hospitably as a guest, is to enter into a covenant which involves moral obligations. A covenant between two parties means, negatively, that they must think or do no evil against each other's body or estate, and positively, that they must co-operate in active good deeds towards each other in every way.[17]

In all their relationships Africans assume a reciprocity of responsibilities and duties determined, in large part, by traditional understandings, beliefs, and practices. Such responsibilities and duties were exercised within a context that bestowed primary value on activities of constituting, reconstituting, preserving, and enhancing the community, which in turn constituted, reconstituted, preserved, and enhanced the lives of all. Like all principles of action, this principle of reciprocity was not abstracted from the concrete relation. Being relative to the relation itself, the principle could not be set in motion apart from an accurate assessment of the status of each person in the relationship. For example, whenever two persons of the same tribal group met, it was necessary for them to converse with each other in order to determine who was senior and who was junior. The answer to that question defined the relationship and determined who should take initiative in relation to the other. Once that question had been settled the corresponding responsibilities and duties became clear.

Being of higher or lower status was not a pejorative judgment but an empirical fact which, in many cases, was invariable. This structure pertained to both primary and secondary associations. For example, age was and continues to be a natural principle of differentiation among African peoples; that is, in the order of social status elderly persons were prior to younger people. Similarly, older siblings had a place of primacy over the younger ones.

Persons of higher status in a relationship could therefore initiate action towards persons of lower status but, as a rule, not the reverse. If the latter wished to approach the former, he or she would need to do so very subtly. Usually the help of a mediator (someone of higher status than the one to be approached) was needed to intervene and seize the initiative on his or her behalf. Further, it was assumed not only that the person of higher social status would be the initiator of action towards the other but also that the former would always act in a morally responsible manner, in such a way as to ensure communal harmony. Thus, in the African context, it was assumed that all actions by persons of higher social status toward those of lower status were justified since it was thought that wrongdoing could not originate from the top, only from below. Such is true of most hierarchies. Family disputes were settled in much the same fashion as disputes were settled elsewhere in the tribal community. Some person in authority would adjudicate the case after hearing both sides of the dispute and then render a decision.

The principle of reciprocity operative in all African relationships pertained primarily to the relations between persons and only secondarily to the possible objects of exchange. This can be seen most clearly in the traditional African marketplace, which has always required immense amounts of time to effect a sale since the issue at stake was never solely the buying and selling of commodities abstracted from the relationship between the buyer and the seller. Rather, serious bargaining either constituted or reconstituted a relationship between the two. Its aim was always to effect an outcome that would be pleasing to both and ensure an ongoing relationship between the two.

Africans express their goodwill through the giving of gifts. Almost any encounter may present such an occasion. Yet Africans feel under no moral obligation, however, to extend their benevolence to people outside their own communal context. Whenever they choose to do so they must first of all grant honorary family status to the outsider and then respond accordingly. This is vividly evidenced in the act of receiving visitors. For example, traditionally, the Yorubas expressed this desire in the form of a welcoming ceremony which centered around the breaking and sharing of the cola nut. The host would break the cola nut and pass it around to those assembled, each of whom would take a piece. After all had been served they would eat together. The act of eating together signified goodwill on the part of all and was a sign of genuine harmony. With the context so defined the relationship could precede accordingly. Some say that the guest is virtually made an honorary member of the family and, depending on his or her status elsewhere, assumes similar status in that context. This welcoming ritual of goodwill is experienced more intensely in the common meal, where everyone present eats from a common dish.

Idowu argues that good character is the culmination of Yoruba morality. He claims that good character alone separates humans from the lower animals. Apart from good character persons do not exist. What appears is merely the empty shell of a person. Thus moral training is the primary responsibility of the family, which it undertakes in association with other symbiotic associations, not least being the sacred diviners and oracles on whose teachings Idowu's argument is based.[18]

Good character is known and praised by the community at large. Character constitutes a person's reputation, which is his or her most precious asset because reputation connotes the moral quality of one's life. In traditional societies evil people were ostracized because they had betrayed their right of membership. Accordingly, Idowu lists the following elements of good character: (1) chastity before marriage on the part of the woman, (2) hospitality, (3) kindness involving generosity, (4) retributive justice, (5) truth telling and rectitude, (6) honesty, (7) covenantal faithfulness, (8) honor and respect for the elderly.[19]

Although Idowu's aim was to list and describe the traditional moral virtues of the Yoruba people alone, he has in fact mapped the moral universe of all traditional African societies. Implied in his analysis and clearly observed everywhere is the deep sense of responsibility the family assumes in training its children in the normative traditions and customs of the community. Indeed, the family is held responsible for the moral recalcitrance of its members. In earlier times, those who persisted in disobeying the laws and rules of the community were banished from the family and the tribal community. In all of these matters, a common moral universe underlies Africa's many diverse cultures.

The African American Family: Typical Features of Moral Significance

Let me make it clear in the beginning of this section that it is not my intention to present a sociology of the contemporary African American family. Rather, as a social ethicist in quest for the continuity of moral and religious values among African peoples, my purpose is to describe how the value of African family life was preserved throughout slavery and how it continues to be the primary basis for all moral and religious development in the African American community. The various societal conditions presently threatening its ongoing life lie beyond the purpose of this inquiry.

The devastating experience of slavery indelibly bruised the consciousness of Africans throughout the diaspora. By no fault of their own, they had been permanently uprooted from the security of their communal and familial belonging and exposed to an alien environment of humiliation and deprivation. Given the centrality of community in their lives, no one can possibly imagine the intense pain they must have experienced in being cut off from their tribal solidarity and familial identity. Yet, in this abysmal cauldron of hatred and abuse, the slaves gradually built their own culture of meaning and value that expressed the moral and religious strivings of their souls.

Undoubtedly the conditions of slavery nullified the structural arrangements for viable family life. Viewed and treated as property, slaves were afforded none of the conditions that contributed to the moral development of human beings. Rather, their entire life was proscribed by the arbitrary dictates and odious interests of their owners. Slave marriages were generally disallowed and even when permitted they had no standing in civil law. Further, married slaves had no self-determining space even in the slave quarters. Both partners were the legal property of their owners, as were their children and, as such, their owners could do with them as they pleased. Accordingly, if allowed to live together, their life in the slave quarters was respected no more than that of the other livestock. Either they themselves or their children could be separated, brutally beat, sexually abused, sold, or even killed at any time. The scope and intensity of the brutality are almost inconceivable. That which had been the most sacred institution in African life, marriage, had become wholly desecrated by the ravages of slavery. Yet, even under these inhuman circumstances, African slaves found ways to preserve many of their family values and, in doing so, they succeeded in retaining their humanity.

Certainly the argument that the slaves preserved many important features of their African moral ethos contradicts that of the prominent sociologist E. Franklin Frazier. His influential position, set forth in his pioneering study, *The Negro Family in the United States,*[20] claimed that no significant measure of African culture survived the experience of slavery. Contrary to his analysis, I contend that in preserving their humanity under the most threatening conditions imaginable, African slaves maintained in their consciousness the most fundamental values of family life in which they had been nurtured prior to their capture, namely:

(1) the natural cohesion of blood relatives,
(2) the undying presence of maternal bonding,
(3) deep respect for the practical wisdom of the elderly,
(4) the power of the elderly to bless or curse,
(5) deference of the younger to the older siblings and the responsibility of the latter for the former,
(6) unquestioned obedience to the authority of parents and the elderly,
(7) a communal ethos of generosity and unselfishness, and
(8) belief in life after death and the reunion of the entire family with God in the spirit world.

All of these values were deeply rooted in traditional African cultural beliefs and practices. The conditions of bondage failed to erase them from their consciousness. Herbert G. Gutman's important sociological study[21] of the slave family provides support for this thesis by showing that, in spite of everything else, a high degree of intergenerational family relationships did occur during slavery. This finding has made all the difference in our understanding of the slave family. In fact, it marks a veritable watershed in the history and sociology of the African American family. Further, it sharply contradicts the findings of all previous studies of the subject. Since the intergenerational feature is essential for the transmission of family values from one generation to the next, Gutman provides adequate evidence to support the view that slaves were able to transmit their own peculiar family values to succeeding generations. His study further adds plausibility to our argument that the moral values of the slaves were not rooted in the moral code that existed between the slave-owner and the slave. Instead, the slaves brought their moral character with them into slavery as indelible evidence of their humanity. The process of adaptation to this alien environment implied syncretizing their own values with those encountered in this alien context. Gutman summarizes the process well:

> But a social process of "creolization" (the transformation of the African into the Afro-American) was already well under way by the time the federal Constitution was adopted and before the invention of the cotton gin. Culture formation among the slaves, which began before the War for Independence and well before the plantation system spread from the Upper to the Lower South, blended together African and Anglo-American cultural beliefs and social practices, mediated through the harsh institution of enslavement. Most slaves involved in the spread of the plantation system and of the developing Afro-American culture over the entire South in the six decades prior to the Civil War were the children and the grandchildren of that adaptive eighteenth-century slave culture, a culture neither African nor American but genuinely Afro-American.[22]

Clearly, Gutman's very innovative and helpful findings center on the nature of Afro-American family values as an amalgam of African and American elements, an adaptational process that he claims was largely completed by the time of the War for Independence, a claim he bases on statistics provided by Philip D. Curtin. The latter argued that over half of all the slaves in North America had arrived by that time, when they had undergone what Richard Hofstadter called a "reluctant adaptation."[23] After citing the comment of Roger Bastide that "To make life possible . . . . they hammered out a new cultural pattern of their own, shaping it in response to the demands of their new environment," Gutman writes:

> That happened everywhere and meant developing standards for perceiving, believing, evaluating, and acting—in short, ordering new experiences that drew upon but could not replicate old cultures. Adaptation for freshly enslaved Africans involved a violent detachment from older cultures, and the emergence of a new culture.[24]

Gutman proceeds to quote C.L. James in the following statement:

> The slave . . . brought himself; he brought with him the content of his mind, his memory. He thought in the logic and language of his people. He recognized as socially significant that which he had been taught to see and comprehend . . . . He valued that which his previous life had taught him to value; he feared that which he feared in Africa.[25]

Most importantly, Gutman acknowledges the views of anthropologists Sidney W. Mintz and Richard Price that "deep-level cultural principles, assumptions, and understandings . . . shared by the Africans in any New World colony" probably served as a "limited but crucial resource" in the early adaptation of African slaves and were "a catalyst in the processes by which individuals from diverse [African] societies forged new institutions."[26] Finally, Gutman concludes that "initial enslavement often mixed together men and women from diverse African societies but did not blot out their consciousness of the social and cultural practices and beliefs associated with these cultures."[27] Accordingly, scattered evidence shows some of these continuities with African cultural values: the practice of polygyny and abstinence from sexual intercourse from the time of pregnancy through to the end of the weaning period; naming children after kinfolk; belief that after death their spirit would return to Africa and join family members in the realm of ancestral spirits.

As discussed above, one cannot overestimate the importance of kinship in African self-understanding. Personal identity and self-esteem are integrally tied up with one's kinship relations. As in Africa, slaves also extended the use of kinship names to members of the larger community. Thus, more often than not they called all older people aunts and uncles and called young people, brothers and sisters. As in Africa this pattern of relating helped to transform kinship obligations into the larger area of social obligations, which served as a basis for communal formation. The history of slavery is replete with examples of slaves sharing their meager material resources with others and always extending a helping hand to those in need.[28] As Gutman rightly states, "Kin obligation among Afro-Americans survived enslavement, and enlarged social obligation emerged out of kin obligation."[29]

One of the most important findings of Gutman's study is the naming-practices of the slaves, which are significant indicators of kinship relations. Though the naming processes of African Americans did not mirror those of their African forebears completely, they do suggest that the slaves viewed their children as significantly related to the larger kinship network. They typically named their children after grandparents, great-grandparents, uncles, aunts, cousins, and even after themselves. This process enabled the slaves to remember their kinfolk from one generation to the next. Yet it also implies that those relatives after whom the children were named also played important roles in the socialization of the children. Clearly the affective tie between grandparents and grandchildren is virtually a universal trait among Africans and African Americans alike. The affective ties between uncles and aunts and their nephews and nieces are also a common feature among the two groups.

Gutman quotes Frederick Douglass and the Yankee schoolteacher Lucy Chase describing the great respect slaves characteristically had for their elders, whether or not they were blood relatives. The following quotation from Douglass states the matter very clearly:

> "Uncle" Toby was the blacksmith, "Uncle" Harry the cartwright, and "Uncle" Abel the shoemaker, and these had assistants in their several departments. These mechanics were called "Uncles" by all the younger slaves, not because they really sustained that relationship to any, but according to plantation etiquette as a mark of respect, due from the younger to the older slaves. Strange and even ridiculous as it may seem, among a people so uncultivated and with so many stern trials to look in the face, there is not to be found among any people a more rigid enforcement of the law of respect to elders than is maintained among them.[30]

According to Gutman, Chase illustrated the same point in the following way: "We had two servants with us. One was a boy and the other a girl. The boy who was younger always called the girl Aunt."[31]

E. Franklin Frazier rightly points out, however, a significant fact about the slave experience, namely the permanence of the bond between the mother and her children: a bond not subject to the impact of external conditions regardless how inimical to family life they might have been. "Consequently, under all conditions of slavery, the Negro mother remained the most dependable and important figure in the family."[32] Further, Frazier cites considerable evidence to prove that slave-mothers "developed a deep and permanent love for their children, which often caused them to defy their masters and to undergo suffering to prevent separation from their young."[33]

As in the African context, slave religion was closely related to the family and its well-being. The slave's reappropriation of Christianity as a religion capable of serving their good (in contradistinction to that of their slaveholders) is evidenced in the family imagery that they used in their spirituals. Both in Africa and in slavery, the affective bonding of children with their mothers was more intense than with any other member of the family. In quoting the nineteenth-century scholar Wilhelm Schneider W.E.B. DuBois' quotation in his book, *Black Folk: Then and Now,* quickly received the appreciation of every school child throughout the African diaspora:

> No mother can love more tenderly or be more deeply beloved than the Negro mother. "Everywhere in Africa," writes Mongo Park, "I have noticed that no greater affront can be offered a Negro than insulting his mother." "Strike me," cried a Mandingo to his enemy, "but revile not my mother." The Hero swears "By my mother's tears." The Angola Negroes have a saying, "As a mist lingers on the swamps, so lingers the love of father and mother."[34]

It should not be surprising then to discover that many of the lyrics of the slave songs expressed their reverence for motherhood, their sorrow about separation from her, and their longing for reunion. Dreams of the latter signified their greatest of joy. For example, one of the verses in the spiritual, "Soon I Will be Done with the Troubles of the World," describes the slave's vision of heaven:

I want to meet my mother,
I want to meet my mother,
I want to meet my mother,
I'm going to live with God.

Similarly, the slaves added verses which included similar references to their brothers, sisters, etc. Thus, we can easily see the slave's imagination incorporating into the Christian view of heaven the African understanding of the ancestral abode. Similarly, many other spirituals reveal the slave's longing to meet his/her mother:

Gonna meet my dear old mother,
Down by the riverside,
Down by the riverside,
Down by the riverside,
Gonna meet my dear old mother,
Down by the riverside,
Gonna study war no more.

Finally, no other spiritual evokes greater pathos than:

Sometimes I feels like a motherless child,
A long ways from home.

In these and other ways, African slaves devised many creative expressions of family life and its meaning for them. Under the conditions of forced separation from family members in Africa, they struggled relentlessly to keep alive old memories of family belonging, and they did so in much the same way as their forbears in Africa had preserved the memory of their ancestors. The memory itself constituted the reality, which was for them a constant source of hope and inspiration. Thus slave literature is replete with memories of and longings for the comfort and security of home and family.

As in Africa, no other family event is more significant among African peoples in the diaspora than funerals. Every person, including the very poor, desires a large, stately funeral. Immediately following the Civil War, the founding of insurance companies comprised one of the more lucrative business operations for African American entrepreneurs. From the earliest days, the churches of freed slaves formed mutual support societies, which ensured adequate burials for their members as well as the provision of material assistance in times of need. Then and now, the entire community rallied round the bereft family throughout the dying process, provided food, shelter, assistance with household chores, and any other helpful expressions of their sympathy and good will. Sitting with the dying round the clock has always been practiced, due to the widespread belief that none should die alone as well as to a strong belief that the dying are very close to the spirit realm and, hence, a special blessing might be received from them just before they cross over.

African and African American funerals have never been private affairs for family members alone. They have always been community events of great importance. Not only do they remind everyone of their own mortality, but they are also enshrouded in mystery. For example, many if not most believe that the spirit of the recently deceased is alive and vested with peculiar powers that can be used for their benefit or for their discomfort, depending on the nature of the relationship between them and the recently departed one. Belief that the spirit lingers in the home for a time after death continues to be widespread among contemporary African peoples. (Bujo writes that it is commonplace among many African tribes to give the departed a place at meals for several days following death. Similarly, in African American churches following the death of the pastor, a deacon, or choir member, the person's seat is often draped for a period of time during which no one is allowed to sit in it.) Often belief in the ongoing consciousness of the departed has been the basis for considerable psychological anxiety and fear both in Africa and in the diaspora. One of the purposes of the wake among African Americans is to offer prayers and sing songs in order to help the spirit of the deceased find its comfortable resting place.

Clearly every family member makes a special effort (often involving considerable sacrifice) to attend the funerals of close relatives. Only sickness or extraordinary long-distance travel can justify their absence. Further, immediate family members have the moral obligation to remember the deceased periodically in some public manner. During slavery and thereafter many objects of value were buried with the deceased, and family members had to stay in mourning for extended periods of time. In North America that meant that they were supposed to wear black clothing and participate in no merriment throughout the specified mourning period. Further and most importantly, no one would dare say anything derogatory about the dead and, more often than not, would accompany any mention of the dead with a short benediction, such as, "May God have mercy on his/her soul."

All of these viewpoints and practices are strikingly similar to those in traditional African cultures. Various beliefs and practices associated with burials may well comprise the single most important connecting link between African traditions on the continent and those in the diaspora. Current archaeological studies of slave burial practices in North America may well reveal much helpful information concerning the social values and religious beliefs of the slaves and, possibly, their connectedness with similar beliefs and practices on the continent.

W.E.B. DuBois once wrote that because of slavery the black churches in America antedated the black family as an institution. Such a view is not commensurate with the argument set forth in this chapter. Rather, I have argued that the African family was not completely destroyed even under the most devastating conditions of slavery. Yet I do acknowledge the important symbiotic relation of black churches and black families, a relation that was eventually joined by subsequent social institutions such as black schools, mutual aid societies, racial improvement associations, and business ventures.

Yet, insofar as social obligations among African Americans were rooted in the linguistic extension of kinship relations into the wider community, the churches eventually became the principal institutional bearers of that tradition. Their symbiotic relation with the family coupled with their use of kinship language in their internal relations greatly facilitated their functions as an extended family. The importance of this fact cannot be overestimated.

Analogous to the patriarch in the traditional African family, the pastor has always been the regal[35] head of the African American community in much the same way as traditional African kings exercised primary authority in the tribal community. Historically, the pastor was almost invariably a man. He was expected to govern the whole church with dignity, firmness, and justice. He was expected to direct the spiritual life of the members through preaching, pastoral care, instruction, and example. Clearly his people expected him to be exemplary as father and husband. Most importantly, they expected him to embody the community's most basic moral and spiritual values and participate with the community in all of its struggles, sorrows, and triumphs. The pastor's primary function, however, was his mediation between God and themselves as well as being the chief intermediary between the black community and the white power structures. His authority transmitted a feeling of security to those who suffered constant insecurity from the threatening conditions and hostile treatment that characterized their daily lives. Although African American churches have had great difficulty in considering the transference of pastoral authority from men to women, some few are presently demonstrating their capacity to adapt themselves appropriately to this inevitable prospect. Much fear concerning the possible loss of spiritual power attends this most pressing issue. Unfortunately, the immense fear surrounding the subject is not abated by either the widespread prejudices of male chauvinism among the clergy or by the refusal of many women to exercise courageous independence by demanding a full-scale critical evaluation of the matter.[36] Until this conflict is satisfactorily resolved, African American churches and the communities they serve will continue to deny the leadership potential in their midst, a denial that has deep moral and religious significance.

As with all regal offices, however, church members do not share equality with their clergy, and this is evidenced in all their personal encounters with them. Faithful stewardship, loyal devotion, and responsible obedience have been the virtues of the laity. Correspondingly, integrity of character, dependable service, and the just exercise of authority have been the prominent virtues of the clergy. Contrary to what is generally thought about monarchs, the personalities of these clergy have not been characterized by harsh severity but rather by warm, friendly amiability and a beneficent spirit. As a consequence, they have tended to exercise their authority in indirect ways. Their clerical titles of "Reverend," "Pastor," and in the past even "Father," along with their liturgical functions make their status unmistakably clear to all. For example, parenthetically, Dr. Martin Luther King, Jr., was affectionately referred to by his closest associates as "de Lawd": a metaphor very much in keeping with the regality of his office. In short, the gentle, respectful, benevolent authority of the African American pastor pleasantly contrasts with the insensitive, disrespectful authorities daily encountered by African Americans in their dealings with white people. Apart from the warmth of the relationship, their authoritarian style of leadership has been both then and now strikingly similar to that of kings in both traditional and modern African societies.

In addition to the pastor's kingly role, his wife is usually referred to as the "first lady," an apt metaphor borrowed from the protocol of the White House. The demonstration of the church's loyalty and devotion to the pastor is ritualized in regular celebratory events traditionally called the pastor's anniversary, which many celebrate annually and others at five-year intervals. In many modern-day urban areas these occasions may involve formal dinners in hotel ballrooms, tributes from governmental officials, lavish gifts from organizations and individuals, or the presence of specially invited dignitaries.

If any should doubt the claim I am making about the regal character of the black pastor, they need only observe the proceedings at any one of the national conventions of black churches. There they will easily see the regal way in which the president or the presiding bishop is treated, beginning with the motorcade from the airport to the hotel, the services provided in the presidential suite and the presidential procession on the floor of the convention. Similarly, in election years, enormous energy has always been expended for many months by clergy and laity alike, waging vigorous campaigns for votes. Such activities give credence to E. Franklin Frazier's description of the black church as a "nation within a nation."

Many churches also bestow honorable status on older women, who are often called church mothers. They usually show leadership in the women's work of the church, especially missionary societies and auxiliaries of various kinds. These women constitute the spiritual pulse of the laity, and their faithfulness can be relied upon in all spheres of the church's work. They are viewed as having all the marks of saintliness and are rightly referred to as the pillars of the church. Some churches install them as deaconesses. In any case, they attend to the sick and shut-ins, aid in the preparation of holy communion, prepare candidates for baptism, serve the funeral meal for bereft families, and a host of other things. Interestingly, as in traditional African societies, black churches are more readily disposed toward reserving particular positions of honor for elderly women while denying similar positions to younger women. This may have some correlation with the traditional African view of post-menopause women as sexually undifferentiated. In light of the moral claims for gender equality, however, none of these traditional practices should be viewed uncritically.

During the first half of the twentieth century, many social theorists assumed that good, stable family life required patriarchal rule. In fact most of those who analyzed the black family, including their most prominent exemplar, E. Franklin Frazier, assumed that the so-called upper classes among the white citizenry set the standard for healthy family life, the marks of which were differentiation from the lower and middle classes, on the one hand, and patriarchal authority, on the other hand. Thus, Frazier wrote:

> Before the rapid urbanization of the Negro population, during and after the first World War, Negro communities were divided on the whole into two main classes. The upper class was made up of a small group of families who, because of their higher standards of morality and superior culture, were differentiated from the great mass of the population.[37]

According to Frazier the primary characteristics of these upper-class black families were their mixed blood, uncritical appreciation for the cultural style of whites, disdain for the lower classes, and high regard for patriarchal governance in the family. With respect to the latter, he argued that it was not unusual during slavery for the husband to purchase his wife and then delay emancipating her for a long while. In that way, he was able to secure his rule over her and the children and thus become a model family man, which had not been possible under the conditions of slavery. Interestingly, Frazier developed this argument to demonstrate how changing economic conditions following slavery gradually enabled the husband to gain ascendency over matriarchal rule in the family. During slavery the male had been denied a place of authority in the family and, hence, the slave family was pathological. His new status was a product of his economic standing. That is to say, male authority over the family and interest in it were not dissimilar from the control and interest any owner has in his or her property.[38]

Unfortunately, Frazier's efforts to theorize about the black family leave little to commend themselves in our day. His well-intended arguments against racism led him to claim an absolute, irrevocable cleavage between the culture of African Americans and that of Africans on the continent. In doing so, he was forced to make the slaveowner's culture the model for all African American cultural values, and thus he victimized the subject he was trying to redeem. Similarly, the only normative resource he could draw upon for his analysis of the twentieth-century black family was the patriarchal family of the white upper classes, of which the so-called black upper class seemed to be a poor facsimile.

5

PERSON

The Embodiment of Moral Virtue

The African View of Personhood

African understandings of *person* are always expressed in social terms because the process of becoming a person can only occur within the confines of the family, which, as we have seen, includes both contemporaries and predecessors. No one has described more adequately the importance of plurality in the experience of African persons than Elia Tema, who writes:

> An African is never regarded as a loose entity to be dealt with strictly individually. His being is based on or coupled with that of others. Next to—or behind—or in front of him there is always someone through whom he is seen or with whom he is associated. The concepts of plurality and belonging to is always present, e.g., a person is always viewed as: "Motho wa batho" (person of persons or belonging to persons). "Motho weso" (Our person or person that is ours).[1]

All scholars in African studies agree on the importance of others in the self-understanding of African peoples. First and foremost, of course, the African person is defined as a member of a family, and so the African person is never alone either in self-concept or in the perception of others. In fact, one can rightly claim that the African person is related to the family as the part of a living organism is related to the whole. As the former cannot live apart from the latter, so the life of a person is wholly dependent on the family and its symbiotic functions of biological lineage, communal nurture, and moral formation.

We must note, however, that in traditional societies not every birth was celebrated as a good thing. Whenever evil spirits were thought to have intercepted the process of gestation, appropriate rituals of expiation were necessary in order to rectify the causes and secure the community against any further evil consequences. Immediately following delivery, familial elders seriously analyzed the meaning of the birth through the most careful investigation of all relevant circumstances attending the event. Frequently the help of professional diviners was sought to ensure accurate analysis of the signs and instructions for the child's upbringing, that is, what to avoid and what to encourage. After the elders were satisfied that the birth was a good one, the process of naming the child constituted the first act of incorporation. That act bestowed personhood on the new life, which was tantamount to announcing its spiritual and moral worth to the family. Mercy Oduyoye writes, "A newborn child is not a person until the naming ceremony has been performed. Before then it is a nonentity."[2] Traditionally this ceremony constituted the beginning of a person's life. The act of naming not only incorporated the child into family membership but it also defined the child's personality, affirmed his or her destiny, and established his or her particular status in the family. Accordingly, Oduyoye writes, "It is not anybody who can name a child, for naming is an exercise of sovereignty, a privilege of proprietorship and a determination of role in life."[3] Among the Yoruba people, for example, the first son born after the death of the father (often the grandson) is considered to be the father reincarnated; hence he is named *Babatunde,* which means "father has returned" and signals that fact to all Yorubas. His place in the family and in the larger community is determined accordingly. When a grandmother has returned in a female birth, the child is named similarly.

The husband of one of my students from Kenya (a member of the Kikuyu clan) explained to me that his son was the first male child born after the death of his father, and so the child's name also indicates that the father has returned. He illustrated the import of this fact by saying that from time to time the child may choose to speak to him as his father and, whenever that happens, ironically, he the biological father is duty-bound to listen to the child as his father incarnated. In other words, the child may in fact chastize his father, which under normal circumstances would be taboo.

In short, the act of naming manifested the family's blessing since the life had been judged to be wholly good, and the family's blessing was also an act of thanks to the ancestral spirits for this event. Had the birth been judged to be evil, the traditional family would have rejected the infant.[4] This often happened with births judged to be misfortunes, and each society had its own views of what constituted such evil. In such circumstances the child was not permitted to survive, and the evil force that had intercepted the process was exorcised through appropriate rituals.

Thus one can easily see in the naming of African children the immense respect parents have for their individuality. If the child has come into the world through the intercession of some deity, the child's name will bear witness to that fact. For example, "Esubiyii, 'Esu gave birth to this one,' or Ogunbiyii, 'Ogun gave birth to this one,' . . ."[5] Parents and family members therefore treat babies with the greatest of care, often indulging them as the most precious of all beings. This is due in large part to the belief that babies have come from the world of spirit, and for a long while they are closer to the spirits than to world of the living. Since they will become acclimatized to this world gradually, it is the responsibility of parents, elders, and others to determine who he or she is as well as his or her likes and dislikes. For example, Drewal reports that "When a child is irritable, cries a lot, and does not sleep, the parents know, according to Ositola, that its ancestral spirit is pinching its body, anxious to gain recognition."[6] Such an explanation gives cosmological import to the mother's careful attention to the baby's needs.

The names of children are the expressive bearers of their place in the family. Accordingly, their names depict the nature of their personalities and destinies insofar as the latter can be known. Further, they also aid parents and others in their enforcement of moral habits by reminding the children about the meaning of their names and, in the case of reincarnation, admonishing them of the obligation they have for developing their character in accordance with that of the particular ancestor they represent.

All African names are meaningful. They tell the story of the child's birth and destiny. Much can be known about a person by understanding his or her name. While revealing the family's understanding of the person's value, the name eventually shapes the person's own self-understanding. I recall participating as a panelist at a conference at the University of Ibadan, Nigeria, in 1984 on the subject "Religion and Modern Youth." One of the panelists was a prominent local chief and his address surprised many. He contended that one of the greatest problems facing contemporary youth was that they had been improperly named by urban parents disconnected from their familial and tribal traditions. He went on to argue that the function of children is to live up to their names. He admonished all concerned to draw upon traditional wisdom before naming their children in order to avoid crucial errors. In his judgment, proper naming not only acknowledged the child's destiny but also empowered the child to actualize it.

Interestingly, however, during that same period I visited an Ibo family at the University of Ibadan a few days after the birth of one of their children. I inquired about the baby's name and, to my surprise, the parents responded by saying that they did not yet know the child's name because they were waiting to hear from the family elders back in the father's native village. Upon receipt of the message they planned to return to their village for the naming ceremony. Thus, not all urban dwellers were ignoring the traditional wisdom in naming their children.

It is important to note, however, that under the conditions of colonialism, African Christians usually gave their children so-called Christian (more accurately, Western) names in addition to their traditional names. Indeed, during much of the colonial era virtually no African could be baptized into Christianity without receiving a "Christian" name. I think it right to assume that from the perspective of colonizers in general and of Christian evangelists in particular, the adoption of Western names connoted a high degree of psychological and social conquest. But, from the viewpoint of the colonized and especially the evangelized, it merely signified their capacity to assimilate Western cultural elements into their own traditions. In doing so, they preserved African cultural values alongside those of their Western intruders. Instead of being vanquished as the latter had hoped, African names were preserved as fundamental signs of personal and communal identity. Similarly, "Christian" names were incorporated into the same structure of meaning.

Since those who name African children refer to them henceforth by the names given them, it was completely compatible with African cultural traditions for the foreigners to call Africans by the Western names they had acquired at baptism. But within the privacy of their family relations their indigenous names were invariably used. I recall an experience I had many years ago in Nigeria when a former student of mine had invited me to his home during my stay in the country. Having chosen not to use his Yoruba names (apart from his surname) while studying in the United States, he was known to me only by his "Christian" name, Jacob. Upon arriving at his family compound while he was absent, I discovered relatives who did not speak much English. When I inquired about Jacob they looked genuinely puzzled. After calling for a school boy who spoke English, it eventually became clear to them whom I was seeking. I soon discovered that while his "Christian" name was known by those who had direct dealings with foreigners either through the educational system, the churches, or travel abroad, others, including various members of his family whom I first encountered, knew him only by his Yoruba names. This is a vivid example of the bicultural experience of colonized Africans. Such practices continue throughout modern-day Africa mainly for pragmatic reasons. That is to say, giving children Western names can facilitate more relaxed associations with Western peoples, who often have great difficulties in pronouncing traditional African names.

African Views of Personal Destiny

Insofar as the act of naming determines personality and affirms destiny, the questions raised by anthropologists and ethnologists about social determination are appropriate because the latter would seem to preclude all notions of individual responsibility. Meyer Fortes' question aptly expresses this issue: "If personhood is socially generated and culturally defined, how then is it experienced by its bearer, the individual?"[7] He goes on to claim that this is the ancient problem of the relation of the so-called inner person to the socially determined person. In other words, can a person be self-aware if the meaning of his or her personhood is wholly bestowed from without?[8] Apart from such self-awareness, how can the person be held responsible for actions that are not freely chosen?

The question of external determination refers directly to the widespread African view of destiny which, as Awolalu[9] recognizes, bears striking similarities to the Calvinist doctrine of predestination. In his view, and that of all others, the person is thought to choose his or her destiny before leaving the realm of spirit to assume human life. Again, Fortes provides a clear definition of the function of destiny:

> Destiny is thought of as a component of a person's personhood. It is supposed to be chosen by himself or herself pre-natally (while he was still "with Heaven above") and therefore to be already effective from his birth. Destiny distinguishes and indeed creates him as an individual encapsulated in his social being but endowed with a personal variant of the normal career pattern for someone of his status, as individual as his physical appearance and personality yet, equally, like every other man or woman in his society.[10]

Awalalu prefers to be more specific and defines destiny in terms of spirituality: an integrative principle governing the person's life and expressing its quality and purpose. Thus, he prefers to speak of a person's destiny as his or her "personality-soul":

> According to the oral traditions, the personality-soul derives directly from the Supreme Being. It is this personality-soul that really makes a person whatever he is. It accounts for the peculiar characteristics of the individual. Indeed, it is the "ruler" of the individual. It serves as man's double or guardian angel who is associated with him from birth, to warn and help him through this life and guide his fortunes . . . . We can further say that it is the personality-soul that animates the body, gives vitality to it, and pervades it with life.[11]

The African understanding of destiny precludes any radical individual autonomy in human action either in its initiation or its consequences. Since all matters pertaining to destiny are governed by the ancestors, they alone are ultimately responsible for the person's actions and achievements. At this point a paradox occurs in that it is widely assumed that both the individual and the ancestors are responsible for the person's actions. This paradoxical relation is best understood as a matter of mutual regulation. Each has reciprocal duties and obligations towards the other. As discussed above, harmony and peace throughout the community signify the good will of the ancestors. Misfortune or sickness, disease or accidents, are viewed as ancestral punishments either for wrongdoing in general or for inattentive devotion to them, in particular. The omnipresence of the ancestors in all the affairs of daily life is both comforting and disquieting because ancestors act in unpredictable ways.

As mentioned above, destiny is chosen in the realm of spirit just before the child is born. Oduyoye refers to destiny as the person's double self who accompanies one throughout life as an invisible companion.[12] The ancestors know the child's destiny and they alone are its rulers. Although destiny is viewed as irrevocable, most Africans believe that it can be modified to some extent. To that end, various rituals of divination are often undertaken to "sweep away" a bad destiny.[13]

Whenever the elders of a family consider it reasonable to blame a person's destiny for some wrongdoing, they are duty-bound to assume responsibility for seeking the services of a diviner. The diviner can intercede with the ancestors and invoke their help in effecting some measure of alteration in the person's destiny. Clearly, the person does not face this crisis alone but rather has the participation of the whole family in atoning for the moral issue at hand. The principal actor in these circumstances, however, must be the father (the eldest male member of the family) since he alone has the authority to initiate direct communication with the ancestors. Yet the father does not have that authority until after his own father has become an ancestor. Since only elderly men have such authority to intercede directly with the ancestors, the importance of the first-born son cannot be overestimated. He is the direct successor to paternal authority in the family lineage.[14] The same applies to the first-born daughter, who similarly inherits her mother's authority. Each assumes the authority of the respective parent only after the latter has passed on to the ancestral realm and all burial rites have been properly undertaken. The patriarchal principle of male authority over that of women permeates the realms of history and of spirit. In each sphere of life, however, female authority is supreme in its own jurisdiction. That is to say, male authority has no jurisdiction over female domains. Thus the presence of goddesses and female ancestors in the realm of spirit constitutes a significant resource for all women. Further, post-menopausal women have always been viewed as equal partners with men both in the home and the larger community. These facts may account for the limits of patriarchy in Africa, where it appears to be restricted primarily to the male-female relations in the home while being virtually inoperative as a functioning principle in the larger society, where women have occupied most offices at one time or another.

It is important to note at this point, however, that African societies have had priestesses and prophetesses from time immemorial. This is a subject that needs much more intensive study and especially by women scholars, who may have greater access to these leaders since their functions often pertain to the peculiar problems of women. In his discussion of indigenous African churches Kofi Appiah-Kubi writes, "There are also some women founders of churches; for example, Alice Lanshina of Lumpa church in Zambia, Captain Abiodum of Cherabim and Seraphim, and Alice Tania of the Church of the Twelve Apostles in Ghana."[15] Similarly, P.R. McKenzie has written an intriguing essay on the prophetess of Yemoja, whose ministry took place in Abeokuta, Nigeria, around the middle of the nineteenth century. He writes:

> The healing ministry of an unnamed priestess of Yemoja, exercised near Abeokuta, and described by Thomas King in 1855, appears to have received less attention than it deserves. It took place, of course, a good half century before the emergence of the typical West African prophet-figures of the kind much studied of late . . . . There appears to be little doubt that the priestess initiated a remarkably popular healing ministry. King's report on her activities, written after a ministry of four months, makes this clear. "People of all ranks," he noted, "have flocked thither. All the

> chiefs with their wives in turns, with the exception of the Ogobonna (the Balogan of Ikija), have been over to pay her a visit. The wives of the palace are not behind in going there, though the king himself (Okukenu, the Alake) has not." Nor was the movement confined to Abeokuta. "The inhabitants of all the neighboring towns . . . come down in great multitude." . . .
>
> The priestess was by all indications basically a devotee of Yemoja, the popular mother-goddess of the waters, including the Ogun river at Abeokuta. Traditionally Yemoja's concern is to help women anxious to have children . . . .[16]

Clearly persons may rightly blame their destiny for things that go awry in their lives. In that respect, destiny relieves the individual of complete responsibility for any particular moral crisis while ensuring the participation of the whole family, including the ancestors, in its expiation. In all of this the communal nature of person is made fully apparent.

Africans also believe that destiny can be modified by the quality of one's character, for which the person has major responsibility. Thus a good destiny must be supported by good moral character, or otherwise the divinities will have their revenge by replacing the good destiny with a bad one. Similarly, bad character or the ill will of witches, sorcerers, and other evil people can cause a happy destiny to deteriorate. Among the Yorubas and others, people are regularly admonished to seek out the oracle divinity, who has the capacity to help preserve good destinies and rectify unhappy ones. Through such assistance persons can learn what to do and what to avoid.[17] Accordingly, cultic devotion to the oracle divinity is widespread throughout Africa so that happy destinies might be preserved and unhappy ones rectified.

So a strong belief in predestination need not nullify personal responsibility for moral development. Rather, Idowu writes, "With the element of character involved, a person is not allowed to expect an automatic fulfillment of a good destiny. He must co-operate to make his destiny successful by acquiring and practising good character."[18] The individual person is not a passive bearer of personhood. Rather, individual self-awareness is evident in the person's internalization of the community's expectations. Although the person's name is a significant indicator of this self-other relationship, various other societal avenues both assist and express the person's destiny. These include occupation, initiation rites, taboos, ritual observances, proverbial teachings, folk tales and stories, social rank, and membership in secret societies.

In situations in which a person's bad destiny is impervious to alteration, that person may be judged to be morally recalcitrant and hence incapable of functioning positively as a member of the community. Such a situation is shameful to all concerned, and traditionally the family had the responsibility of expunging the person from membership. Such a person was exiled from the family and the tribal community and, more often than not, sold into slavery. In these and related ways, the community's moral code was rigorously enforced.[19] Since the malfunctioning person was believed to be both a spiritual and moral liability, communal cleansing necessitated an act of expulsion. Mercy, forgiveness, compassion, and similar attitudes had no efficacy in restoring the equilibrium between the community and the realm of spirit. Thus traditional African societies strictly followed traditional customs in praising those who were morally good (for example, bestowing upon them various kinds of rewards in the form of material gifts, honorary titles, etc.) and punishing those who were morally wicked.[20]

The symbiotic functions of various societal practices contributed immensely to the ongoing task of moral formation, which was not complete until the end of the person's life. Hopefully, by the time the person became an elder he or she would have attained wisdom, viewed as the accumulated communal knowledge underlying all of life's experiences. This connoted the capacity to guide and judge others. In fact, old age implied not only the attainment of such wisdom but also the temporal proximity of elders to ancestorhood, which greatly enhanced their authority. These factors were the basis for the African reverence of elders whose words of blessing or curse[21] were extremely powerful. Even in our day, no African person makes any important decision in his or her life without first seeking the blessing of the familial elders. Few would go against the advise of their elders.

Since the person is an integral part of the community, the latter assumed major responsibility for the former's moral development and spiritual devotion. As a result, the individual person was never alone but continuously advised, chastised, and encouraged by members of the family and the larger community. The art of moral training implied that every activity should serve the good of the community. In other words, all practices were thought to have a moral goal, and it was thought that persons should be formed in such a way as to desire that goal more than anything else. To do otherwise would be tantamount to serving one's own selfish interest and thereby relegating the community to a secondary place in one's scheme of importance. Selfishness was viewed as one of the greatest evils because it reverses the moral code.

Even casual observance of Africans on the continent will reveal their deep devotion to the community's well-being as manifested in their willingness and even eagerness to render service to the family and the larger community. In fact, one soon discovers that receiving the community's praise is for them the highest possible reward. Thus whenever persons fare well they feel duty-bound to share their bounty with the community. So-called successful Africans choose to build large homes in order to accommodate many family members who will be certain to come to stay for extended periods of time. One will also observe that they willingly bear responsibility for aiding family members in all sorts of circumstances: helping to pay educational expenses for nephews, nieces, cousins; contributing to marriage dowries, funerals, or anniversaries. While living with a pastor in Soweto, South Africa, a few years ago, I saw that on several occasions he was called upon to make a contribution to the "unveiling of a tombstone" (a most significant memorial event that is expected to take place sometime within the year following the death of an esteemed family member) in order to help purchase the necessary sheep for the communal meal. I was impressed by the seriousness with which the pastor attended to such matters. Clearly he viewed this as important a part of his ministry as anything else he did.

Because the person is an essential part of family and the larger community, each significant event in the individual's life is at one and the same time an important occasion in the life of the whole community. As the latter is affected for good or ill by the unfolding drama of the individual's life, times of happiness and grief are invariably shared by the community. Consequently it is rare for Africans to experience loneliness. Mbiti aptly describes this communal reality:

> What then is the individual and where is his place in the community? In traditional life, the individual does not and cannot exist alone except corporately. He owes his existence to other people, including those of past generations and his contemporaries. He is simply part of the whole. The community must therefore make, create or produce the individual. Physical birth is not enough: the child must go through rites of incorporation so that it becomes fully integrated into the entire society. These rites continue throughout the physical life of the person, during which the individual passes from one stage of corporate existence to another. The final stage is reached when he dies and even then he is ritually incorporated into the wider family of both the dead and the living.
>
> Just as God made the first man, as God's man, so now man himself makes the individual who becomes the corporate of social man. It is a deeply religious transaction. Only in terms of other people does the individual become conscious of his own being, his own duties, his privileges

> and responsibilities towards himself and towards other people. When he suffers, he does not suffer alone but with the corporate group; when he rejoices, he rejoices not alone but with his kinsmen, his neighbors and his relatives whether dead or living. When he gets married, he is not alone, neither does the wife "belong" to him alone. So also the children belong to the corporate body of kinsmen, even if they bear only their father's name. Whatever happens to the individual happens to the whole group, and whatever happens to the whole group happens to the individual. The individual can only say: "I am, because we are; and since we are, therefore I am." This is a cardinal point in the understanding of the African view of man.[22]

Though difficult for Western minds to grasp, Africans have no conception of person apart from the community. This means more than the maintenance of a symbiotic relation between the individual and the community. Such implies a prior separate state. No such separation is possible in African thought. The two are related as opposite sides of the same coin. The one implies the other.

Contrary to the thinking of many Western peoples, this communal view of personhood does not imply the devaluation of individuality. Rather it implies that the value Africans bestow on individuals is not the primary good. Instead, in the order of moral importance, the corporate community always assumes priority over individual members. Thus under certain conditions the person may be sacrificed for the well-being of the corporate body in much the same way as a modern-day person might choose to undergo a surgical procedure to amputate a body part. Because the latter is highly valued, such a procedure is never encountered casually. Invariably, its justification lies in its purpose, namely, promoting the health of the whole body. Similarly, the sacrifice of a person for the common good is always a very serious undertaking because the purpose of the sacrifice has very high value. Modern warfare may be viewed as another analogy. Under such conditions, courageous persons willingly risk their lives for the common good, and their deaths are honored as national sacrifices. Also in the African context, individual persons may well accrue considerable personal honor by virtue of their self-sacrificing activities.[23] In Africa the highest moral good is that of serving the common good with one's material and spiritual resources. Consequently, Africans have had no difficulty in understanding the sacrificial view of the atonement upheld by many Christians.[24] Such a view of human sacrifice is deeply rooted in African traditions. Indeed, Africans have always been baffled by Christian missionaries condemning their traditional practices of human sacrifice while proclaiming the sacrificial death of Jesus Christ.

Clearly, the communal evaluative process that begins at birth continues throughout life because the community has more than a casual interest in the destiny of all its members. In fact, the destiny of each person affects the well-being of the whole community for better or for worse. Thus nothing is taken more seriously by African communities than the moral nurture and guidance of children, who belong to the whole community. The community is teacher, parent, guardian, advocate, legislator of all. As Mbiti writes:

> In African societies, the birth of a child is a process which begins long before the child's arrival in this world and continues long thereafter. It is not just a single event which can be recorded on a particular date. Nature brings the child into the world, but society creates the child into a social being, a corporate person. For it is the community which must protect the child, feed it, bring it up, educate it and in many other ways incorporate it into the wider community. Children are the buds of society, and every birth is the arrival of "spring" when life shoots out and the community thrives. The birth of a child is, therefore, the concern not only of the parents but of many relatives including the living and the departed. Kinship plays an important role here, so that a child cannot be exclusively "my child" but only "our child."[25]

African societies characteristically rejoice when a woman becomes pregnant. In many contexts the marriage is not considered consummated until pregnancy occurs. Mbiti says that that alone marks the woman's complete integration into the husband's family. Contemporary young married couples living abroad often choose to delay having children, much to the dismay of their parents in the homeland.

No greater tragedy befalls a woman than infertility.[26] The childless woman not only has nobody of her own blood to maintain her immortality after death, but she fails to be a vehicle in the cyclical process of life by which the unborn enters the community's life destined to enhance its quality. "In the birth of a child, the whole community is born anew; it is renewed, it is revived and revitalized."[27] The child is in fact owned by the community, which provides structures for guiding and monitoring its moral and social development. Many of these structures are in the form of rites of passage, which normally include initiation and puberty rites, marriage and procreation, public titles and office, death and the ancestral world. All of these are sacred events confirmed by traditional ceremonies in which individual persons covenant with the community to be faithful in exercising all their respective duties, obligations, and responsibilities. Many contend that the individual person becomes fully born only after having passed through all of these rites of passage. In other words, to be fully born is to be fully actualized which can only occur in community. Total alienation from the community is tantamount to losing one's personhood and becoming a mere thing.

It is an understatement to say that traditional African cultures valued tribal community more highly than the family and, similarly, valued the family more highly than the individual person. The reason for such ranking is rooted in the necessary dependency of individual persons on the family. In fact, apart from the family the person could never be. As we have seen, personhood is a status that is bestowed upon one after birth and not a natural right by virtue of biological birth alone. Similarly, the African family has no meaningful reality apart from the tribal community. In each case the part-whole relationship is the appropriate analogy. That is to say, the one is related to the other in a reciprocal relation of interdependence wherein each contributes to the well-being of the other. Yet it is self-evident to all that in the temporal order the whole both precedes and supercedes the part. That is to say, the tribal community has priority over the family and the latter over the individual, not unlike the relation of any living organism to its biological parts. While the whole can survive a loss of the part the reverse is unthinkable. Thus, Africans contend that the value of person is derivative from the community and measured by his or her contribution to the latter's well-being. Individual rights and liberties are always determined within the communal context.

Let me reiterate the central importance of the ancestral spirits in the life of the family and each of its members. Because the spirits' role and function comprise the fundamental basis of human reality in African life, many contend that a person does not become fully actualized until he or she has passed through historical life and entered the realm of the ancestral spirits. Such an outcome necessitates a long and happy life blessed with many children and grandchildren who fare well. All such conditions are necessary prerequisites for what Africans call "a good life and a good death." That alone guarantees one access to ancestorhood. Premature deaths caused by accidents, disease, or wrongdoing are rejected by the ancestors, and the deceased is severed from the family lineage forever. No greater disaster can befall one than that. All who die childless are condemned to a similar fate.

Conflicting Views of Liberty and Authority

At this point it is possible to discuss one of the principal conflicts between Western and African understandings of personhood: a conflict that has been a constant source of difficulty in the post-colonial relationships of African and Western peoples. More specifically, this conflict has had a profound effect on the process of nation-building in contemporary Africa and on the self-understanding of African peoples throughout the world. Additionally, this conflict is also a peculiarly American problem. In his discussion of the rights that citizens have, Ronald Dworkin argues that an individual right against the state is the heart of constitutional theory in the United States.[28]

As seen above, however, traditional African cultures were ordered in accordance with the principle of community that was hierarchically arranged with the community of ancestors as the primary ruling power, followed respectively by the descending authorities of tribal and familial communities. We have also seen that the African person can only be understood in that tripartite communal relation. Interdependent relations among persons, families, tribe, and ancestors comprise the nature of African humanity. Since each is a part of a larger whole, all are related to one another reciprocally. That is to say, the purpose of each is to contribute life to and to receive life from all of the others. No one community can exist severed from the others. In other words, each part of the whole social organism is necessary. As the value of the individual derives from the community, the goal of the community is to promote the life of the individual. Thus, individual rights and liberties cannot be determined apart from this communal context and the necessary responsibilities and obligations implied by membership in it.

This type of thinking is difficult for the Western mind to appreciate because the latter alters the relation by giving moral primacy to individual persons and lesser value to either the family or the larger community. Such thought virtually reverses the African understanding of the relation of person and community. Although there are numerous exceptions to the rule (the most obvious being that of military conscription which, as we have indicated, is a kind of sacrificial offering for the good of the whole community), much of Western society has tended to view the sanctity of the individual person as the highest moral good. It is viewed as inviolate under all circumstances. Accordingly, both the U.S. Constitution's Bill of Rights and the United Nation's Declaration of Human Rights are derivative from that principle, subscription to which has contributed enormously to the expansion of civility among diverse peoples.

Clearly, the Western justification of individual autonomy was long in the making. In differing ways modern proponents have drawn their source material from the Renaissance, the Protestant Reformers and the philosophy of the Enlightenment. Yet, to view those major philosophical and theological revolutions as simply supportive of individualism and inimical to corporate authority would be a gross oversimplification and quite misleading. Rather, on the positive side, I claim that one finds in each of those movements radical new thinking about the importance of personal decision and responsibility as well as the value of individual liberty and conscience. Most particularly, one finds in all of them a deep suspicion toward and a profound criticism of all external authorities, whose powers they believed required constant restraint. Although each of the above movements made positive contributions toward developing normative understandings of community, their novelty centered on the relationship of the individual person to external authority and, more specifically, the importance of protecting the former from the arbitrary whims of the latter. Although leaders in these movements were not the first to think seriously about this relationship, I think it fair to say that they were the first to argue for the primacy of the individual over traditional authorities. Thus, in this respect, the founders of these movements may be viewed as unwitting progenitors of modern democracy, that is, of government by the consent the people under the principle of "one man, one vote."

Yet the new interest in the value of individuality soon led others to radicalize the principle by divorcing it completely from all forms of external authority. This modern tendency led to various political philosophies of limited government and the eventual reign of the doctrine of *laissez-faire* in economic relationships. While the norm of individuality is a positive contribution to human society, I agree with Cornel West about its distortion into "those doctrinaire individualisms which promote human selfishness, denigrate the idea of community, and distort the holistic development of personality."[29] In short, the modern Western world gradually became heir to a tradition that is greatly suspicious of every form of external authority. Western philosophy, theology, and political science, whether conservative or liberal, are replete with thought that elevates the importance of the individual over that of the community. Although this tradition has been a significant corrective for all societal systems that diminish the value of individuality, it in turn has spawned many unresolved problems that can be helped by those whose traditions view community as the fundamental condition for personhood.

It is well known that in all matters of faith and morals the free-church tradition of Protestantism has emphasized the primacy of the individual over the corporate community. While the community may seek to influence the thought and practice of individuals, it tends to have very little legislative authority with which to force compliance, due to the voluntary nature of its membership. Further, outside the domains of established churches, morality and religion tend to be relegated to the private sphere of life, subject to little or no governmental interference. This has the effect of aiding the secularization of the public realm, making it void of religion and any morality emanating from it. Accordingly, in the United States a recent nominee for the Supreme Court (Judge Clarence Thomas) felt justified in saying at his confirmation hearing before the U.S. Senate Judiciary Committee that his personal moral beliefs were irrelevant to his function as a judge because, in his judgment, a judge should be morally neutral. He interpreted neutrality to mean that a judge should allow no preconceived views to influence his or her judicial judgment. In other words, this prospective Justice of the U.S. Supreme Court was saying that individual moral commitments should not influence the decisions of judges. Rather, judges should compartmentalize their moral commitments and act apart from them. The extent to which that is possible was not pursued by the Senate committee, thus implying possible agreement on their part. Yet such a distorted position as Thomas' is understandable in a secular nation built on the constitutional doctrine of the separation of church and state and where religion and morality are viewed as purely private matters. In spite of the nation's motto, "In God We Trust," printed on every denomination of its currency, the judge's position implies that from the point of view of the law, no principle (divine or otherwise) should stand above the Constitution. Obviously, if morality has no place in the public realm, a serious question arises concerning the quality of the law as well as of the government. More specifically, one might rightly ask about the relation of so-called personal morality and that of public officials. This puzzle for Americans gained public visibility during the Watergate scandal of 1972–74 with a partial response in the establishment of various centers for the study of ethics throughout the nation. Rarely, if ever, has any of these centers been associated with the study of religion, a fact that seems to imply its irrelevance.

All such bifurcation of thought concerning person and community, morality and religion, individual liberty and communal authority, is alien to traditional African societies. Yet in many contemporary African countries leaders have struggled with the idea of constructing secular states as apparent pragmatic solutions to Islamic-Christian conflicts. Interestingly, traditional African religions have always been more tolerant of diverse religions than either Islam or Christianity. Nevertheless, those who are fully shaped by the wholism of traditional culture find it virtually impossible to design secular states with any measure of deep conviction because any and all such endeavors are wholly alien to their basic understandings of human life. In my judgment, this may be one of the most prominent reasons for the failure of constitutional secular governments in post-colonial Africa.

African American Views of Personhood

The self-understanding of African Americans has long been characterized by their struggle for freedom: an activity in which they have been continuously engaged from the earliest days of slavery up to the present time. In one way or another, all their moral strivings have reflected that struggle. Nowhere has this been more evident than in their religion, music, and song. There and elsewhere they have nurtured the hope and worked tirelessly for a radically new social order fully shaped by a nonracist moral principle.[30]

Consonant with the understandings of their African forebears, African Americans have always known that persons cannot flourish apart from a community of belonging. They have also known that any community that oppresses its members is no community at all but, rather, a seething cauldron of dissension, distrust, and bitterness. Thus they have had no difficulty in discerning a moral contradiction at the heart of the American republic: a contradiction caused by the primacy of racism as an organizing principle in the nation's public life.[31]

Contrary to the opinions of some, African Americans have continuously claimed that morality attends everything humans do both privately and publicly. Consequently, they have never been able to conceive of societal structures or their leaders as morally neutral in the exercise of their duties. Nor have they been able to view their resistance to racism in anything other than moral terms. As a racially despised minority in the so-called new world, they always knew that their survival both as individuals and as a group depended on their capacity to deal constructively with the immorality of racism. That capacity eventually came to expression in two principal styles of action that scholars have named *protest* and *accommodation.* The goal of protest activities was to effect some measure of systemic reform in the public practice of racism, while accommodationist activities aimed at helping African Americans adapt to those public practices. While the latter did not imply any affirmation of racism per se, compliance with its conditions made African Americans unwitting collaborators with the perpetrators of racism. Freed slaves of the antebellum period constituted the vanguard of the protest tradition. They became the progenitors of black abolitionism, integrationism, and nationalism, the three major benchmarks of African American resistance. Their leaders have continuously enriched the nation's moral discourse by their tireless efforts to keep the issue of racial justice on the public agenda.

It should not be surprising to discover that the African American understanding of personhood is integrally related to the communal struggle for racial justice. That quest is deeply rooted in the African experience of tribal community, the basic condition for familial and individual life. Thus, as a principal means of survival, African slaves and ex-slaves devoted enormous amounts of energy toward building a measure of community through various kinds of social bonding. As discussed above, the slaves eventually reconstructed their experience of tribal community under the principle of racial unity. In similar ways they also preserved some of the essential elements of African family life. It is astonishing that such achievements occurred in the midst of conditions that were wholly inimical to human life.

Under the conditions of slavery African Americans also maintained, in large part, their traditional understandings of person. Since the latter necessitated community, the slaves used every opportunity at hand to build social cohesion. They did so by demonstrating a spirit of good will not only toward one another but also toward their slaveowners. Although the practical goal of surviving the cruel conditions of slavery was a clear motivation for the cultivation of such a beneficent spirit, the art of doing so also constituted one of the basic building blocks of community. While the slaves clearly knew that no good could result from the display of mean and bitter attitudes toward arbitrary masters, it was reasonable to assume that a good disposition could yield positive results.

Such thinking had deep roots in the traditional way Africans on the continent had responded to the conditions of slavery. In those contexts, slaves could reasonably expect eventual integration into the family structure of their owners. Such an expectation, however, depended wholly on their disposition. That alone determined their qualification for inclusion in the family. The essential qualities of such a disposition included cooperation, loyalty, and good will. Clearly, accommodationism marked the traditional African orientation to slavery.

Thus the basic adjustment of African American slaves to their situation was influenced to a great extent by their traditional views of slavery and its causes. The latter had been viewed as some combination of punishment for wrongdoing, military conquest, family or tribal deprivation, or predestination. Most believed that accommodating to their plight afforded them a greater hope of survival since neither successful escape nor victorious rebellion seemed possible. Those who refused to accommodate suffered greatly. Yet accommodationism did not exclude various types of indirect resistance, especially in their moral and religious convictions.[32]

Narratives by and about African American slaves are replete with stories pertaining to their many humane attributes, which, incidentally, their oppressors usually viewed as evidence of their "childlike" nature. Invariably those attitudes of care, compassion, empathy, and good will were manifested primarily in their relations with children and, especially, with their master's children. In fact, the loving care that slave women extended to their master's children contributed to the formation of the stereotypical name, *mammy:* a name that connoted the warmth, nurture, and affection of the most esteemed, long-term, female household servant. In caring for their master's children, often to the neglect of their own, slave women had an indelible effect on the emotional development of both. As in traditional African villages, the maternal bonding of slaves on the American continent was not limited to their own children but extended to all children with whom they were associated. Similarly, even when pregnancy resulted from the rape of their masters, slave women bonded fully with the infants they delivered. As in Africa the slaves subjected their own children to harsh disciplinary measures both as a sign of retaining the typical African authoritarian relationship over their children and more especially as a proven means of passing on to the next generation the traditional wisdom of child development and moral formation. Clearly, their relations with children helped them preserve the basic remnants of traditional African family life, namely, the capacity to nurture, the experience of maternal bonding, respect for and obedience to parental authority.

Apart from the relationship of slave women to children, the African impulse for social bonding was expressed regularly in their clandestine meetings in the bush arbors,[33] as well as in their work songs (the earliest form of slave music),[34] dancing,[35] story-telling,[36] humour,[37] and countless other ordinary activities of daily life. Yet a deliberate effort was made to conceal from their masters all such efforts to humanize their world. As a result, slaveowners knew very little about the slave's world of meaning and value. They could only impute their own erroneous interpretations to the practices they observed, practices that were usually ladened with layers of double meaning.

The lack of consistent family life within a wider supportive community made it very difficult for the slaves to preserve their African traditions in any complete way. Nowhere was this loss experienced more deeply than in the desecration of the family, which was the principal locus for the moral formation of persons. The traditional wisdom gained from intergenerational family life was a loss that the slaves deeply mourned. Naming ceremonies, puberty rites, age-group associations, secret societies, public festivals, royal courts, professional priests, musicians, dancers, sculpturers, traders, and countless other rituals, guardians, role models, and teachers were no longer present as moral exemplars for the young and moral enforcers for the larger community. In time, many of these varied functions were transferred to new expressive forms. Eventually they integrated the latter into their religion, which they had effectively concealed[38] from their masters during the period of slavery.

As the African understanding of person is intrinsically related to traditional understandings of family and community, so too is the African American. Undoubtedly influenced in many ways by the American philosophy of individualism, African Americans have nonetheless never embraced the latter in any complete way. Although they developed a more distinctive understanding of person than that of their African counterparts, the two share much in common with each other. More specifically, the African American understanding of person exhibits the basic marks of wholism that emanate from its traditional African source.

In light of the fact that African American scholars have not written treatises on individuality, it is my view that one of the best ways to grasp their understanding of person is through an examination of African American music since the latter comprises one of the most basic expressions of African American philosophy. In fact, their music reveals the person-community relationship more clearly than anything else. During the past few decades much academic progress has been made in demonstrating how African American music is descended from traditional African music. Mary Ellison states the matter clearly:

> Blues is descended in a remarkably direct way from African music. Both the musical pattern and the lyrical content are based on African models. While African music is too diversified to lend itself well to generalizations, certain characteristics are common to most of the areas from which slaves were shipped to America. Call and response, rhythmic counterpoint, polyrhythms, and melodic and harmonic sophistication are frequently encountered, as are virtuoso solo performances on instruments closely similar to the guitar and the harmonica. Even more universal are the slurred and flatted notes and melisma so characteristic of the blues, and the tonal structural qualities of certain African songs are often startlingly like the blues . . . .
>
> Most constant of all, however, was the African musician's commitment to meaningful lyrics that reflect every human response to life, from common daily experiences to more abstract problems. During and after the slavery period, music in Africa was an integral and functional part of life, and a song was composed to enrich every occasion and emphasize every mood. Music was not only an essential means of communication but also an expression of the most fundamental feelings and facts. William Ferris, historian of the blues, commented, "African griots, slave singers, and country and urban bluesmen share a common musical tradition."[39]

Ellison provides abundant evidence in support of her thesis that African American music in all of its varied forms (spirituals, blues, rhythm and blues, jazz, gospel, rock, funk, rap, disco, reggae) is characterized by its resistance to racial injustice. In fact, it is widely assumed by many, including Ellison, that African Americans use music as a popular and effective means for social commentary and prophetic utterance. Accordingly, she draws the startling conclusion: "Music has explored the range of human choices for black people with a lucidity and honesty rarely achieved by politicians."[40] Such a sentiment is similar to that of Diallo and Hall, who also speak about the power of African music to convey meanings: "Words alone do not convey the meaning. The music and the gestures of dance also impart meaning."[41]

My argument shares much in common with that of Ben Sidran, however, who claims that "black culture assimilated white culture by accepting its forms while drastically altering its content."[42] He proceeds to demonstrate this claim by arguing that African American individualism differed greatly from Western individualism in that the former never separated the individual from the community. This made all the difference in their respective moral and psychological understandings. Thus, to a great extent, African Americans have been alienated from the value system of Euro-Americans.

Sidran also argues that because of the orality of both African and African American cultures, the former was transmitted to the latter through speech patterns and music.[43] "Black musicians have traditionally been in 'the vanguard group' of black culture."[44] Further, with respect to social realities, they have never been escapists. Rather, they have always sought to unite their art with life's experiences in order to reconstitute the latter.[45]

One way of seeing how the African understanding of person was preserved in African American music is to look at the way the soloist (an unknown concept in traditional African music) functioned in African American music. Like the traditional African griot, the soloist typically tells the story of the community while telling his or her own story and by telling it in such a way that his or her unique individuality becomes evident. All who hear the story can identify with it; and the moans and groans, cries and shouts testify to the reification of the lived experience. The prominent use of the first-person pronoun in many of the blues and gospel songs serves to personalize the experiences of the whole community.

Yet African American soloists do not tell the story in a stylized way. Rather, they express their own individuality through various forms of improvisation both vocal and instrumental. Whenever they sing and play the blues, gospel, funk, soul, or rap, African American musicians invariably improvise. Most of these artists agree that classical players and singers of black music are inauthentic unless they are unable to depart from the written score and offer their own improvised contributions. Only in the latter does the player demonstrate his or her unique individuality. Yet the one who improvises is never separated radically from the band which accompanies his or her performance. In a jazz band each artist eventually rises from the band for a "break-out" improvised performance and then returns to resume his or her place in the harmonious unity of the band's rhythm. In African American thought and practice, this solo-band relation in music is analogous to the person-community relation in their philosophy. "The large Negro bands, however, attempted to maintain a 'group feeling' that was a function of individual personalities."[46] A peculiar feature of black music is that individuality is not totally submerged in a fixed, stylized way in any of the sections of the band or the chorus.

The soloist's improvised contribution is a very disciplined activity occurring within the confines of a unified composition to which the whole band adheres. The composition itself allows for a broad range of individualized creativity within certain prescribed limits. "The ability to perform music at the peak of emotional involvement, to be able to maintain the pitch of the involvement, and continue the process of spontaneous composition separates black entertainment from almost all of Western tradition."[47] Solo improvisation not only encourages competition (one of the principal characteristics of urbanism); it is also expressive of the liberty of the individual to do as he or she pleases. The soloist's creative flourish may be viewed as a signification of an individualized protest against all external constraints. Clearly the type of individualism encouraged by improvisation contributes to the esteem of all who participate because no single normative criterion of excellence exists in black music. Rather, everybody can be the best at doing something, namely, his or her own thing. In writing about early twentieth-century music in New Orleans, Sidran says the following:

> The individuation within black music, the necessity for each man to have his own "sound," tended to ease this competitive pressure by enabling more people to "do well"; there was no narrow category of good music or good performance. The importance of the individual was second to that of the group in New Orleans, yet this period can be seen as the beginning of a trend, which parallels that of urbanization, wherein the group sentiment is more often than not shaped by individual innovation. The urban environment encouraged the individual psychologically to stretch out much further than had been allowed in rural society.[48]

All students of black music agree that the black musician has always been a cultural leader. In the period prior to their professionalization as paid entertainers, black musicians played a leading role in shaping the cultural ethos of the community at large. Being spiritually inclined, the music was dependent upon a communal response commensurate with its motivational impulse. Hence black music can be rightly understood as the joint creation of the musician and the audience in a continuous interaction very much like the typical "call-response" communicative relationship between the black preacher and his or her congregation.

It is not difficult to see both the autonomous and unifying functions of African American music. As cultural leaders, individual musicians share much in common with African American preachers. Deeply rooted in the oral traditions of their people, their primary function has been that of serving the good of their community in its quest for freedom and its implications for human dignity and empowerment. To that end individual performers have contributed all their energy. In fact, the criterion of excellence has always been the same for African American preaching and music alike: the ability to persuade the people to affirm and celebrate redeeming features in both the substance of the story and the creative powers of the storyteller. The latter always assumed great importance because he or she had the capacity to give new life continuously to a much-repeated oral narrative in need of tireless transmission from one generation to another. Yet it was crucial that the novelty and complexity of each art form be readily perceptible to its ordinary listeners. Otherwise it would surely die. Further still, the moral leadership of both the preacher and the musician has always been determined by the communal purpose served by each, namely, to encourage their people to remain in the struggle for freedom.

Interestingly, African American music has been an important arena for the emergence of female musicians, many of whom gained immortality as truly great artists.[49] Although male instrumentalists have dominated African American music, notable exceptions occurred during the World War II era, when the Sweethearts of Rhythm, an all-women's band (which included some white members camouflaged as mulattos) gained worldwide fame. In the contemporary period many all-women bands in reggae[50] music have appeared both in the U.S. and elsewhere. Many other bands now boast a growing number of women instrumentalists. Yet, in spite of the history of predominantly all-male bands, female vocalists have made their distinctive mark on virtually every genre of black music in every period. Names like Billie Holiday, Shirley Horn, Peggy Lee, Bessie Smith, Ella Fitzgerald, Nina Simone, Lena Horne, Sarah Vaughan, Mahalia Jackson, Clara Ward, the Supremes, and Aretha Franklin have become legendary even in their own time. Sweet Honey in the Rock, led by Bernice Johnson Reagon, an a cappella quintet has achieved world renown in our day while not compromising either the textual base of its mission or its creative genius. Clearly the music of the African American churches, long dominated by women both as instrumentalists and vocalists, has been a training ground for the wider world of black music. Comprehensive studies of African American women musicians are much needed, as are studies of the African American impact on Euro-American music. Both have been greatly neglected.

Many have written about the healing powers of music among African peoples. In fact, some have claimed that the terms *musician* and *healing* are synonymous. Diallo and Hall have written accordingly about the groups they studied:

> In the Minianka villages of Fienso and Zangasso, the musicians were healers, the healers musicians. The word musician itself implies the role of healer. From the Minianka perspective, it is inconceivable that the responsibilities for making music and restoring health should be separate, as they are in the West.
>
> In the Miniankan view and practice of music, harmony is the central concept—the fitting combination and pleasing interaction of parts in a whole. The encomposing whole for our present purposes is the Minianka cosmos, with its invisible and visible dimensions. The entire Minianka village social structure and culture seek to sustain the lives of the people in harmony with one another, the Creator, the ancestors, the spirits of the bush, and nature. Kle-kolo, the path of the Creator, is the path of harmony. Weaknesses of human character, such as envy, jealousy, and hatred, are sources of disharmony. They cause people to stray from Kle-kolo, set people against one another, and make them vulnerable to harmful influences from invisible spirits, which can be additional sources of disharmony. This is the cosmos in which Minianka musicians play their instruments and heal. . . .
>
> Music thus can be a potent force for maintaining or restoring human harmony with the cosmos. This is its ultimate purpose in Minianka culture.[51]

Since the function of music in Minianka culture is similar for the whole of Africa, I contend that it has played a similar healing role for African Americans from the days of slavery up to the present day, speaking the language of the gods in song, music, and dance as a traditional method of restoring the cosmic equilibrium that had been seriously ruptured by the experience of slavery. As with their African forebears, music accompanied all the events of their daily life, including work, worship, festivity, sickness, death. Most importantly, the text and rhythm of the music conveyed transcendent meanings of hope, which may well be the greatest healing power in the midst of life-threatening situations.

Since the desire for freedom has always been the paramount moral goal of African Americans, none can escape its impact. In fact, the style of life that African Americans choose to adopt both as individuals and as a group reflects their response to that desired goal. Since none would dispute that the goal implies an ongoing struggle, all would agree with the sentiments expressed by Frederick Douglass in 1857:

> If there is no struggle, there is no progress. Those who profess freedom and yet deprecate agitation are men who want crops without plowing. They want rain without thunder and lightning. They want the ocean without the awful roar of its mighty waters. Power concedes nothing without a demand. It never did and it never will.[52]

Further, and most importantly, African American understandings of person, family, community, and God are integrally related to one another. The understanding of each is determined primarily by their experience of an existential dialectic, namely, between their collective desire for freedom, on the one hand, and the reality of not having it, on the other hand. It is certain that the moral formation of persons cannot occur apart from that dialectic. Rather, as in warfare, all must assume a political stance in relation to their primary mission in life. For example, insofar as the African American tradition can be divided into two or more major philosophical or political responses to that struggle, then moral development follows accordingly. Children are morally formed in accordance with the basic philosophical or political commitments held by those who assume primary responsibility for their upbringing.

Commensurate with their African roots, African Americans have borne no small disdain for the philosophy of individualism and the cultural spirit it has fostered. They have had similar contempt for the logical extension of such a philosophy in the moral development of self-centered persons who pursue their own autonomous purposes with little or no regard for the well-being of others. Such persons, morally shaped in accordance with the principle of individual autonomy, differ sharply from those who are formed in consonance with a historical principle of communal belonging. The thought of the former sacrificing either their own lives or even a substantial part of their property for the good of others is totally repulsive to them. By contrast, the communal traditions of African Americans (deeply rooted in Africa and preserved through slavery in the family, music, and religion) have made it psychologically impossible for the vast majority of them to embrace fully the basic value system of white Americans. Consequently, the predominant moral and religious values of the two groups differ sharply, a difference clearly manifested in their respective thought about person, family, community, and religion, as well as their understandings of music, property, and politics.

Finally, the African American understanding of person is directly correlated with the latter's contribution to the community's well-being. In other words, a person's social status is measured by the meaningfulness of his or her service to the community. For many generations the highest moral achievement among African Americans was that of being dubbed by the community "a race leader." That entitlement was and continues to be confirmed by countless numbers of recognition ceremonies held annually all over the nation for the purpose of distributing coveted prizes and awards to various individuals for their voluntary services to the African American community. Such occasions ratify the consensual belief that the moral integrity of individuals is determined finally by their selfless devotion to the well-being of the community.

6 ETHICS

African and African American Social Ethics

The African Factor in the African American Experience

Africans and African Americans share a common worldview, which comprises a cosmological whole and unites all of life in and among the realms of spirit, history, and nature. Hence, it follows that all knowledge in their daily lives should presuppose this fundamental holism. Accordingly, the present inquiry into the nature of African and African American ethics rightly began with a deep probe into the common features of traditional African cosmologies and a constructive description of how they were retained in the North American Diaspora. That task provided the foundation on which I have constructed a plausible argument in support of the claim that African spirituality (the dynamic and integrating power that constitutes the principal frame of reference for all individual and collective experiences) was preserved in recognizable form among the North American Diaspora. This does not mean that it was preserved exactly as it had been several centuries ago in Africa. Rather, since all living traditions necessarily change over time, African traditions not only adapted themselves to their new environment but also altered it in many important ways. Thus, I have demonstrated that basic African religious and moral values were preserved in Western cultural forms. The result has been the gradual emergence of an African American culture that contains an amalgam of African and American elements.

In describing and analyzing African spirituality (that is, the African factor in the North American experience), I have sought to identify the basic building blocks for an African and African American social ethic. I have concluded that the basic elements for such an ethic are derived from and reflective of the dynamic structural unity among the four constitutive spheres of African experience, namely: God, community, family, person. Furthermore, I have argued that those four spheres of experience are fully interdependent. No one of them can flourish apart from all the others. Their interdependence is manifested in a variety of reciprocal functions, much like the interrelations among the parts of a living organism.

Similarly, the interdependence of individuals and the community has major implications for all human activities. For instance, since individuals are parts of the community, the latter must assume responsibility for both the good and the bad actions of the former. Thus, the community celebrates the good that individuals do and, whenever their bad actions offend either some divinity or ancestor, the community must repent of those actions by offering propitiatory sacrifices to counteract the ill effects of the deed.[1] Africans never view wrongdoing as strictly an individual matter.

Throughout this study I have taken care to explicate the nature of the changes that many African traditions have undergone in the diaspora. In doing so, I have argued that the African slaves utilized various European cultural forms for the transmission of African values. In fact, they wove various African meanings into those new cultural forms through creative processes of improvisation, practices that Henry Louis Gates has defined as analogous to the African and African American vernacular traditions of *signifying.*[2] Admittedly, the means by which African values were transmitted to the so-called new world differed in accordance with the conditions of slavery. For example, in those areas where African slaves far outnumbered their captors and had minimal face-to-face contact with them, many African traditions were easily preserved with little modification. Numerous examples of these are extant in various parts of the Caribbean Islands and, most prominently, in Brazil. In other areas, however, and especially in the United States, where they were rigorously controlled and stringently forbidden to continue African customs, slaves were forced to conceal the latter from their owners by camouflaging them in cultural forms that usually conveyed double meanings, one for the eyes and ears of slaveowners, the other for the slaves.

Virtue Theory

As we have seen above, the preservation and promotion of community is the paramount goal of African peoples in all spheres of life. It is a practical goal that is deeply rooted in their cosmological thought and constitutive of all personal and public life.[3] Thus, it is not only descriptive of public reality but also normative for every part of it. In other words, it is the determinative measure of value for all human activities. In fact, the purpose of all the realms of life (spirit, history, and nature) is to preserve and promote the well-being of the community, the breadth of which varies in accordance with the nature of particular political alliances between and among various tribal groups. In the descending order of power from the supreme God, through the subdivinities, ancestral spirits, communal and familial leaders, to the youngest child, the highest good of each is the same, namely, the preservation and promotion of the community's well-being.

The anthropocentric nature of African cosmological thought and the holism it entails imply a sacramental view of life in general and of human life in particular. Yet African anthropocentrism does not imply either the superiority of humans over other forms of life or a denial of the supremacy of the deity over all existence. Nor does it constitute a rationale justifying wanton exploitation of humans over natural resources. It merely means that humans are at the center of a sacred cosmos in which they are expected to assume immense responsibilities for the preservation of its unity. The integral relationships between humans and invisible superior powers require a reciprocity of functions between them both. In return for their devotion and faithfulness, humans can expect the protection of both the divinities and the ancestors from a variety of unfriendly cosmic forces. In other words, it is the responsibility of humans to take the initiative in maintaining good communal relations with the invisible world of spirits. If they exercise their responsibilities well, they will receive appropriate compensation in the form of a good life. If they fail to do so, they will suffer misfortune. Insofar as humans are faithful in their devotion to the invisible spirits, they can rightly expect reciprocity. Hence, it is common for Africans and African Americans alike (whether they be traditionalists, Christians, or Muslims) to offer prayers in the form of petitions for the basic conditions of life: health, food, shelter, and protection from all forms of evil including social abuse, political oppression, and economic deprivation. In fact, Africans view religious devotion and good moral habits as necessary conditions for the prevention and the solution of most practical problems in daily life. It is virtually inconceivable for Africans to think of human existence apart from its dependent relationship on God, the divinities, and the ancestral spirits. Consequently, there are no atheists among them.

This sacramental view of life does not claim any primordial cosmological fault in the nature of humanity as such. In fact, African cosmologies have nothing comparable to a doctrine of original sin[4] that condemns the whole of humanity. This does not mean that Africans view all humans as morally good. Nothing could be further from the truth, and evidence to the contrary is quite abundant. Rather, in contrast to those who are born with good destinies, it is widely believed that some people are bearers of various types of bad destinies. Some of them are capable of modification; others not. In either case, with the combined help of professional diviners and much concentrated effort on their own part, humans may, to a certain extent, overcome many aspects of a bad destiny. Thus the notion of destiny, whether good or bad, does not imply human passivity. Instead it informs persons about the possibilities that they are either capable or incapable of realizing.

Clearly, the holistic worldview of Africans implies a sacramental view of life. Additionally, the practical goal of community as the highest good, coupled with the reciprocal relationships between persons and invisible spirits, signal the pragmatic nature of all African thought in relation to each of the realms of life, namely, spirit, history and nature. As a matter of fact, Africans are not easily disposed to speculative thought because the latter tends to have little or no empirical basis. Rather, much of African thought, including that of theology and ethics, arises out of the problems of daily experience, and it is pursued for the purpose of discovering practical solutions for everyday problems. In short, African theology and ethics are practical sciences in the service of the community's well-being. Hence, both are intrinsically political.

Having identified the paramount goal of African and African American thought and practice, let us now discuss the necessary capacities and moral attributes needed for its realization. As we will see, both the capacities and the moral attributes have their empirical bases in the worldviews of African peoples. The ethic I wish to explicate was signalled in the thesis I proposed in chapter 1 above, namely, that among African peoples on the continent and in the diaspora good moral character constitutes the nature of the moral life, and it is both rooted in and derived from God the creator and preserver of all that is.

To advance this argument in as clear and concise a way as possible, I have decided to adopt the following illustrative method. First, I will draw upon the inspirational resources provided by the momentous events of the present period in South Africa, namely, the inauguration of Nelson Rolihlahla Mandela as the first president of that republic to be elected by universal franchise. The whole world agrees that Mandela is an extraordinary person and a leader *par excellence*. His moral character accounts for both. Certainly there appears to be no doubt in his mind or in that of his followers that the good for himself and the good for the community are the same, even though the community's realization of its good is greater because its sphere of responsibility includes all the people. Evidence of this philosophy permeates all of his speeches. In my judgment, no African embodies that ethic more completely in our day than Nelson Mandela, whose strength of character has inspired countless millions both on the continent and around the world. As my argument unfolds, relevant dimensions of his life and moral development will be explicated.

Second, I will also illustrate this ethic by drawing on the resources of the long struggle of African Americans for citizenship rights in the United States and, more specifically, the moral attributes of Martin Luther King, Jr., whose personal integrity and leadership skills have been immortalized not only in the United States but globally. President Mandela and Dr. King are moral exemplars of the African and African American ethic respectively. They share a common spirituality, and their names have become worldwide metaphors for the struggle for the realization of a unified multiracial (commonly called in South Africa "nonracial") community. Interestingly, one discovers very little substantive discussion of either African or African American culture in the writings or speeches of either of the two. Yet the immense impact of their respective cultures on each of them is unmistakable.[5] In my judgment, because of their interest in providing grounds for an expansive community, they saw little need to focus attention on the specificity of their particular cultures. Yet nothing in their respective teachings violates the basic values implicit in their respective African and African American cultures.

The form of the African and African American social ethic I wish to explicate is that of moral virtue (that is, moral excellence), which is deeply rooted in and reflective of the peculiar spirituality I have discussed and analyzed throughout this book. The basis of this ethic in the common worldview of African and African American peoples separates it significantly from other traditions of virtue ethics that draw their source material from different cultural situations in order to address the moral issues implicit in those contexts.[6]

As in all theories of moral virtue, African and African American virtues are dispositions that are not innate. They are acquired by habitual practices, preferably begun in early childhood through teaching and practice. In turn, they eventually produce certain types of character that dispose persons to do certain kinds of things. Since habits can be either good or bad, their quality is determined by that of the goal they serve. Thus, the virtues of African and African American ethics are teleological. That is to say, they are determined by the goal of preserving and promoting community, which we have seen is the ultimate goal of all African peoples. Further and most importantly, these peoples find their fulfillment in the pursuit of that goal.

Thus African and African American ethics is primary concerned with the development of a certain kind of moral character, a character that reflects the basic values of their respective communities. Morality pertains to the cultural ethos and, hence, is culturally specific.[7] According to this perspective, there is no universal morality as such, even though some common moral values are widespread among diverse cultural groups. Yet in my judgment morality is univocal only within particular communities. That is to say, it is determined by the norms, values, and goals of particular communities. The resolution of conflictual relationships between and among communities requires that all concerned be in agreement with the norms, values, and goals of some transcendent community in which the conflicting groups share membership. If they do not share such membership, conflicts among them cannot be resolved apart from the construction of some consensual framework.

In virtue ethics the quality of a person's character determines the quality of that person's actions and vice-versa. The circularity of this argument is important because it demonstrates the relation of being and doing. Each implies the other. For example, a person of moral virtue is one who exercises good habits and, conversely, the exercise of good habits constitutes a person of moral virtue.

An important question that arises in every discussion of virtue ethics is the following: "Why should a person become morally virtuous?" Invariably, the answer to that question is, in a word, *self-realization.* That is, like everything else in the world, a person's life has an ultimate goal, the attainment of which marks the person's full growth. If that ultimate goal is the preservation and promotion of community, as we have argued it is for Africans and African Americans, and if the acquisition of moral virtues is the means to that end, then a person becomes morally virtuous in order to make a substantial contribution to the preservation and promotion of the community. Since the African understanding of community is integrally related to God and the entire realm of spirit, the goal of self-realization is a transcendent goal that is sacramental in nature. Its pursuit is what W.E.B. DuBois once called a "spiritual striving."

The ethics of moral virtue is practical in every sense. Its goal is knowledge of the morally good that humans can do in order to become morally good. Thus, knowing the good is for the sake of doing the good and becoming good. In that respect, virtue ethics has much in common with art. Unlike some arts, however, which produce artifacts that lie outside the process of doing, virtue ethics is like music in that its goal is not separate from the practice. As there is no music apart from playing music, there can be no good people apart from the doing of good actions. Good action is always goal-oriented, and its goodness is determined by the extent to which its quality is commensurate with that of the goal it serves. Thus clarity about the latter is the first principle of good action.[8]

Yet practical habits from which moral virtues emerge are not acquired easily. They involve effort and sometimes discomfort. Yet, as learning to play a musical instrument is stressful in the beginning, practice eventually renders the activity seemingly easy because it becomes a habit and thus it can be performed without thinking. That is not to say, however, there is no thought in the habit. Rather, the thought is absorbed into the activity.

A distinctive feature of African and African American ethics is its grounding in a cosmological spirituality that unites three interdependent realms of life, which are usually ranked in hierarchical order—spirit, history, and nature. Thus, all life is sacred. This is a fundamental principle for all African peoples. Unlike in most Western thought, the sacred is not separated from human and natural life but permeates both. As a consequence, the function of human life is a sacred vocation, namely, to preserve and promote the life of the community. That is also the sacred obligation of the entire community and each of its individual members. Further, all the traditions of the community serve that end. Whenever that life-affirming function is thwarted or perverted by some evil force, then appropriate propitiation must be undertaken by the community in compliance with the prevailing wisdom of the elders and diviners. The evil force must be expunged so that the life of the community can continue.

Since the whole of life is sacred and since the moral virtue of individuals and that of the community are the same, African and African American ethics aims at enabling individual persons to become good so that they will also become good leaders in their respective communities. Africans and African Americans cannot conceive of the one apart from the other. Hence the goal of their ethics is the moral development of both the person and the community.

Such an ethic of virtue does not replace or preclude an imperative ethic of duty and obedience as prescribed by law. The latter is always necessary in pluralistic contexts, especially in urban areas as well as in regional and national governments, where one cannot presuppose a communal ethos of shared moral values. Yet laws themselves must rely upon a citizenry that is morally disposed toward respecting and obeying their mandates.

Some African and African American Moral Virtues

Within this framework we note specific virtues that are highly praised by both Africans and African Americans. As we will see, each virtue requires a natural capacity and adequate social conditions that support its development. This does not mean that the virtue is produced by either nature or by social conditioning. On the contrary, each virtue is acquired through the long process of proper habituation through teaching and practice. Many African practices, however, are communal in nature, namely, festivals, rituals, and ceremonial rites of passage, all of which are embued with religious and moral meanings.

Further, each virtue designates both a psychic and communal value. That is to say, each is a value for the individual as well as one for the community. The former connotes personal development; the latter, leadership development. Both are interrelated; the one implies the other. This crucial feature of the African and African American ethic connotes the integral person-community relationship that is basic to the African and African American understanding of each.

Finally, I will try to name the converse of both the moral virtues and their corresponding leadership styles, taking care to illustrate the latter with reference to President Mandela and Dr. King. Let me add, however, that no attempt will be made to be comprehensive in naming all the virtues. In fact, I have no way of knowing how many virtues there may be. Thus, I will name what appear to me to be the most prominent ones.

Beneficence

No virtue is more highly praised among Africans and African Americans than that of beneficence because it exemplifies the goal of community as it is internalized by individual persons and community leaders. That is to say, the individual's disposition is so shaped by the ultimate goal of community that he or she finds contentment in facilitating the well-being of others. For them, the good of others always assumes priority over their own good. During a recent visit to South Africa I decided to telephone my friends in Soweto near the end of the conference I was attending. Knowing that they would inevitably invite me to spend some days with them, I had taken that into consideration in booking my return flight. When they learned, however, that I had been staying in a hotel in Johannesburg for almost a week while attending the conference, they expressed deep sorrow. "That is not the way we treat our friends," my Sowetan host said. In his mind, people stay in hotels only when they have neither family members nor friends in the area. It made no difference to him that transporting me daily to and from the conference would have inconvenienced him and his family. From his point of view, such an inconvenience was the sacrifice he would have gladly made on behalf of his friend and, further, I should not have been concerned about that matter. Further still, he felt embarrassed that his friends might learn about this matter and in some way blame him. He tried to impress upon me that, because we are friends, I am his family's responsibility whenever I visit his country, and I should not deny them that pleasure.

During that same trip, I had also arranged to visit a former student who lived a longer distance away from Johannesburg. Upon arriving, to my surprise I discovered that he and his wife had prepared to give me their bedroom and bath for the whole period, while they and another visiting relative slept with their three children. Once again I was deeply concerned about the inconvenience I was causing the family. From their perspective, though, they were honored by my visit, and they welcomed the temporary sacrifice of convenience because of that honor. The whole experience was reminiscent of the many times my own mother and father willingly gave up their bedroom for the comfort of guests, sometimes guests whom they had not known for very long. It was taken for granted throughout my community that guests were to receive the best the family had to offer.

For well over a century the African United Baptist Association of Nova Scotia was hosted annually by their respective member churches throughout the province. In each location where the association met, the entire black community, including those who were not members of the churches, participated in hosting the out-of-town guests by providing meals and lodging in their small homes. Since virtually none had spare guest rooms, family members often slept on the floor in order to accommodate more guests than the house seemed able to hold. In recent years this traditional practice has gradually changed, as growing numbers delegates can afford to stay in hotels that had been in previous years racially segregated. In spite of the immense amount of work involved by the hosting families, the joy and delight of it all was that the guests should return to their respective homes feeling that they had been treated well. Their turn to reciprocate would eventually come. Such an annual custom corresponded well with the African view of hospitality.

The above examples anecdotally illustrate the virtue of beneficence. The practical adjustments made by all the family members in hosting visitors impart to children a good part of their training in the gradual acquisition of the same virtue.

Development of the virtue of beneficence is always well supported by a good destiny. Beneficent people come into the world blessed by God and destined for greatness. In Africa their names become bearers of their destiny, pointing to the way in which their lives should develop. Similarly, a good destiny is recognized among those African Americans who are named after family members, prominent heroes or cherished celebrities. In each case, it is hoped that the children will live up to their good names and fulfill all the expectations of their families.

Being born with a good destiny implies birth into a family of commensurate value that possesses all the necessary resources needed for the child's moral development. Destiny requires basic, supportive familial conditions of physical security, economic viability, and good will because moral development can only occur in a moral context.

Synonyms for beneficence are many. They include hospitality, generosity, liberality, benevolence, magnanimity, love. All are expressive of practices undertaken by persons whose character is shaped by those practices. The beneficent person is a person of good will, one who joyfully extends hospitality to all alike. In this respect the beneficent person respects all persons. Though morally superior to ordinary people, the beneficent person is quite unaware of his or her moral goodness. Like all moral virtues, beneficence functions as a second nature for the one who is beneficent.

Africans and African Americans expect their leaders to be beneficent. That is to say, they expect them to share their bounty with all their people because nothing is more glorious than the communal enjoyment of its wealth. Private acquisition of property in whatever form for the enjoyment of the individual or a small elite is the converse of a beneficent spirit. Further, by not counting the cost, the beneficent person is not controlled primarily by the principle of efficiency.

President Nelson Mandela embodies the virtue of beneficence. His gracious spirit of good will is abundant, and his magnanimous hospitality to all and especially to his former oppressors is nearly unbelievable. The relationship that developed between him and his warden of twenty years, James Gregory, has seemed equally incredible to the world at large. Yet these and numerous other acts of kindness merely demonstrate the man's beneficent character. Undoubtedly, the source of his moral development was the training he received in three places: (1) the royal family into which he was born; (2) Fort Hare University (the prominent university founded by missionaries in order to give blacks throughout southern Africa access to excellence in higher education), in which he was educated; and (3) the African National Congress, of which he frequently identifies himself as a disciplined member. All of these institutions have embodied the African and African American goal of preserving and promoting community.

In his cultivation of beneficence as a moral virtue, Mandela's character was fully formed long before he was sentenced to prison in his early forties. That spirit continued to express itself throughout those years as he exercised leadership from his prison cell and, eventually, became a worldwide symbol of the underground struggle against apartheid. When he walked out of prison on February 11, 1990, after having served twenty-seven years of a life sentence in pursuit of the rights of citizenship for his people, the world to its astonishment saw and heard a kingly man with a beneficent spirit that was more embracing than most could imagine.

Mandela's beneficent spirit contributes immeasurably to his unmistaken likeness to a traditional African king, who is invariably a statesperson in every sense of the word. Such a leader is good-spirited; dedicates himself wholly to the good of all the people; knows his place in the scheme of things; is a willing servant of the masses; listens carefully to them and knows that ultimate authority rests in those whose needs the leader is charged to serve; is confident of his power; is courageous; is willing to negotiate and compromise with his enemies for the good of the community; and always rules wisely in accordance with the desires and needs of the community; and is open to the idea of an expansive community of ever-increasing diversity.

Martin Luther King, Jr., represented African America's most prominent embodiment of the virtue of beneficence. None doubted that he was born with a good destiny. Accordingly he was named after his father, who had risen from the status of a sharecropper to a nationally acclaimed minister and an esteemed leader in the black community of Atlanta, Georgia. Nurtured and protected by an intergenerational family all of his life, never having been in want of material resources even during the Great Depression, Martin Luther King, Jr., was among the most privileged African Americans of his day. The symbiotic functions of his family, church, and school were continued when he entered prestigious Morehouse College, long committed to the training of African American male leaders embued with a mission of service to the African American community. In that context, King's teachers and moral exemplars were some of African America's most talented academic scholars and "race leaders," not least of which were Benjamin Mays, Howard Thurman, and George Kelsey, to mention only a few.

King's beneficence was also seen in a variety of personal traits, namely, his love of family, his deep loyalty to the well-being of his people, his belief in the equality of all peoples, his embrace of the major traditions of his people as mediated to him through the family, school, church, and college. Further, as a leader of his people in the struggle against racial oppression, which brought America's race problem and his movement to worldwide visibility, King's beneficent spirit was expressed in his unrelenting commitment to the philosophy of nonviolent resistance, his strong belief in the redemptive power of unmerited suffering, his untiring devotion to the principle of loving one's enemies, his consistent view that nobody is beyond the pale of moral transformation, his steadfast faith that love and justice will ultimately prevail over evil.

Finally, King was the founder of the Southern Christian Leadership Conference, which institutionalized the principles that guided the thought and practice of the Civil Rights Movement that he led. King and his organization soon became a source of moral power for peaceful social change in the United States. All who participated in the practices of nonviolent resistance were morally changed by them and gradually formed in accordance with the virtue of beneficence.

The converse of beneficence is, of course, the vice of meanness. Synonyms for meanness are small-mindedness, mean-spiritedness, disdain, contempt of others, self-centeredness, selfishness. The corresponding leadership style is that of the dictator, whose primary purpose is to make the needs of the community subservient to those of his or her own. Such a style is aloof, haughty, disdainful, arrogant, conceited, and wholly destructive of community, quintessential qualities of the philosophy of possessive individualism.[9]

Forbearance

Forbearance is an important moral virtue for Africans and African Americans because both have been bearers of a tragic destiny for many generations. That is, each has had to endure a long-term dehumanizing plight of racial oppression, economic injustice, political disfranchisement, and social ostracism. For generations their children were born into the cauldron of human degradation, cursed by conditions of suffering and deprivation. They did not (and often still do not) have access to the necessary resources with which to effect any radical change in their respective situations. Under such bitter conditions, moral development was closely allied with the struggle for survival, and moral character was gradually formed in accordance with the virtue of forbearance.

Because it helps people to survive dehumanizing conditions, forbearance can be one of the most effective means for preserving and promoting the goal of community. Patience and tolerance are two of its main synonyms. Yet the activities leading to its realization can be easily misunderstood as implying either complacency or contentment with one's situation. Rather, it may in fact be the case that, after careful deliberation about possible responses to a miserable situation, the simple act of *waiting* may be the best of all possible strategies. Doing what is necessary to preserve life under caustic conditions need not be viewed as either mindless submission or cowardice but, instead, as intelligent action. The collective wisdom of those who have lived for generations under such conditions may often be the most credible support for the spirit and practice of forbearance.

Activities that serve the pragmatic goal of survival are often the habits necessary for developing the virtue of forbearance. Under the most oppressive conditions, all forms of resistance are inevitably forced into concealment, as was commonplace during the periods of slavery and colonialism. Yet their subversive activities were often the principal means by which the people preserved their loyalty to the principal goal of their respective communities, the pursuit of freedom. Those who became outwardly rebellious, however, often lost their lives at an early age. Others who continuously resisted engagement with any such dissidence tended to develop character traits that in some respects were almost identical with those of their oppressors. That is to say, they eventually grew to hate their own people and, in different ways, they tended to blame their own race for all of their problems. Thus, to a great extent, they assumed the spirituality of their oppressors.[10]

During his many years in prison, Nelson Mandela chose to concentrate his activities on survival skills for himself, coupled with continuing his leadership from prison in the anti-apartheid struggle. He never lost sight of the goal in the service of which he had been sentenced to life in prison. Nevertheless, he became a person of forbearance by doing whatever he could in many concealed ways to aid his compatriots in the struggle. Since most of his fellow inmates at Robbin Island were political prisoners, it eventually came to be known as a training base for the underground activities of the African National Congress. I have heard several say that they rejoiced in being sentenced to Robbin Island because it was like going to a graduate school of education to study with the world's most esteemed scholar. There they would meet and learn directly from Nelson Mandela for the first time, a man whose name, picture, and words were banned throughout South Africa. Interestingly, all such efforts to obliterate the man's leadership only added to his mystique and in turn helped to unify all elements in the resistance movement.

Often leaders of freedom movements do not make good politicians because they are not easiiy disposed toward compromise. Nelson Mandela is different. On the one hand, he would never compromise on the principle of universal franchise for his people nor grant the government the right to the high moral ground by demanding that the A.N.C. forsake its commitment to armed struggle. With respect to the latter, he said the following soon after his release from prison:

> The renunciation of violence by either the government or the ANC should not be a precondition to, but the result of negotiation. . . . The position of the ANC on the question of violence is, therefore, very clear. A government which used violence against blacks many years before we took up arms has no right whatsoever to call on us to lay down arms.[11]

Yet, on the other hand, Mandela was willing to compromise with then-President F.W. deKlerk in ways so politically astute that the world has been amazed. I claim that his capacity to hold on to certain essential principles while compromising on other matters exhibits the virtue of forbearance, which held him in good stead during his imprisonment and which prepared him well for his later role in negotiating the demise of apartheid.

Similarly, Martin Luther King, Jr., possessed the virtue of forbearance. The initial way in which he and his associates responded to the arrest of Mrs. Rosa Parks reveals the content of the virtue. At first, the Montgomery Improvement Association, headed by King, did not challenge the system of racial segregation as such but merely requested modest improvements in the management of segregated buses. King and most of his followers, having endured racial segregation and discrimination all their lives, had been trained from childhood onward in customary habits of dealing with it. Most felt it was an unchangeable social structure strongly supported by the terrorizing activities of the Ku Klux Klan and bent on coercing compliance with the system through mass fear and intimidation. In my judgment the virtue of forbearance resulted from longstanding practices among African Americans, extending back to the earliest days of slavery on the continent of Africa.

Undoubtedly, one tradition that this virtue inspired was the so-called accommodationist leadership style of Booker T. Washington, whose influencial leadership was a dominant force in the public life of African Americans throughout the first two decades of the twentieth century. That legacy, which Washington himself inherited from his teachers and mentors, has lived on in succeeding generations as symbolized in the many schools throughout the south that continue to bear his name.

In my judgment, the virtue of forbearance also enabled both Africans and African Americans to give their assent to the philosophy of nonviolent resistance long before it was named and articulated as such by Mahatma Gandhi. That is to say, it was not the philosophy of nonviolent resistance that inspired people's acceptance of it. Rather, it was generations of nonviolent practices that culminated in the virtue of forbearance and motivated people's acceptance of it. The novelty of its use by King was that of direct public confrontation with the white power structure rather than the older activities of indirect subversion.

In sum, the leadership of both Nelson Mandela and Martin Luther King, Jr., involved their courageous commitment to uncompromising legal principles vis-à-vis the issues of disfranchisement, racial segregation, and discrimination, on the one hand, and varying forms of pragmatic compromises vis-à-vis public policy strategies, on the other hand.

The converse of the virtue of forbearance is that of impatience or intolerance, which leads to either foolish and impulsive activities on the one hand or acquiescence, on the other hand. The former is likely to contribute to a retaliatory style of leadership while the latter invariably produces reactionary leadership.

Practical Wisdom

Practical wisdom is excellence of thought that guides good action. This virtue pertains to the measure of cognitive discernment necessary for determining what hinders good action and what enables it. It is the fully developed capacity of a free moral agent for making reasonable judgments about the best means for the attainment of penultimate goals as well as the determination of their commensurability with the ultimate goal of the good life. As with all the virtues practical wisdom is acquired by example and practice. For instance, proper training requires exposing children to the influence of persons of practical wisdom. That is, children need to be in the care of such people for a long time to observe them as models and emulate their activities. Children imitate the activities and styles of their primary mentors—parents, older siblings, adult family members, teachers.

Africans and African Americans highly value the wisdom of their elders because of its grounding in a reservoir of experience. Africans are convinced that the normative value of tradition is embodied in those who have lived to see old age and are now close to the transition to the ancestral world. In their upbringing, most African parents assume that their children will be significantly related to the generation of their grandparents and, possibly even that of their great-grandparents. Unfortunately, the conditions of modern urban life have often militated against the full realization of this reality. Similarly, African Americans have assumed the important presence of intergenerational adults in the upbringing of their children. Whenever their children were separated from their grandparents by geography (as when African Americans had emigrated to the cities), many generations of parents sent their children to live with their grandparents during school holidays. Since time is needed for the efficacy of personal influence, spending the summer in the care of one's grandparents enabled the child to learn about their values and to experience the practical import of those values.

Practical wisdom pertains to intelligent discernment. Most importantly, the person of practical wisdom is able to relate the values of the tradition appropriately to particular situations. A good example of this power is the ability to bring proverbial knowledge to bear on particular contexts as a cultural tool of education and enlightenment. Sometimes that ability is acquired even by the young and especially when they are exposed to proverbial teaching, as Sylvanus Udoidem relates:

> Among the Ibibio, if a young person uses many *Nke* [proverbs] to flavour his discussion or drive home his argument, he is often looked upon as *"Eyen Akan-eren"* ("the son of an old man"). This is not meant in a literal or biological sense . . . . What the expression means is that such a speaker has taken possession of the linguistic inheritance bequeathed to his generation by the older ones. Such individuals are considered as being knowledgeable, wise, sophisticated, versatile and having a moral character on whom the elders can rely for the continuity of the shared values of the people.[12]

Like all the virtues, practical wisdom is the excellent exercise of a skill. Since it pertains to the art of discerning the best means to the attainment of goals, it is calculative in nature. The person of practical wisdom must weigh options and choose the best of them. In the process, the person must also calculate the extent to which the substance of the deliberations should be made public or concealed. Poor judgment with respect to either may damage the outcome's acceptability. A person of practical wisdom also knows when to end the deliberative process and make a decision. Discerning the right time to act is an important part of the process.

Practical wisdom is essential for the whole of moral virtue and for all good leadership because it provides the reasoning underlying all the virtues. Practical wisdom enables excellence in judgment. The person of practical wisdom must not only be knowledgeable about the cultural tradition, as a scholar might be. More importantly that person must know how to relate the traditional wisdom of the ages to the particular issues at hand and to do so in such a way that reasonable persons throughout the community will see and approve the integrity of the judgment. Thus, before passing judgment, the person of practical wisdom must listen well to all who have relevant information pertaining to the issue at hand. Such a person must be open-minded. He or she must shun premature closure. Since the problems at hand are likely to be divisive within the community, the person of practical wisdom seeks a solution that reconstitutes the unity of the community without any undue sacrifice.

Undoubtedly, all would agree that both Nelson Mandela and Martin Luther King, Jr., were men of practical wisdom. From an early age, both "drank deeply," so to speak, from their respective cultural traditions. Both were nurtured in intergenerational families, and in those contexts they were exposed in various ways to the best leaders and mentors of their day. Both had the opportunity to exercise leadership in the youth divisions of the communal organizations in which their elders were visibly active.[13] At an early age both gained experience as peer leaders and impressed all who observed them as intelligent, trustworthy young men with great potential for moral leadership. Mandela's practical wisdom was most manifest in his negotiating skills with his former enemies, and King's practical wisdom was most manifest in his crafting and delivery of persuasive public speeches.

The converse of practical wisdom is simply natural instinct, which issues in impulsive activities that are both unreasonable and uncontrolled. Such people are easily provoked to anger, and their leadership style is necessarily erratic.

Improvisation

Moral virtues are like arts. They are formed by habitual practice. Although they adhere to certain common patterns, mere imitation alone can produce neither morally virtuous persons nor great artists. Rather, the practices that produce either the virtue or the art must become like a second nature made distinctive by the individuality of the person. Thus the person becomes formed by the practice and exhibits that form in a novel way. The novelty represents the actor's unique mark.

Although African and African American families have high regard for tradition, they are also lovers of creative ventures and especially those that expand upon a prescribed theme. Such is the nature of improvisation, which reaches its zenith in musical, oratorical, and ceremonial performance. Among African peoples, one sees signs of improvisation almost everywhere, from the mundane affairs of life to the sublime. In all parts of Africa one is constantly amazed by the high degree of human ingenuity that is displayed in the day-to-day activities of ordinary life. The way in which music, dancing, and singing are integrated into the activity of work contributes energy and beauty to the improvisational and cooperative spirit of the people involved. Westerners visiting anywhere in Africa can be constantly surprised in observing the improvisational work of African auto mechanics repairing engine difficulties with limited tools and few if any spare parts. Such improvisational skills are truly inventive. Since poverty constitutes a basic condition for many improvisational practices, African peoples bestow much praise on the authors of invention because, more often than not, their product represents the creation of something new out of virtually nothing.

One of the most significant spheres of creativity in Africa is that of proverbs. The ability to speak in proverbs is a creative art, as is the ability to understand it. Proverbs are examples *par excellence* of improvised activities. They tend both to affirm and to violate customary rules. I think that Udoidem's analysis of the origin and function of proverbs is analogous to the activities that culminate in the virtue of improvisation:

> Proverbs promote the recovery of order through a new context. The creativity that is involved goes beyond proposing new meanings—it reorganizes our vision of reality. A proverb serves as an occasion for creative reflection: it is a framework for collaborative and contributive creativity both for the speaker and the listener. The former gains a new insight into the given situation that necessitates the application of a particular proverb. For the latter, this provides a frame for reflection, creative insight and an awareness of a new reality. A proverb helps the mind to become investigative and creative. . . . Proverbalization is thus a private and relatively unstructured process that results in the creation of new ideas and insights.[14]

Improvisation comprises unpredictable variations on a theme. It brings novelty to bear on the familiar, not for the sake of destroying the latter, but for the purpose of heightening the individuality and uniqueness of the agent and his or her creative ability. Improvisation expresses not only the agent's creativity and spontaneity but also his or her spirit of perceptive wholeness. By keeping the old and new close at hand, the virtue of improvisation embraces and enhances the whole and thus serves to promote and preserve the goal of community.

The art of improvisation appears throughout the cultural history of African Americans to such an extent that some have claimed that a powerful aesthetic quality inheres in the race itself. If aesthetics is understood as the attempt to make life better, then the traditions of African peoples have always aimed at that goal. Dealing constantly with the tragic elements of life, Africans have traditionally sought to make life more pleasant through the cultivation of the visual and auditory arts. Drawings, paintings, sculptures are everywhere abundant, from the most remote village to the densest urban centers. Similarly, music and dance in their intense creative polyrhythmic forms are designed to help the people in every possible circumstance of life. African arts are to enhance the everyday life of the people, not primarily to change their conditions but to enable the people to see and hear and feel beauty. As long as the people enjoy beauty, they do not succumb to the tragic elements in their midst. Their spirits are uplifted, and in that way the arts preserve and promote the well-being of the community.

All creative activities are commensurate with this art of improvisation. Moral formation and political leadership are not exceptions. Nelson Mandela's embodiment of the virtue of improvisation is seen in his consistent activities aimed at remolding both the old system of racial oppression and its perpetrators into a newly expansive "non-racial" community. The vision of the latter includes the former oppressors united in a thoroughly reorganized and reconstituted system. The virtue of improvisation was acquired by Mandela from the teachings and examples of his predecessors and contemporaries alike (several of whom he does not hesitate to name time and again, such as Robert Subukwe, John Dube, Josiah Gumede, G.M. Naicker, Chief Luthuli, Chris Hani, and Oliver Tambo). Clearly, too, Mandela's activities have inspired the improvisational activities of countless others in drama, music, dance, song, as well as numerous types of community organizational work throughout the nation.

Martin Luther King, Jr.'s embodiment of the virtue of improvisation is seen primarily in the excellence of his oratorical skills, whereby he was able to infuse new meanings into old traditions and remake them into suitable bearers of a new public morality. Like Mandela, King acquired the virtue of improvisation from his teachers and mentors. Similarly, a whole generation of people was inspired to improvisational activities by extending the principles of his work to numerous other causes. His work also provided the inspiration for creative advances in the arts and in all levels of political involvement.

The converse of the virtue of improvisation is rigidity, fixity, legalism, dogmatism, all of which connote an incapacity for creativity and an insensitivity to the psychic needs of oppressed peoples. All such leaders can only imitate prescribed patterns. Their leadership is invariably robotic, and their capabilities are limited to the performance of only routinized functions.

Forgiveness

After centuries of racial oppression one can rightly ask why African peoples seem to exhibit such little racial hatred in return for the misery they were forced to endure. Even during the most intense periods of resistance to slavery, segregation, colonialism, and apartheid, they have rarely been consumed by the spirit of hatred. How did they escape such a destiny? This is an important question, worthy of the most careful investigation, although beyond the scope of this study. Suffice it to say that the commitment of African peoples to the goal of community is one of the principal reasons for the lack of racial hatred among them. The goal of their life is to build relationships, rather than prohibit them, which has had an enormous effect on their moral formation.

African peoples have always known the great toll that hatred takes on both the personality of individuals and the life of the community. In the interest of their highest goal, community, they have shunned hatred by cultivating the virtue of forgiveness through the habitual exercise of kindness.

Even in defeat, however, Africans have always admired the technological superiority of European peoples which, like their own powers, they believed to be deeply rooted in the realm of invisible spirit. Thus they knew that all warfare between themselves and Europeans would necessarily be cosmological in nature. Since most of their traditional attempts to expunge the Western invader by force had failed, they felt obliged to forbear and wait for the proper time when it would be possible to rid themselves of European domination by means other than warfare. In the meantime they would do whatever was possible to cultivate the seed of resistance in many and varied concealed ways. By mid-century the right time had arrived and their goal of political independence was close at hand. At the same time a similar circumstance was appearing in the historical struggle of African Americans for racial justice.

The virtue of forgiveness is essential for the ongoing life of community. For countless reasons, humans inevitably fail to do the good that they are capable of doing. The results of those failures can and often do threaten the well-being of others. Traditionally Africans faced such circumstances by seeking effective means for the restoration of the spiritual balance upset by the pernicious activity. Only then could reconciliation occur between the parties involved. As we have seen, since all activities in Africa are integrally related to all the realms of life, the reconciliation had to be similarly inclusive of all the grieved parties.

The breaking of taboos constituted the most severe threat to the community's well-being. In such cases, restoration of the balance required a major sacrifice, usually the life of the wrongdoer. Such an act was not viewed as merely retaliatory but as a necessary and effective means for reconciliation with all the offended persons, spirits, and divinities.

Thus traditional African societies knew much about forgiveness and what it entailed both for individuals and the community alike. Consequently, Africans did not harbor long-term resentments against anybody.

They instead sought to resolve the problems as quickly as possible so as not to be exposed to the spiritual imbalance for too long a time. In their relations with slaveholders and colonialists alike, African peoples entered into various types of communal relationships with them all along the way. As servants they attended to all their oppressors' personal needs, often living with them under the same roof or in the same compound. Through involuntary sexual liaisons African women on the continent and in the diaspora have given birth to a mixed race of people. Eventually small numbers of the conquered ones were formally educated in the foreigner's cultural traditions. These and many numerous other practices knitted the two groups together in an ambiguous way. Yet no such unity, ambiguous as it was, could have been possible without the forgiveness of the African peoples for their long night of sorrow and misery. From then until now, Africans have striven for the expansion of community in which the two races might be able to live together in mutual respect. It may be that many of the continuing problems between the two rest in the fact that the Europeans never asked the Africans for their forgiveness. That is to say, they never repented of their evil deeds or attempted to compensate their victims for their losses.

Nelson Mandela's approach to the virtue of forgiveness is instructive. Despite serving twenty-seven years in prison for his pursuit of a just cause, he exhibits no detectable signs of racial hatred. Rather, the spirit of dignity and good will that he revealed to the world on the day of his release from prison was the same spirit that African peoples have been extending to their oppressors for many generations. It did not surprise Africans anywhere that he had the capacity to forgive his oppressors and to negotiate with them in good faith. He laid down only one condition, however: that those with whom he negotiated would be persons of integrity. He believed that then-President deKlerk was such a person. It was a belief about which he had some second thoughts at one point in the process, when the progress of the negotiations was seriously threatened by reports of the complicity of the South African police force in fomenting violence. Mandela's confidence in deKlerk was soon restored by the latter's reactions to those charges. Clearly some measure of repentance is a precondition for the efficacy of forgiveness.

Similarly, Martin Luther King, Jr., was imbued with the virtue of forgiveness. When his home was bombed for the first time, while his wife and baby daughter sat in a room next to the blast, he calmed the angry crowd that gathered, imploring them not to fight violence with violence but with the spirit of nonviolence, which functioned for him as a philosophy of forgiveness. Time and again he reiterated his teaching that African Americans were called to hate the evil but not the evildoer; that they should never give up the idea that evildoers are capable of moral transformation.

The virtue of forgiveness has been reflected in the leadership style of both men. It is no accident that Mandela's new government took as its motto *reconciliation and unity,* invoking two key political principles that signal the ultimate goal of the new South Africa. These political principles gained credibility in large part because of their embodiment in the character of Mandela himself.

The virtue of forgiveness was reflected in the leadership style of Martin Luther King, Jr., who often seemed to foretell that he would be assassinated some day. Yet his many speeches, including his final sermon the night before his death, were replete with the spirit of forgiveness, admonishing his followers not to fight hate with hate but with love and forgiveness. The way of love and forgiveness is not, as often thought, the way of weakness but of strength because it is not a natural response but rather a response that manifests a second nature.

The converse of the virtue of forgiveness is the vice of hatred, which repudiates any possibility of reconciliation with one's enemies and which views one's enemies as demonic. The leadership style that emanates from such a vice is isolationist, chauvinist, and belligerent, easily disposed to acts of retaliation.

Contrary to such acts, which accept evil on its own terms, the virtue of forgiveness facilitates rising to a higher moral ground. For forgiveness to be workable, however, the instruments of violence must be tightly controlled through adequate structures of justice. King's practice of nonviolent resistance was practical because he could rely on such structures through the actions of the Supreme Court and the National Guard. But the African National Congress, fully committed to nonviolent resistance for fifty years, finally concluded that it was no longer workable because of the lack of such structures of justice for restraining violence. Thus, after the Sharpville Massacre in 1960, the African National Congress reluctantly decided that it was forced by the structures of violence to engage in armed struggle. In reflecting on that period, Mandela writes:

> The government knows only too well that there is not a single political organization in this country, inside or outside Parliament, which can ever compare with the ANC in its total commitment to peaceful change.

> Right from the early days of its history, the organization diligently sought peaceful solutions and, to that extent, it talked patiently to successive South African governments, a policy we tried to follow in dealing with the present government.
>
> Not only did the government ignore our demands for a meeting; instead it took advantage of our commitment to a nonviolent struggle and unleashed the most violent form of racial oppression this country has ever seen. It stripped us of all basic human rights, outlawed our organizations, and barred all channels of peaceful resistance. It met our demands with force and, despite the grave problems facing the country, it continues to refuse to talk to us. There can only be one answer to this challenge: violent forms of struggle.
>
> Down through the years oppressed people have fought for their birthright by peaceful means, where that was possible, and through force, where peaceful channels were closed.[15]

Mandela's words clearly demonstrate the necessary conditions for the workability of nonviolent resistance. Neither Mahatma Gandhi nor Martin Luther King, Jr., faced such ruthless disregard for human life as did Mandela and his African National Congress. Neither Gandhi nor King and their respective movements were banned from civil society.

Justice

A word must now be said about justice and whether it is for Africans and African Americans one of the moral virtues. I claim that it is the supreme virtue because it is the sum of all the virtues. On the one hand, it inheres in each of them by determining the moral impact of their practices on others. On the other hand, it is the totality of the moral quality contained in all the virtues. In other words, one cannot be just without possessing all the other virtues because complete justice would be diminished by the lack of any one of them. Thus, the virtues of beneficence, forbearance, practical wisdom, improvisation, and forgiveness and those that are not treated here are all practical activities, the exercise of which contributes not only to one's own good but, more importantly, to the good of the community. The latter is the ultimate goal of justice. In all human activities, African peoples are concerned primarily with two forms of justice: (1) the individual's obligations to the community as mediated through the many dealings individuals have with one another and (2) the community's obligations to its members and itself. Aristotle classified these two concerns as commutative and distributive justice, respectively, the former pertaining to civil law and the latter to the common good.

It is beyond the task of this study to present a full-scale African and African American understanding of justice. Suffice it to say, however, that the ultimate goal of justice is also the preservation and promotion of community. A distinctive feature of the African view of distributive justice is the substantive role that the community is expected to assume for the well-being of its members. Many have referred to this concern in traditional African society as African socialism or, more precisely, African communalism. Both terms connote a high degree of communal ownership of basic material resources required by all citizens for a viable life.

Because of the high moral value Africans place on community as the ultimate goal of all their activities and because of its integral relatedness to the various realms of life, most Africans are favorably disposed to the basic principles of socialist governments while reluctant to transfer any particular political structure from a foreign cultural context to their own. Their orientation to socialist principles, then, owes nothing to the philosophy of Karl Marx or the ideology of communism as practiced by the former U.S.S.R. or by other modern governments. Rather, its grounding lies in the cosmological thought of traditional African societies. Such thought is fundamentally different from that Western Enlightenment political philosophies, which are primarily interested in protecting individual rights and private property. The latter philosophies necessarily presuppose contractual societies that, unlike communal societies, cannot take for granted the protection of individuals. Theories of human rights are necessarily constructed, and their legalization becomes foundational for all such contractual societies. An inevitable problem emerges, however, whenever the latter seeks to impose its moral system of thought onto countries not constituted according to theories of political contract.

As with all the virtues, African understandings of justice are regulated by the demands of their ultimate goal, namely, the preservation and promotion of community. Such a goal requires a basic structure of inclusive equality, wherein the well-being of all the community's members is assured. This does not imply any form of absolute egalitarianism since the hierarchical ordering of African societies insists on many levels of inequality based on moral and political distinctions with respect to the differing contributions each makes to the well-being of the whole community.

In terms of his leadership, Nelson Mandela's proposed program of Reconstruction and Development reflects his commitment to a communal understanding of justice. Though he has pledged himself to a free-market economy, the precise economic theory that will inform his government is not yet fully known. Yet I predict that his government will never draw sharp lines of demarcation between formal laws of rights and opportunities, on the one hand, and public policies of material assistance and entitlements, on the other hand.

At the time of Martin Luther King, Jr.'s death, he was preparing to lead a march on Washington protesting the plight of the nation's poor and calling upon the government to assume responsibility for the elimination of poverty. His organizing the nation's diverse poor into the Poor Peoples' Campaign, along with gleanings from numerous speeches, informal conversations, and close personal associations have provided evidence for some scholars to claim that he was a so-called closeted socialist.[16] In my judgment, King's political philosophy was based on his strong belief in the "beloved community" as the final goal of all human endeavor. In his philosophy, government has an obligation to provide for the legal protection as well as the material necessities of its citizenry.

Public and Private Ethics

The foregoing analysis of six African and African American virtues, namely, beneficence, forbearance, practical wisdom, improvisation, forgiveness, and justice, has demonstrated their deep roots in the cultural traditions of African peoples. Although not comprehensive, I hope that discussion of six of them is adequate to illustrate the theory of African and African American ethics.

Demonstrating the personal and public character of African and African American ethics has been a necessary methodological requirement because the ethic we have sought to explicate is primarily a public one. Its *telos* or goal is inherently public, namely, the preservation and promotion of community. By illustrating the embodiment of all six virtues in two major international figures, President Nelson Rolihlahla Mandela and Dr. Martin Luther King, Jr., I have made a plausible argument in support of my claim that these two persons, one African and the other African American, shared a common worldview and embodied a common morality. Further, they have both greatly inspired countless millions around the world to embrace their respective visions of social justice as well as their moral endeavors for its realization. Further still, I have endeavored to show how each of the virtues they embodied expressed itself in their public practices. By doing so, I hope I have signalled the implications of this ethic for public policy and especially how each was able either to reappropriate or reconstitute the Eurocentric traditions of their respective societies.

Yet I cannot overemphasize the fact that my intent in drawing upon Mr. Mandela and Dr. King is to illustrate an African and African American ethic that is in no way limited to these two leaders. I hope that none will misunderstand this aim.

All of the virtues that we have discussed are royal virtues. That is, they are the virtues befitting the character of most traditional African kings and queens, who, as we have seen, are wrongly understood as despots. They were, rather, mediators between the tribal community and the world of spirit. Their traditional role was always to strive to maintain all the proper relationships between the many and varied forces on which the community's well-being depended. Further and most importantly, these royal virtues have always been widely distributed within African communities, laying claims on each member to aspire to their realization in his or her moral development. Every member of the community was expected to develop the moral nature of a good king or a good queen. A community of such moral integrity guaranteed its preservation. Thus the ethic has pragmatic value.

Finally, given the negative disposition Americans have had toward royalty, at least since the American Revolution, it is important to say a word in defense of the term *royal* because African traditions cannot be understood or appreciated apart from a clear grasp of this reality. Admittedly, there are good kings and bad kings, good queens and bad queens. Although not all traditional African societies had monarchies, alternative structures provided similar forms of authority. Sometimes the paramount authority was located in a council of chiefs. Under such circumstances, the function of the council was not unlike that of the traditional king. In any case, societies were hierarchically ordered, with numerous checks and balances against despotism, which was always considered the worse form of evil that could possibly befall a people. Whenever despots emerged, however, traditional societies had effective ways for the removal of such persons from office, usually by ceremonial sacrifice. Many military coups in modern-day Africa should be understood in this light. When political corruption becomes so extensive as to stifle the strivings of the masses for a viable life, the latter have often rejoiced and praised the military for bringing them relief from their suffering. But when the military merely replaces the despotism of the former by its own arbitrary governance, then the condition of the people can worsen.

American scholars have long been puzzled in their attempts to explain the immense authority exercised by the typical African American pastor. Since the vast majority of African American churches have a congregational type of polity, it is all the more puzzling to explain why the pastor has as much authority as he or she does. Unfortunately, the widespread use (by sociologists and others) of Max Weber's category of charismatic leadership to explain this phenomenon has become almost commonplace. In my judgment, such a concept fails to do justice to the phenomenon. A far more adequate explanation for the pastor's status lies in an understanding of African kingship and the way its moral substance has been transmitted to America through the role and function of African American religious leaders. Their congregations assume the space of a tribal community and they themselves embue the tribal chief or king with a wide breadth of authoritative powers.

The Christian Factor in African and African American Social Ethics

In the beginning of this book I suggested that Christianity and Islam were too guest religions on the African continent that are continuing to undergo the process of syncretism with traditional African cultural thought and practice.[17] Presently that process is being called by many names, the most frequent being "Africanization," "enculturation," "indigenization," and "decolonization." Regardless of the name, however, the goal is the same, namely that of enculturating Christianity so that Africans will cease viewing it as a lingering legacy of the cultural imperialism of European colonialism. Unlike Islam, however, and though undertaken unwittingly, Christians' practice of translating Christianity into African languages has greatly facilitated that process.[18]

Traditionally, Africans on the continent and in the diaspora have searched the biblical scriptures for positive references to African peoples.[19] From the earliest times they have taken great comfort in the text that has been a keystone for all African Christian nationalism, namely, Psalm 68:31, "Princes shall come out of Egypt; Ethiopia shall soon stretch out her hands unto God." In varying ways this text became the justifying source for the so-called Ethiopian Movement that swept the African continent from the 1880s onward. A century earlier it had been a source of inspiration for the African American Independent Church Movement. The principal aims of both movements were two: resistance to racism, slavery, and colonialism, on the one hand, and advocacy for the independence of African churches from European control, on the other hand. Unfortunately, both movements were greeted by their opponents with extreme measures of political, legal, and military repression. The British, for example, imprisoned and executed several Christian prophets of this movement, including Prophet John Chilembwe of Malawi, who was executed in 1915 and Prophet Simon Kimbangu (founder of the Church of Jesus Christ of the Prophet Simon Kimbangu), who was imprisoned in the former Belgian Congo from 1921 until his death in 1951.[20] Most independence movements in Africa and nationalist movements in the diaspora have claimed some measure of inspiration from Psalm 68:31.

The African American Independent Church movement emerged with the founding of the African Methodist Episcopal Church, the African Methodist Episcopal Zion Church, and the African Episcopal Church, all in the 1790s. In 1805 Thomas Paul organized the African Baptist Church in Boston and, along with a group of Ethiopian traders who had resisted the segregated seating patterns of the white Baptist Church in New York, he organized the Abyssinian Baptist Church in New York City in 1808. The following year, the First African Baptist Church in Philadelphia was founded. The spirit of this African American Independence Movement as affirmed by the vast majority of African Americans was commensurate with that of the Ethiopian movement a century later.

The founding of the Liberian settlement of repatriated American slaves in 1820, as well as the colonization of Sierra Leone by returned slaves from Nova Scotia in 1792, contained similar nationalist elements that reflected the spirituality of their peoples in their common quest for an independent space in which to pursue their goal of community-building.

Ethiopia's almost unique status, having been one of only two African countries never to have fallen under the yoke of European colonial rule, added immense significance to her near-sacred status among African peoples everywhere. Further, the import of Ethiopianism was enhanced by the symbol of its throne and the resplendent majesty of its Emperor, who traced his descent back through Queen Cleopatra to the Queen of Sheba, the wife of King Solomon. Additionally, the Emperor's titles included that of Defender of the Faith and Head of the Ethopian Orthodox Church, which tradition claimed had been founded by St. Thomas the Apostle.

No visit by any head of government has ever captured the imagination and pride of African Americans like that of his imperial Majesty Haile Selassie's visit to New York City in the 1930s. His gift to Abyssinian Baptist Church of a six-foot silver Cross is firmly embedded in the pulpit area of the present edifice. In Trinidad, Jamaica, and other parts of the Caribbean the Rastafarian Movement[21] once claimed the Emperor Haile Selassie as the Living God of his followers, the Ras Tafari. The movement claims that salvation comes only to those who are repatriated to Africa and live under the sovereign rule of African governments. The Rastafrians also claim continuity in philosophy and theology with Marcus Garvey's Back to Africa Movement, clearly the largest African American social movement ever to arise in the United States. During its rapid ascent to national visibility in the 1920s, it spread throughout the United States, Canada, and the Caribbean with the blessing of Bishop Alexander MaGuire and his newly founded African Orthodox Church, a branch of which still survives in my native town of Sydney in the province of Nova Scotia. All contemporary black nationalist and Pan-Africanist movements exhibit many similarities with the Garvey Movement.

Inspired by the independence of Ghana in 1957 under the charismatic leadership of Kwame Nkrumah, black consciousness movements in the United States emerged and soon spread to Canada and linked up with similar movements in South Africa in the late 1960s and early '70s. All exhibited the common goals of freedom and empowerment for African peoples. The spirit of these movements has permeated African cultures everywhere, redeeming them from centuries of conquest by the restoration of political independence and the recovery of personal dignity. The many and varied corresponding activities of African peoples on the continent and in the diaspora have been both complementary and encouraging resources for one another.

Greatly enabled by the rapid technological developments in communications, African peoples are in closer contact with one another than was ever thought possible even a quarter of a century ago. Only in the twentieth century have Africans come to the Americas voluntarily, and in the last half of the twentieth century they have been coming in ever-increasing numbers. Similarly, in recent decades, large numbers of African Americans have been traveling back and forth to Africa in large numbers. The full cultural impact of such face-to-face encounters is hard to estimate. Suffice it to say that the cultural impact is already being felt in music, dance, religion, and the visual arts. Clearly African peoples are rapidly discovering the enormous cultural resources they may yet contribute to the enrichment of one another's lives.

Most Africans on the continent now claim Christianity as their own. Even though the gradual process of enculturation continues unabated in the independent African churches,[22] it is often greatly hindered by the various controlling forces that many former mission churches continue to exert on their denominational counterparts in Africa. Yet the handwriting is on the wall, so to speak, and sooner or later, like African American Christianity, African Christianity will also emerge full-blown as a distinctive contribution to the newly emerging world Christianity that has no one normative center in any particular cultural context.

Postscript

In spite of the many methodological issues that have restrained many scholars from undertaking this type of study, I am confident that I have made a plausible case for the continuity of moral and religious experience between African peoples on the continent and those in the North American diaspora. It is my hope that this inquiry will be viewed as a significant stimulus for many similar studies in the future.

Undoubtedly, African Americans have a deep and abiding interest in the subject matter of this book because it concerns our identity as a people. One of the many devastating effects of both slavery and institutionalized racism on the psyches of our people was the widespread dissemination of erroneous propaganda about African humanity: propaganda that pervaded the Western world for many centuries. Interestingly African Americans always knew that the absorption of either negative or ambivalent attitudes toward Africa would mirror similar attitudes about themselves. Hence, our destiny as a people seems to have been one of constantly reconstructing our self-understanding in the face of overwhelming negative odds. The moral and spiritual health of our people, then and now, depended on the creative power of human ingenuity to forge positive meanings out of negative experiences. Happily, our foreparents did not despair in the face of their misery but, rather, acted and thought in such ways as to preserve and enhance all possible life-giving forces. These included, first and foremost, the cosmological worldview that they brought with them into slavery: a worldview that was destined to be modified though not obliterated by their encounter with this new world. Thus I have sought to explicate the commonalities of moral and religious experience that underlie the many cultural differences among our African forebears.

Though dependent throughout on the findings of many scholars principally in anthropology, ethnography, and history, I have taken great care not to become captive to their social-functionalist methodologies. Rather, I have adopted the heuristic use of a phenomenological method[1] which permits an empathic yet critical engagement with the subject matter at hand. Throughout this study I have assumed that centuries of slavery, racial segregation, and disfranchisement greatly enabled African Americans in retaining the most prominent elements of an African worldview that constituted their only reliable frame of meaning. Hence, all encounters with the world of their Western captors were interpreted through that frame of reference. Accordingly, they transmitted African meanings through a vast variety of Euro-American cultural forms. In this work I have sought to explicate the nature of that process and to demonstrate its import for the construction of an African and African American theory of moral virtue.

This study is written primarily for African peoples in the North American African diaspora because the problem that impels this inquiry is the need to explicate the nature of the African factor in that experience. I cannot overemphasize one point, however, namely that the argument of this book is in no way biologistic. No gene accounts for the preservation of the African factor. Further, it is also important to note that this study does not imply that the preservation of the African factor is unique to Africans alone. Rather, I would hypothesize that studies of other immigrant groups would yield similar results.

Though many anthropologists and historians have made notable contributions to our understanding of African cultures, and though several comparative studies have focused on the impact of traditional African religions on African American Christianity, this book comprises the first such extant study in religious social ethics. In providing a constructive theory of moral virtue, I have laid the foundation for an African and African American religious social ethic which, in keeping with its African lineage, is intrinsically empirical, political, and theological.

Thus, this is a study in religious social ethics. Its goal has been that of providing a framework for a moral theory that fits the relevant historical data. Having done that, it is appropriate to ask about the implications of our theory for public policy. In brief, a moral theory of virtue requires a set of social conditions that will facilitate the realization of its desired ends, namely, the development of morally virtuous people. In other words, moral development is dependent on a community's capacity to facilitate it. If for any reason a community fails to provide an environment that is conducive for the development of moral virtues the converse will certainly occur. That is to say, the moral character of the community will be reflected in the moral development of its children. So it should not be surprising to anyone that a community that allows children to have easy access to dangerous weapons such as handguns will yield a generation of children easily adept at using such weapons for their own purposes. Thus a theory of moral virtues implies a morally virtuous society. Conversely, moral development is necessarily arrested by conditions of family instability, economic impoverishment, wanton violence in the streets, poor education, the lack of symbiotic familial and social organizations deeply committed to the well-being of children. Thus a theory of moral virtue implies comprehensive public policies aimed at preserving and enhancing the community's well-being as a societal construct. Young people have the opportunity to develop into morally virtuous persons only when good symbiotic relations pertain among those responsible for their moral health: stable families, trustworthy schools, concerned churches, and various sociopolitical organizations. In short, a theory of moral virtue implies the need for a comprehensive public policy promoting the moral development of its citizenry.

Lest readers misunderstand my intent, let me hasten to say that it is far from that of romanticizing traditional African cultures. Any lack of criticism of the latter in this book is justified by my claim that moral criticism must be prospective rather than retrospective. That is to say, the past can be criticized morally only by employing relevant moral criteria from that period. In appropriating the past for the present, however, one is justified in subjecting that past to the reigning moral criteria of the present. Accordingly, I have raised relevant criticisms about the function of patriarchy in contemporary African and African American communities.

Finally, I need to say a word about the particular moral exemplars I have chosen to highlight in chapter 6, namely Dr. Martin Luther King, Jr., and President Nelson Rolihlahla Mandela. Let no one suppose that my selection of two prominent men implies any particular gendering of the moral virtues. On the contrary, all Africans and African Americans, male and female, are expected to develop the same moral virtues and manifest the same type of moral character.

Further, though all saints are morally virtuous persons, not all morally virtuous persons are saints. Hence, the discovery of moral blemishes in one's personal life does not necessarily rob one of his or her exemplary moral status since one's contributions to the well-being of the larger community may well outweigh the former. In my judgment, this certainly applies to both King and Mandela as well as to countless others. Yet I do not hold to any radical moral cleavage between one's private and public life.

Notes

Preface

1. In my judgment, the term *black loyalist* is a misnomer because the primary loyalty of these ex-slaves was to their own cause of freedom rather than the British crown, to which the white loyalists were deeply committed. Treated as pariahs by the white settlers and denied the promises made to them by their British liberators, blacks encountered misery rather than the joys of freedom in Nova Scotia. Several historians have studied this event, the most prominent being the following: Robin Winks, *The Blacks in Canada: A History* (New Haven: Yale University Press, 1971); James W.St.G. Walker, *The Black Loyalists: The Search for a Promised Land in Nova Scotia and Sierra Leone, 1783–1870* (Halifax: Dalhousie University, 1976); Frank Stanley Boyd, Jr., *McKerrow: A Brief History of Blacks in Nova Scotia, 1783–1895* (Halifax, Nova Scotia: Afro-Nova Scotian Enterprises, 1976); Bridglai Pachai, *Peoples of the Maritimes: Blacks* (Nova Scotia: Four East Publications, 1987).

2. Albert J. Raboteau, *Slave Religion: The "Invisible Institution" in the Antebellum South* (Oxford: Oxford University Press, 1978), 139–40.

3. See Grant Gordon, *From Slavery to Freedom: The Life of David George, Pioneer Black Baptist Minister* (Hantsport, Nova Scotia: Lancelot Press for Acadia Divinity College and the Baptist Historical Commission of the Atlantic Baptist Convention of the Atlantic Provinces, 1992).

4. *Christian Responsibility in an Independent Nigeria: A Report Prepared for the Christian Council of Nigeria* (Lagos: Christian Council of Nigeria, 1960).

1. Africa: Revolution in Understanding

1. Carol Gilligan's highly acclaimed book, *In a Different Voice* (Cambridge, Mass.: Harvard University Press, 1983) offers sharp criticism of the inherent male bias in Lawrence Kohlberg's moral theory, which she argues skews his understanding of self and morality to such an extent that the theory can in no way do justice to women and their moral development. For a splendid discussion of the racist principle of discrimination, see "A Genealogy of Modern Racism" in Cornel West, *Prophesy Deliverance: An Afro-American Revolutionary Christianity* (Philadelphia: Westminster Press, 1982), 47ff.

2. Iris Marion Young, *Justice and the Politics of Difference* (Princeton, N.J.: Princeton University Press, 1990), 7. Some representative works of the period are the following: Harold Cruse, *The Crisis of the Negro Intellectual* (New York: William Morrow & Co., 1967) and *Rebellion or Revolution* (New York: William Morrow & Co., 1968); Paulo Freire, *Pedagogy of the Oppressed* (New York: Continuum Publishing Corp., 1970); Nathan I. Huggins, Martin Kilson, Daniel M. Fox (eds.), *Key Issues in the Afro-American Experience* (New York: Harcourt Brace Jovanovich, 1971); Albert Memmi, *The Colonizer and the Colonized* (Boston: Beacon Press, 1965); Frantz Fanon, *The Wretched of the Earth* (New York: Grove Press, Inc., 1968) and his *Black Skin, White Masks* (New York: Grove Press, 1967); S. P. Fullinwider, *The Mind and Mood of Black America* (Homewood, Illinois: The Dorsey Press, 1969); Gayraud S. Wilmore, *Black Religion and Black Radicalism: An Interpretation of the Religious History of Afro-American People* (New York: Anchor Press/Doubleday, 1973).

3. See Cornel West's commentary on postmodernism in his *The American Evasion of Philosophy: A Genealogy of Pragmatism* (Madison, Wisc.: University of Wisconsin Press, 1989), 236, where he writes: "Much of the current 'postmodernism' debate, be it in architecture, literature, painting, photography, criticism, or philosophy, highlights the themes of difference, marginality, otherness, transgression, disruption, and simulation."

4. E. Bolaji Idowu, Chair of the Department of Religious Studies in the University of Ibadan, Nigeria, was the first African religious scholar in this period to undertake such a study. Although his *Olodumare: God in Yoruba Belief* (London: Longmans, 1962) was perhaps more theological than anthropological, it represented a serious ethnographical study that revealed considerable new material published there for the first time. Five years later John S. Mbiti published his classic study, *African Religions and Philosophy* (Garden City, N.Y.: Praeger Publishers, 1969), which aimed at discussing traditional African religions as a whole. In 1965 a solid historical treatise in African religious history was published by J.F.A. Ajayi, *Christian Missions in Nigeria 1841–1891: The Making of a New Elite* (Evanston, Ill.: Northwestern University Press, 1965). In this study the author presents his work as a self-conscious effort to represent the post-colonial African historical consciousness.

5. Cornel West, *Prophesy Deliverance,* 47.

6. P. Olisanwuche Esedebe, *Pan-Africanism: The Idea and Movement, 1776–1963* (Washington, D.C.: Howard University Press, 1982), 18.

7. St. Clair Drake, *Black Folk Here and There: An Essay in History and Anthropology* (Los Angeles: Center for Afro-American Studies, University of Calif., 1987), 14.

8. Michael Omi and Howard Winant, *Racial Formation in the United States: From the 1960s to the 1980s* (London, Routledge, 1986), 14–15. For a full treatment of this subject, also see Drake, *Black Folk Here and There,* 20ff.

9. Ibid., 60.

10. It is interesting to note that senior civil servants in the colonial regime in West Africa received a six-month home leave every eighteen months in order to

recuperate from the stresses and strains of West African climatic conditions. I myself witnessed this during my stay in Nigeria in 1961–64 as well as during an earlier visit in 1958.

11. See V.Y. Mudimbe, ed., *The Surreptitious Speech:* Presence Africaine *and the Politics of Otherness, 1947–1989* (Chicago: University of Chicago Press, 1993), xiii.

12. Ndabaningi Sithole, *African Nationalism* (London: Oxford University Press, 1959), 30

13. J. Ki-Zerbo, ed., *General History of Africa, vol. 1: Methodology and African Philosophy* (Berkeley: University of California Press, 1989), 24.

14. In 1947 Alioune Diop gave birth to the anti-colonial journal *Presence Africaine* for the purpose of retrieving African culture, restoring the dignity of African peoples, and enabling both culture and peoples to assume their rightful place in the scholarly world.

15. In one of his several weighty books, the historian John Henric Clarke has written a splendid biographical introduction to Diop. See Cheikh Anta Diop, *Civilization or Barbarism: An Authentic Anthropology,* trans. Yaa-Lengi Meema Negemi, and ed. Harold J. Salemson and Marjolijn de Jager (Brooklyn, New York: Lawrence Hill Books, 1981), xiii–xxi. See also an extensive analysis of the development of Diop's argument in Drake, *Black Folk Here and There,* 137–41; 152–53; 310–15. See also a splendid and informative memorial essay by Mamadou Diouf and Mohamad Mbodj, "The Shadow of Cheikh Anta Diop," in Mudimbe, *The Surreptitious Speech,* 118–135.

16. See Molefe Asante, *The Afrocentric Idea* (Philadelphia: Temple University Press, 1987).

17. J. Ki-Zerbo, ed., *General History of Africa, vol. 1:* viii.

18. For a full discussion of this subject, see ibid., 54ff, "The Oral Tradition and Its Methodology."

19. Patrick Manning, *Slavery and African Life: Occidental, Oriental, and African Slave Trades* (Cambridge: Cambridge University Press, 1990), 165.

20. See William Pierson, *Black Legacy: America's Hidden Legacy* (Amherst: University of Massachusetts Press, 1993).

21. Cornel West, *The American Evasion of Philosophy,* 139.

22. W.E.B. DuBois, *The Souls of Black Folk: Essays and Sketches* (New York: Fawcett, 1961 [1903]), 17.

23. Drake, *Black Folk Here and There,* 4.

24. Alain Locke, *The New Negro,* . . .

25. See Arnold Rampersad's "Introduction" to the 1992 edition of *The New Negro* (New York: Atheneum MacMillan Publishing) for a description of the academic and social context of the founders of the Harlem Renaissance. In this essay Rampersad notes that the Board of Trustees of Howard University would not grant Professor Alain Locke permission to teach a course on race in spite of the fact that he had graduated from Harvard University, studied as a Rhodes scholar at Oxford before continuing his studies at the University of Berlin and

the Collège de France in Paris. Clearly the constraints against African American scholars were many and varied. Nevertheless, creativity was not stifled.

26. Alain Locke, *The New Negro,* 5.

27. Examples of these are the Harlem Renaissance writers: Alain Locke, Jean Toomer, James Weldon Johnson, Claude McKay, Langston Hughes, Charles S. Johnson, Jessie Fauset, Countee Cullen, W.E.B. DuBois, Kelly Miller, Zora Neale Hurston, Arna Bentemps, to mention only a few. On the African continent scholars such as Edward Blyden, J. Olumide Lucas, Samuel Johnson (Pastor of Oyo), are notable examples.

28. James H. Cone, *Black Theology and Black Power* (New York: Seabury, 1969).

29. The first major criticism of Cone's theology appeared in J. Deotis Roberts, *Liberation and Reconciliation: A Black Theology* (Philadelphia: Westminster Press, 1971). His appreciation for black theology is seen in his identification of himself as a black theologian who affirms the black theology project in principle while disagreeing with certain aspects of Cone's thought in particular.

30. This should not be surprising, given that his Ph.D. dissertation in the joint program at Garrett Theological Seminary and Northwestern University was on Karl Barth's anthropology.

31. An excellent case study of this society is found in a book written by one of its principal founders. See Charles Shelby Rooks, *Revolution in Zion: Reshaping African American Ministry* (New York: Pilgrim, 1990).

32. Gayraud S. Wilmore, *Black Religion and Black Radicalism: An Interpretation of the Religious History of Afro-American People* (New York: Doubleday, 1972).

33. James H. Cone, *The Spirituals and the Blues* (New York: Seabury, 1972).

34. Several recent publications by African American ethicists illustrate this orientation: Walter Fluker, *They Looked for a City: A Comparative Analysis of the Ideal of Community in the Thought of Howard Thurman and Martin Luther King, Jr.* (Lanham, Md.: University Press of America, 1989); Robert Michael Franklin, *Liberating Visions: Human Fulfillment and Social Justice in African-American Thought* (Minneapolis, Minn.: Fortress Press, 1990); Enoch H. Oglesby, *Born in the Fire: Case Studies in Christian Ethics and Globalization* (New York: The Pilgrim Press, 1990).

35. Those who have given serious attention to African studies and whose works are greatly appreciated by African American religious scholars are the following: Albert J. Raboteau, *Slave Religion: The "Invisible Institution" in the Antebellum South* (New York: Oxford University Press, 1978); Gayraud S. Wilmore, *Black Religion and Black Radicalism;* Leonard E. Barrett, *Soul-Force: African Heritage in Afro-American Religion* (Garden City, N.Y.: Doubleday, 1974); Henry H. Mitchell, *Black Belief: Folk Beliefs of Blacks in America and West Africa* (New York: Harper & Row, 1975); Robert E. Hood, *Must God Remain Greek? Afro Cultures and God-Talk* (Minneapolis: Fortress Press, 1990;

Enoch Oglesby, *Born in the Fire.* In addition, some younger African American religious scholars have been involved in dialogical work with theologians in South Africa. Prominent among these are the following: Dwight N. Hopkins, *Black Theology USA and South Africa* (Maryknoll, N.Y.: Orbis Books, 1989); Josiah U. Young, *Black and African Theologies: Siblings or Distant Cousins* (Maryknoll, N.Y.: Orbis Books, 1986).

36. For a discussion of this meeting, see Rooks, *Revolution in Zion,* 143.

37. Ibid., 144.

38. Some of the principal pioneers and representative works in this movement are the following: Katie G. Cannon, *Black Womanist Ethics* (Atlanta, Ga.: Scholars Press, 1988); Jacqueline Grant, *White Women's Christ and Black Women's Jesus: Feminist Christology and Womanist Response* (Atlanta, Ga.: Scholars Press, 1989); Delores Williams, *Sisters in the Wilderness: The Challenge of Womanist God-Talk* (Maryknoll, N.Y.: Orbis Books, 1993); Renita J. Weems, *Just a Sister Away: A Womanist Vision of Women's Relationships in the Bible* (San Diego, Calif.: LuraMedia, 1988); Cheryl Townsend Gilkes, "Mother to the Motherless, Father to the Fatherless: Power, Gender, and Community in an Afrocentric Biblical Tradition," in *Semeia: An Experimental Journal of Biblical Criticism* 47 (1989): 57–85; Emilie M. Townes, *A Troubling in My Soul* (Maryknoll, N.Y.: Orbis Books, 1993). See also Townes' *Womanist Justice, Womanist Hope* (Atlanta, Ga.: Scholars Press, 1993); Toinette M. Eugene, "Moral Values and Black Womanists," *Journal of Religious Thought* 44 (Winter-Spring 1988): 23–34.

39. Some prominent twentieth-century representatives of this style are E. Franklin Frazier, John Hope Franklin, Carter G. Woodson, Rayford W. Logan.

40. This term is borrowed from St. Clair Drake, whose book *Black Folk Here and There* is largely a critical and appreciative analysis of this style of scholarship, variously expressed in such theoretical designations as Egyptology, Pan-Africanism, and Afrocentricity.

41. A few prominent twentieth-century representatives of this style are Cheikh Anta Diop, Chancellor Williams, Ivan Van Sertima, Yosef ben-Jochannan, John S. Mbiti, Mercy Amba Oduyoye.

42. As one who spent a lifetime studying African religions and is fully aware of their diversity, Noel Q. King writes that he is constantly amazed by the amount of spiritual unity that exists in Africa in the midst of its diversity. See his book *African Cosmos: An Introduction to Religion in Africa* (Belmont, Calif.: Wadsworth Publishing Co., 1986), 2, as well as his bibliographical source materials.

43. Winthrop S. Hudson, "The American Context as an Area for Research in Black Church Studies," *Church History* 52 (1983), 170–71.

44. Ibid., 171.

45. Ibid.

46. Frantz Fanon, *Black Skin, White Masks* (New York: Grove Press, 1967).

47. See my essay entitled, "Expanding and Enhancing Moral Community: The Task of Christian Social Ethics," in *Issues of Justice: Social Sources and Religious Meanings,* ed. Warren R. Copeland and Roger D. Hatch (Macon, Ga.: Mercer University Press, 1988).

48. It is important to note here that law is ambiguous because its source can be either external or internal. For example, as with every association, the members of the academic community agree upon internal covenants of governance which, in turn, require the protection of civil law.

49. Mercy Amba Oduyoye, *Hearing and Knowing: Theological Reflections on Christianity in Africa* (Maryknoll, N.Y.: Orbis Books, 1986), 36.

50. J. Ki-Zerbo, ed., *General History of Africa, vol. 1,* x.

51. Mechal Sobel, *Trabelin' On: The Slave Journey to An Afro-Baptist Faith* (Westport, Conn.: Greenwood Press, 1979).

52. One of the earliest and most prominent proponents of this theory was Melville Herskovits, whose book *The Myth of the Negro Past* (New York: Beacon Press, 1958) is virtually a classic in the field of African cultural studies. See also Lawrence W. Levine, *Black Culture and Black Consciousness: Afro-American Folk Thought from Slavery to Freedom* (New York: Oxford University Press, 1977); Albert J. Raboteau, *Slave Religion;* John W. Blassingame, *The Slave Community: Plantation Life in the Antebellum South* (New York: Oxford University Press, 1979).

2. God: The Source and Ground of All Life

1. John S. Mbiti, *African Religions and Philosophy* (Garden City, N.Y.: Doubleday & Co., 1970), 2–3. See also J. Omosade Awolalu, *West African Traditional Religion* (Ibadan, Nigeria: Onibonoje Press & Book Indus. Ltd., 1979), chs. 6 & 7; E.G. Parrinder, *West African Religion* (London: Epworth Press, 1961); *idem, African Traditional Religion* (London: S.P.C.K., 1968); E.B. Idowu, *African Traditional Religion: A Definition* (London: SCM Press, 1973), as well as his *Olodumare: God in Yoruba Belief* (London: Longmans, 1962).

2. J. Omosade Awolalu, *Yoruba Beliefs and Sacrificial Rites* (Essex, Eng.: Longman Group Ltd., 1981), 3.

3. Mbiti, *African Religions and Philosophy,* 20.

4. See ibid, 17–18.

5. Emefie Ikenga Metuh, *God and Man in African Religion: A Case Study of the Igbo of Nigeria* (London: Geoffrey Chapman, 1981), 35.

6. *The Christian Century* 97 (August 27-September 3, 1980), 817.

7. Ibid., 818.

8. Gabriel M. Setiloane, *African Theology: An Introduction* (Johannesburg, S. Afr.: Skotaville Publishers, 1986), 29.

9. Ibid., 29.

10. Mbiti, *African Religions and Philosophy,* 38.

11. Evan M. Zuesse, "Perseverence and Transmutation in African Traditional Religions," in Jacob K. Olupona, ed., *African Traditional Religions in Contemporary Society* (New York: Paragon House, 1991), 174.

12. For a good discussion of this subject and a splendid list of Yoruba names for the deity, see Modupe Oduyoye, "Names and Attributes of God" in E.A. Ade. Adegbola, *Traditional Religion in West Africa* (Ibadan, Nigeria: Daystar Press, 1983), 349–57; also see Metuh, *God and Man in African Religion,* ch. 3.

13. Metuh, *God and Man in African Religion,* 34ff.

14. Joseph Akinyele Omoyajowo, "The Role of Women in African Traditional Religion," in Jacob K. Onupona, ed., *African Traditional Religions in Contemporary Society,* 74. For a good summary of the place of women in creation myths, proverbs, and prayers, see John S. Mbiti, "*Flowers in the Garden: The Role of Women in African Religion,*" in ibid., 59–71.

15. Geoffrey Parrinder, *African Mythology* (New York: Peter Bedrick Books, 1986), 23.

16. Ibid., 71.

17. Ibid., 80ff.

18. J. Omosade Awolalu, *Yoruba Beliefs and Sacrificial Rites,* 54.

19. Parrinder, *African Mythology,* 44.

20. Ibid., 101.

21. Ibid., 111ff.

22. Albert J. Raboteau, *Slave Religion: The "Invisible Institution" in the Antebellum South* (Oxford: Oxford University Press, 1978), 86.

23. We are indebted to Evan M. Zuesse for her use of this term. See Evan M. Zuesse, "Perseverence and Transmutation in Traditional Religion," 170.

24. Joseph E. Holloway, ed., *Africanisms in American Culture* (Bloomington and Indianapolis: Indiana University Press, 1990), 37.

25. Lawrence W. Levine, *Black Culture and Black Consciousness: Afro-American Folk Thought from Slavery to Freedom* (New York: Oxford University Press, 1977), 31.

26. Mbiti, *African Religions and Philosophy,* 20ff.

27. Levine, *Black Culture and Black Consciousness,* 32.

28. For a nearly comprehensive account of this process of moving from an African consciousness to a quasi-African American consciousness en route to an African American Christian ethos, see Mechal Sobel, *Trabelin' On: The Slave Journey to an Afro-Baptist Faith* (Princeton, N.J.: Princeton University Press, 1988); see also her subsequent book, *The World They Made Together: Black and White Values in Eighteenth-Century Virginia* (Princeton: Princeton University Press, 1989).

29. This viewpoint is similar to Melville Herskovits' in his effort to show how the slaves translated European words and cultural expressions into African speech patterns and behavior systems respectively. See Raboteau's discussion of Herskovits in *Slave Religion,* 51.

30. Levine, *Black Culture and Black Consciousness,* 53.

31. Holloway, ed., *Africanisms in American Culture.*

32. Kwasi Wiredu, *Philosophy and an African Culture* (Cambridge: Cambridge University Press, 1980), 45.

33. John W. Blassingame, *The Slave Community: Plantation Life in the Antebellum South* (New York: Oxford University Press, 1979), 20–21.

34. Ibid., 20.

35. Eugene D. Genovese, *Roll, Jordan, Roll: The World the Slaves Made* (New York: Pantheon Books, 1974), 211.

36. Jacob K. Olupona, *Kingship, Religion and Rituals in a Nigerian Community: A Phenomenological Study of Ondo Yoruba Festivals* (Stockholm, Sweden: Almqvist & Wiksell International, 1991), 171–72.

37. Margaret Washington Creel, *A Peculiar People: Slave Religion and Community-Culture among the Gullahs* (New York: New York University Press, 1988), 2.

38. Joseph E. Holloway, "The Origins of African-American Culture," in Holloway, ed., *Africanisms in American Culture,* 17.

39. The best available argument in support of this is found in Lamin Sanneh's book, *Translating the Message: The Missionary Impact on Culture* (Maryknoll, N.Y.: Orbis Books, 1989).

40. See Albert J. Raboteau, *Slave Religion,* 98.

41. John Blassingame, *The Slave Community,* 98.

42. This viewpoint is similar to that of Melville Herskovits in his effort to show how the slaves translated European words and cultural expressions into African speech patterns and behavior systems, respectively. See Albert J. Raboteau's discussion of Herskovits in his *Slave Religion,* 51.

43. Some prominent representatives of this type of scholarship are: Levine, *Black Culture and Black Consciousness;* Sobel, *Trabelin' On; idem, The World They Made Together;* Robert Farris Thompson, *Flash of the Spirit: African and Afro-American Art and Philosophy* (New York: Random House, 1983); Creel, *A Peculiar People.*

44. Two prominent scholars of this genre are: Levine, *Black Culture and Black Consciousness;* Sterling Stuckey, *Slave Culture: Nationalist Theory and the Foundations of Black America* (New York: Oxford University Press, 1987).

45. Peter Randolph, "Plantation Churches: Visible and Invisible," in Milton Sernett, ed., *Afro-American Religious History: A Documentary History* (Durham, N.C.: Duke University, 1985), 66.

46. Levine, *Black Culture and Black Consciousness,* 160.

47. For a full explication of this understanding, see Peter J. Paris, *The Social Teaching of the Black Churches* (Philadelphia: Fortress Press, 1985).

48. A more complete analysis of this tradition is found in ibid.

49. See John S. Mbiti, *African Religions and Philosophy,* 268. Also see Benezet Bujo, *African Theology in Its Social Context* (Maryknoll, N.Y.: Orbis Books, 1992), 20.

50. For a full discussion of the function of hierarchy in African ethics see John S. Mbiti, *African Religions and Philosophy,* Chapter 17.

51. Ibid., 268ff.

52. J. Omosade Awolalu and P. Adelumo Dopamu, *West African Traditional Religion* (Ibadan, Nigeria: Onibonoje Press and Book Indus. Ltd., 1979), 77.

53. For a full description of Esu see Awolalu and Dopamu, *West African Traditional Religion,* 82ff.

54. Albert J. Raboteau, *Slave Religion,* 44.

55. Genovese, *Roll, Jordan, Roll,* 246.

56. Sobel, *Trabelin' On,* 232.

57. Mbiti, *African Religions and Philosophy,* 20.

58. In chapters two and five of her recent book *Sisters in the Wilderness: The Challenge of Womanist God-Talk* (Maryknoll, N.Y.: Orbis Books, 1993), Delores S. Williams gives primacy to both the survival and wilderness themes in African American woman's tradition. Similarly this writer has drawn upon the same themes in his discussion of the theology of the black churches in Canada. See his essay, "The Moral, Political and Religious Significance of the Black Churches in Nova Scotia" published as the Fifth Anniversary Lecture by the Black Cultural Centre for Nova Scotia, 1989. Yet it is important to note, however, that the African understanding of wilderness is woeful. See discussion below of Wole Soyinka's play, *A Dance of the Forests,* 53–54.

59. See Delores S. Williams' relevant, constructive analysis of this subject matter in her *Sisters in the Wilderness: The Challenge of Womanist God-Talk* (Maryknoll, N.Y.: Orbis Books, 1993).

3. Community: The Goal of the Moral Life

1. John S. Mbiti, *African Religions and Philosophy* (Garden City, N.Y.: Doubleday, 1970), 3.

2. Ibid., ch. 8.

3. Margaret Washington Creel, "Gullah Attitudes toward Life and Death," in Joseph E. Holloway, *Africanisms in American Culture* (Bloomington and Indianapolis: Indiana University Press, 1990), 88.

4. J. Omosade Awolalu and P. Adelumo Dopamu, *West African Traditional Religion* (Ibadan, Nigeria: Onibonoje Press and Book Indus. Ltd., 1979), 71.

5. Even under the oppressive conditions of life in the townships of South Africa, this author has observed the prominence of this memorial, which in English is referred to as the "unveiling of the tombstone." These ceremonies occur at the grave site and are followed by the slaughtering of sheep and much festivity. Family, neighbors, and friends share in the expense and frequently the churches are also involved in some way.

6. Westerners visiting African countries are frequently amazed by the space purchased in daily newspapers for memorializing renowned family members. These often entail full-page ads.

7. For a full discussion of this subject, see Mbiti, *African Religions and Philosophy,* 266ff.

8. 'Zulu Sofola, "The Theatre in the Search for African Authenticity," in Kofi Appiah-Kubi and Sergio Torres, eds., *African Theology en Route* (Maryknoll, N.Y.: Orbis, 1981), 132–33.

9. Mbiti, *African Religions and Philosophy,* 21.

10. Ibid., 21, 23.

11. Ibid., 28–29.

12. This is one of the most difficult problems facing any African woman who fails to marry or to bear children. Few things in the Western context can compare with the profound social stigma and personal guilt that stems from such a circumstance. Although various alternative arrangements serve to protect and conceal the infertility of men, no such arrangements are available to women.

13. For a comprehensive study of this goddess, see Judith Gleason, *Oya: In Praise of an African Goddess* (San Francisco, Harper Collins Publishers, 1992).

14. For evidence in support of this argument, see Lawrence W. Levine, *Black Culture and Black Consciousness: Afro-American Folk Thought from Slavery to Freedom* (New York: Oxford University Press, 1977), 37.

15. Robert Farris Thompson, *Flash of the Spirit: African and Afro-American Art and Philosophy* (New York: Random House, 1983), 7.

16. Basil Davidson, *The African Genius: An Introduction to African Social and Cultural History* (Boston: Little, Brown & Co., 1969), 191.

17. Ibid., 192–93.

18. Ibid., 193.

19. J. A. Adedeji, "The Egungun in the Religious Concept of the Yoruba," in E.A. Ade. Adegbola, ed., *Traditional Religion in West Africa* (Ibadan, Nigeria: Daystar Press, 1983), 124ff.

20. For a comprehensive case study of African kingship, see Jacob K. Olupona, *Religion and Kingship in a Nigerian Community: A Phenomenological Analysis of Ondo Yoruba Festivals* (Stockholm: Almqvist & Wiksell International, 1990).

21. Reference his study, *The Negro Church* (Atlanta: Atlanta University Press, 1903).

22. For discussion of the roots of this style of charismatic leadership in the oral traditions of Africa and its predominance in the African American churches, see C. Eric Lincoln and Lawrence H. Mamiya, *The Black Church in the African American Experience* (Durham, N.C.: Duke University Press, 1990), 13–14.

23. See K. Onwuka Dike, *Trade and Politics in the Niger Delta, 1830–1885* (Oxford: Clarendon, 1959), for one of the earliest scholarly analyses of this important phenomenon in the West African slave trade. Also see Patrick Manning, *Slavery and African Life: Occidental, Oriental and African Slave Trades* (Cambridge: Cambridge University Press, 1990), ch. 5.

24. Manning's *Slavery and African Life* is an excellent study of the impact of the African slave trade.

25. Ibid., 87.

26. Ibid., 86.

27. Ibid., 149ff.

28. This writer has had the uneasy experience of visiting Fort Jesus in Mombasa on the east coast of Kenya, a massive stone structure built by the Portuguese in the fifteenth century for the warehousing of slaves.

29. Howard Thurman, *Deep River: Reflections on the Religious Insight of Certain of the Negro Spirituals* (New York: Harper & Brothers, 1955), 43–44.

30. Frederick Douglass, "Slaveholding Religion and the Christianity of Christ," in Milton C. Sernett, ed., *Afro-American Religious History: A Documentary Witness* (Durham, N.C.: Duke University, 1985), 104–05.

31. All over the south and in many parts of the north, low-key celebrations of the Emancipation Proclamation are still held on January 1, often in churches and frequently sponsored by or in association with the National Association for the Advancement of Colored People. In fact, the so-called African-American national anthem, "Lift Every Voice and Sing," was composed by James Weldon Johnson to be sung at one such celebration in Jackson, Florida, in 1900. Similarly, in several places in Canada annual celebrations of the end of the slave trade in the British Colonies continue to be held.

32. This corresponded with the time when the Fisk Jubilee Singers had begun making the spirituals the subject matter for the concert stage by adhering to all the canons of theatrical performance. Here the songs not only served the pragmatic function of all cultural arts in bringing aesthetic pleasure to concert audiences, but they also demonstrated that the folk-materials of slaves (i.e., both lyrics and tunes) could be arranged musically by descendents of slaves for the aesthetic appreciation of theater audiences everywhere in the world and, more especially, the royal houses of Europe. Also, this was thought to be an effective means for eradicating racial prejudices of various sorts from the minds of white people.

33. In the United States, this resulted in the formation of the Association for the Study of Afro-American Life and History, founded by Dr. Carter G. Woodson in 1915, who began publishing the quarterly *The Journal of Negro History* in 1916. Under Woodson's initiative Black History Week has been celebrated annually since 1926. These were premier events in the continuing effort to encourage learned studies and reflections on all dimensions of the African American past.

34. Davidson, *The African Genius,* 51; also see E. Bolaji Idowu, *Olodumare: God in Yoruba Belief* (London: Longmans, 1962), ch. 3.

35. Davidson, *The African Genius,* 52.

36. Charles H. Long, *Significations: Signs, Symbols, and Images in the Interpretation of Religion* (Philadelphia: Fortress Press, 1986), 106.

37. Ibid., 176.

38. Joseph E. Holloway, ed., *Africanisms in American Culture* (Bloomington and Indianapolis: Indiana University Press, 1991), xix.

39. Ibid.

40. This problem has often been cited as one of the worst legacies of the slave past, namely, African American self-hatred manifested in numerous ways, not

least being the color-line within the African American community and the various cosmetic treatments of skin bleaches, surgical procedures, etc.

4. Family: The Locus of Moral Development

1. John S. Mbiti, *African Religions and Philosophy* (New York: Doubleday, 1970), 135.

2. Diane Kayongo-Male and Philista Onyango, *The Sociology of the African Family* (London and New York: Longman, 1984), 6.

3. For an explanation of this custom, see Kayongo-Male and Onyango, *Sociology of the African Family,* 7.

4. Ibid., 7.

5. John S. Mbiti, *Love and Marriage in Africa* (London: Longman, 1973), 192.

6. See Awa Thiam, *Black Sisters Speak Out: Feminism and Oppression in Black Africa* (London: Pluto Press, 1977).

7. Ibid., 8.

8. W.E. Burghardt Du Bois, *Black Folk: Then and Now* (New York: Henry Holt & Co., 1939), 118.

9. John S. Mbiti, *African Religions and Philosophy,* 268. In the opening pages of his book *African Theology in Its Social Context* (Maryknoll, N.Y.: Orbis Books, 1992), 20, Benezet Bujo discusses the hierarchical ordering of life in Africa, beginning with God the dispenser of all life. He writes, "Life is participation in God, but it is always mediated by one standing above the recipient in the hierarchy of being. This hierarchy belongs both to the invisible and to the visible world. In the invisible world, the highest place is occupied by God, the source of life. Then come the founding fathers of clans, who participate most fully in the life of God. Then come the tribal heroes, deceased elders, other dead members of the family, and various invisible beings, including earthly powers, although these belong partly also to the visible world . . . . They include the king, and the queen-mother, as well as those who wield or represent royal power; the chiefs of clans and the oldest members of families; heads of households; family members."

10. Mercy Amba Oduyoye clearly distinguishes between matriliny and matriarchy, which are often confused by Westerners. The former exercises no political power. In fact, in her own Akan tradition, which is matrilineal, women inherit through their older brother. See her *Hearing and Knowing: Theological Reflections on Christianity in Africa* (Maryknoll, N.Y.: Orbis Books, 1986), 122–23.

11. See Christine Oppong, *Middle Class African Marriage* (London: George Allen and Unwin, 1981), 91–93.

12. There are female ancestors as well, but they are not as powerful as the male ancestors.

13. E. Bolaji Idowu, *Olodumare: God in Yoruba Belief* (London: Longmans, 1962), 151.

14. Mbiti, *African Religions and Philosophy,* 139.

15. Ibid., 174.

16. Ibid., 175.
17. Idowu, *Olodumare,* 149–50.
18. Ibid., 144ff.
19. Ibid., 157–168.
20. E. Franklin Frazier, *The Negro Family in the United States* (Chicago: University of Chicago Press, 1939).
21. Herbert G. Gutman, *The Black Family in Slavery and Freedom, 1750–1925* (New York: Vintage, 1976).
22. Ibid., 34.
23. Ibid., 329.
24. Ibid.
25. Ibid.
26. Ibid.
27. Ibid.
28. Ibid., 224–29.
29. Ibid., 229.
30. Ibid., 218.
31. Ibid.
32. Frazier, *The Negro Family in the United States,* 32.
33. Ibid., 49.
34. DuBois, *Black Folk,* 106.
35. I have chosen to refer to the African American pastor as *regal* or *kingly* instead of patriarchal in order to express more richness of leadership style. Clearly, the notion of kingship is a broader and deeper metaphor than that of patriarchy, which applies more to the conditions of family relationships (especially those between men and women) than those of the wider community, which is the pastor's rightful sphere of work. Although the metaphor of kingship may irritate some Americans, Africans will have no difficulties in seeing the functional continuities with their own traditions.
36. The patriarchy of the African American churches has come under scathing attacks by womanist theologians, a representative example of which is found in Delores S. Williams recent book, *Sisters in the Wilderness: The Challenge of Womanist God-Talk* (Maryknoll, N.Y.: Orbis Books, 1993), ch. 7 and 8. Note especially her description of the universal Hagar's spiritual church as an exemplary African American egalitarian religious tradition, 225–228.
37. Frazier, *The Negro Family in the United States,* 296.
38. Ibid., ch. 9.

5. Person: The Embodiment of Moral Virtue

1. Elia Mashai Tema, "Pastoral Counseling Encounter with African Traditional Values and the Acculturation Process," (unpublished Master of Theology thesis in the Department of Systematic Theology, Theological Ethics and Practical Theology, University of South Africa, February 1979), 21.

2. Modupe Oduyoye, "Man's Self and Its Spiritual Double," in E.A. Ade. Adegbola, ed., *Traditional Religion in West Africa* (Ibadan, Nigeria: Daystar Press, 1983), 285.

3. Ibid.

4. Often what was judged evil by one tribal group was judged a blessing by another. For example, the Yorubas view the birth of twins as a special blessing from the ancestors, and they were named accordingly Idowu and Kayinde. But the Ibos viewed twins as a curse, and traditionally they were killed.

5. Margaret Thompson Drewal, *Yoruba Ritual: Performers, Play, Agency* (Bloomington: Indiana University Press, 1992), 52.

6. Ibid., 56–57.

7. Meyer Fortes, *Religion, Morality and the Person: Essays on Tallensi Religion* (Cambridge: Cambridge University Press, 1987), 250.

8. Fortes mentions such prominent figures as Marcel Mauss, Emile Durkheim, C.H. Cooley, George Herbert Mead, and Margaret Mead, all concerned about this question. See Ibid, 250.

9. J. Omosade Awalalu and P. Adelumo Dopamu, *West African Traditional Religion* (Ibadan, Nigeria: Onibonoje Press and Book Indus., 1979), 161.

10. Fortes, *Religion, Morality,* 149.

11. J. Omosade Awalalu and P. Adelumo Dopamu, *West African Traditional Religion,* 156–57. The authors then proceed to give an extensive account of this concept of destiny or personality-soul among many African peoples. See 157–71.

12. Modupe Oduyoye, "Man's Self and Its Spiritual Double," 273ff.

13. Fortes presents a lengthy description of this process in *Religion, Morality and the Person,* 147f.

14. Fortes subjects the relationship of father and eldest son to a psychological analysis in his chapter on "The First Born." See ibid., 218ff.

15. Kofi Appiah-Kubi, "Indigenous African Christian Churches: Signs of Authenticity," in Kofi Appiah-Kubi and Sergio Torres, eds., *African Theology en Route* (Maryknoll, N.Y.: Orbis Books, 1981), 124.

16. P.R. McKenzie, "Was the Priestess of Yemoja Also among the Prophets?" in *Orita: Ibadan Journal of Religious Studies* 9 (June 1975), 67–68.

17. Ibid., 162ff.

18. E. Bolaji Idowu, *Olodumare: God in Yoruba Belief* (London: Longman's 1962), 181.

19. See J.N. Kudadjie, "How Morality Was Enforced in Ga-Adangme Society," in E.A. Adegbola, ed., *Traditional Religion in West Africa* (Ibadan, Nigeria: Daystar Press, 1983), 171ff.

20. Ibid., 172–73. For an excellent discussion of the methods of policing in traditional Nigerian societies, see Tekena N. Tamuno, "Traditional Police in Nigeria," in ibid, 177–93. This article also discusses the role of women in policing the criminal offenses of women.

21. For a detailed discussion of the power of speech and especially of the curse among Nigerian peoples, see Modupe Oduyoye, "Potent Speech" in ibid., 203ff.

22. John S. Mbiti, *African Religions and Philosophy* (Garden City, N.Y.: Doubleday, 1970), 141.

23. J. Omosade Awolalou and P. Adelumo Dopamu say that among Africans the most valued sacrifice is a blood sacrifice, and in that category human sacrifice is the greatest because of the worth of human persons. They view this as not unique to Africans but widely adhered to in antiquity, including by the Jewish and Christian religions. Accordingly, Africans have had no difficulty in grasping the meaning of Christ's sacrifice. See their *West African Traditional Religion,* 33–35. Similarly, those close attendants of the king, who are destined to accompany him into his grave, are very highly respected by the entire community and live a life of royal privilege.

24. See J. Omosade Awolalu, *Yoruba Beliefs and Sacrificial Rites* (Essex, U.K.: Longman, 1979).

25. Mbiti, *African Religions and Philosophy,* 143.

26. Ibid.

27. Ibid., 150.

28. Ronald Dworkin, *Taking Rights Seriously* (Cambridge, Mass.: Harvard University Press, 1978), 269ff.

29. Cornel West, *Prophesy Deliverance: An Afro-American Revolutionary Christianity* (Philadelphia: Westminster Press, 1982), 17.

30. For a full explication of this principle as institutionalized in their churches, see the author's *The Social Teaching of the Black Churches* (Philadelphia: Fortress Press, 1985), ch. 1.

31. See Alan B. Anderson and George W. Pickering, *Confronting the Color Line: The Broken Promise of the Civil Rights Movement in Chicago* (Athens, Georgia: The University of Georgia Press, 1986).

32. Albert J. Raboteau, *Slave Religion: The "Invisible" Institution in the Antebellum South* (Oxford: Oxford University Press, 1978), 290ff.

33. For a description of these meetings by a contemporary theologian, see Dwight Hopkins, *Shoes That Fit Our Feet: Sources for a Constructive Black Theology* (Maryknoll, N.Y.: Orbis Books, 1993), 18–20.

34. See Ben Sidran, *Black Talk* (New York: Holt, Rinehart and Winston, 1971), 15–16.

35. For a good discussion of the ring shout, see Sterling Stuckey, *Slave Culture: Nationalist Theory and the Foundations of Black America* (New York: Oxford University Press, 1987), 85–88.

36. Ibid., 77–78.

37. For an excellent discussion of the peculiarities of African American humour, its presence in black music, and its descent from Africa, see Henry Louis Gates, Jr., *The Signifying Monkey: A Theory of African-American Literary Criticism* (New York: Oxford University Press, 1988), 51–60.

38. I prefer to use the term *concealed* in relation to the slave church rather the term *invisible* which is more often used by sociologists and historians. The term *concealed* implies much more deliberate activity on the part of the slaves than the

term *invisible* does. Further, to speak of its invisibility is to view the matter from the perspective of slaveowners.

39. Mary Ellison, *Lyrical Protest: Black Music's Struggle against Discrimination* (New York: Praeger Publishers, 1989), 2. In addition, Ellison lists the following prominent scholarly studies of black music: Eileen Southern, "African Retention in Afro-American Music (U.S.A.) in the 19th Century"; David Evans, "African Elements in Twentieth Century United States Black Folk Music"; Portia Maultsby, "Africanisms Retained in the Spiritual Tradition," all in D. Heartz and B. Wadie, eds., *Report of the Twelfth Berkeley Congress 1977* (American Musicological Society, Barenreiter Kasel, 1981), 88–98, 53–66, and 75–82 respectively; Eileen Southern, *The Music of Black Americans: A History* (New York: W.W. Norton & Co., 1971), 3–24; Paul Oliver, *Savannah Syncopators: African Retentions in the Blues* (London: Studio Vista, 1970), 10–101.

40. Ellison, *Lyrical Protest,* 1. It should be noted that the ongoing debate about the moral quality of rap music vividly reveals conflicting viewpoints about the political message that rap music should convey.

41. Yaya Diallo and Mitchell Hall, *The Healing Drum: African Wisdom Teachings* (Rochester, N.Y.: Destiny Books, 1989), 71–72.

42. Sidran, *Black Talk,* 25.

43. Ibid., 12.

44. Ibid., 6.

45. Ibid., 28.

46. Ibid., 74.

47. Ibid., 47.

48. Ibid., 43.

49. See chapter 5, Mary Ellison, *Lyrical Protest,* for one of the best analytical descriptions of freedom and independence as expressed by African American women in song.

50. Ellison, *Lyrical Protest,* 11.

51. Diallo and Hall, *The Healing Drum,* 79–80.

52. Ellison, *Lyrical Protest,* 47.

6. Ethics: African and African American Social Ethics

1. For a full discussion of this ritual, see J. Omosade Awolalu, *Yoruba Beliefs and Sacrificial Rites* (London: Longman, 1979), 152-56.

2. Henry Louis Gates, Jr., *The Signifying Monkey: A Theory of African-American Literary Criticism* (New York: Oxford University Press, 1988), 63-64.

3. This insight is supported by the work of Robert Michael Franklin. His book *Liberating Visions: Human Fulfillment and Social Justice in African-American Thought* (Minneapolis: Fortress Press, 1990) constitutes an important ethical inquiry into the lives of four major African American leaders in order to explicate the integral relatedness of the personal and public dimensions of their respective thought and action.

4. If *original sin* refers to violation of things that are forbidden by God, then the African understanding of taboo may be its closest equivalent. E. Bolaji Idowu names adultery, beating one's parent, and breaking a covenant as tabu. See his *Ododumare: God in Yoruba Belief* (London: Longmans, 1962), 144ff.

5. In my judgment most African American ethicists have discerned the importance of culture for African American ethics. Hence many of their works have assumed the form of cultural analyses in search of the basic elements of an African American social ethic. This judgment applies to the following: Garth Baker-Fletcher, *Somebodyness: Martin Luther King, Jr., and the Theory of Dignity* (Minneapolis: Fortress, 1993); Lewis V. Baldwin, *There Is a Balm in Gilead* (Minneapolis: Fortress, 1991); Lewis V. Baldwin, *To Make the Wounded Whole* (Minneapolis: Fortress, 1992); Katie G. Cannon, *Black Womanist Ethics* (Atlanta, Ga.: Scholars Press, 1988); John H. Cartwright, "The Religious Ethics of Howard Thurman," in *Annual of the Society of Christian Ethics,* ed. by A. Anderson (1986): 79-99; Riggins R. Earl, Jr., *Dark Symbols, Obscure Signs: God, Self, and Community in the Slave Mind* (Maryknoll, N.Y.: Orbis Books, 1993); Toinette M. Eugene, "Moral Values and Black Womanists" *Journal of Religious Thought* 44 (Winter-Spring, 1988): 23–34; Walter E. Fluker, *They Looked for a City: A Comparative Analysis of the Ideal of Community in the Thought of Howard Thurman and Martin Luther King, Jr.* (Lanham, Md.: University Press of America, 1989); Robert Michael Franklin, *Liberating Visions: Human Fulfillment and Social Justice in African-American Thought* (Minneapolis: Fortress, 1990); Enoch H. Oglesby, *Ethics and Theology from the Other Side: Sounds of Moral Struggle* (Wash., D.C.: University Press of America, 1990); *idem, Born in the Fire: Case Studies in Christian Ethics and Globalization* (New York: Pilgrim Press, 1990); Peter J. Paris, *The Social Teaching of the Black Churches* (Philadelphia: Fortress, 1985); *idem, Black Religious Leaders: Conflict in Unity* (Louisville, Ky.: Westminster/John Knox Press, 1992); Cheryl J. Sanders, "Slavery and Conversion: An Analysis of Ex-Slave Testimony," (unpublished Th.D. thesis, Harvard Divinity School, 1985); Archie Smith, Jr., *The Relational Self: Ethics and Theory from a Black Church Perspective* (Nashville, Tenn.: Abingdon, 1982); Erwin Smith, *The Ethics of Martin Luther King, Jr.* (Toronto: Edwin Mellen Press, 1981); Emilie M. Townes, *Womanist Justice, Womanist Hope* (Atlanta, Ga.: Scholars Press, 1993); also see Marcia Y. Riggs, "'A Clarion Call to Awake! Arise! Act!' The Response of the Black Women's Club Movement to Institutionalized Moral Evil," and M. Shawn Copeland, "'Wading through Many Sorrows': Toward a Theology of Suffering in Womanist Perspective," in Emilie M. Townes, ed., *A Troubling in My Soul: Womanist Perspectives on Evil and Suffering* (Maryknoll, N.Y.: Orbis Books, 1993); Theodore Walker, Jr., *Empower the People: Social Ethics for the African-American Church* (Maryknoll, N.Y.: Orbis Books, 1991; Gayraud S. Wilmore, *Black Religion and Black Radicalism: An Interpretation of the Religious History of the Afro-American People,* 2nd ed., (Maryknoll, N.Y.: Orbis Books, 1983); Preston N. Williams, "Contextualizing the Faith: The

African-American Tradition and Martin Luther King, Jr., in Ruy Costa, ed., *One Faith, Many Cultures* (Maryknoll, N.Y.: Orbis Books, 1988).

6. This does not preclude certain similarities between African and African American virtues and those of other traditions. Readers will detect some correspondences with Aristotle's ethics and especially the relation of the latter to the major science of his *Politics.* But readers will quickly discern major methodological differences between our ethic and that of Stanley Hauerwas, whose Christian ethics assumes no direct responsibility for political engagement. See especially his books *Character and the Christian Life: A Study in Theological Ethics* (San Antonio, Tx.: Trinity University Press, 1985) and *The Peaceable Kingdom: A Primer in Christian Ethics* (Notre Dame, Ind.: University of Notre Dame Press, 1983). Further, although I have much admiration for Alasdair MacIntyre's major work, *After Virtue: A Study in Moral Theory* (Notre Dame, Ind.: University of Notre Dame Press, 1984), I am convinced that his pessimism about the incommensurability of virtue ethics in a pluralistic society is contradicted by the transformative actions of leaders like President Nelson Mandela and Dr. Martin Luther King, Jr., both of whom have been exemplars of virtue ethics as well as effective negotiators for social change in their respective pluralistic societies.

7. All virtue ethics require a primary moral goal that is reflected in a set of canonical virtues. Virtues are types of moral excellence. All citizens and especially all public officers are expected to possess that set of moral virtues, which are further bolstered and encouraged by official respect and praise. They are acquired by proper training and habitual practice.

The Western tradition of virtue ethics is derived from Plato and Aristotle. Plato's virtues, later called the cardinal virtues by Christian tradition, are four, namely, temperance, courage, prudence, and justice. Plato's virtues were ideal forms. Building on the ideal Platonic virtues, Augustine claimed that God was the source of the virtues and their final end. Augustine viewed the moral life as faith in Jesus Christ and obedience to the dictates of God. By identifying God with the true end of human action, ethics becomes deductive inquiry that begins with the being of God rather than the strivings of humans. From this line of Platonic thinking the Christian virtues were understood as supernatural and transcendent of human strivings.

Aristotle's ethics was quite different; his method was inductive rather than deductive. In his view ethics involved a scientific inquiry into the ethos of particular communities. Thus ethics was culturally specific, dealing with the kind of virtues that the culture nurtured and encouraged. Further, in Aristotle's approach ethics and politics are part of the same inquiry because the final goal of individuals and that of the state are the same. Further, the person of complete virtue was capable of ruling the others because that person was not only morally good but also knew how to effect the good for others.

Thomas Aquinas' method was that of synthesizing the Aristotelian view of the virtues with that of Augustinian tradition by identifying the three Christian virtues of faith, hope, and love as supernatural virtues that complemented the natural cardinal virtues.

Many modern virtue ethicists have much in common with the Platonic and Augustinian tradition. My approach, however, differs from theirs in being more closely related to the Aristotelian tradition, in view of the cultural specificity of African and African American ethics. This does not necessarily imply parochialism. Rather it is my claim that the breadth and depth of community can only be determined politically. The capacity of communities to be open to expansion is also determined by their cultural traditions. Finally, readers will find in this study no attempt to impose any Aristotelian framework of thought onto our subject matter. I have instead discovered a small number of methodological similarities between the ethics of Africans and African Americans and that of Aristotle. Yet the two remain very different in many ways.

8. Again, readers of Aristotle's *Nicomachean Ethics* and *Politics* will easily recognize his shadow in many parts of this text. Since Aristotle's theory of moral virtue has had enormous influence on all subsequent theories of moral virtue, it should not be surprising to encounter his influence here, especially in my discussion of the general features of the theory of moral virtue. Nevertheless, I have tried hard not to impose Aristotle's thought onto that of Africans and African Americans. In order to avoid doing so, I have made every effort to stay within the thought forms of the latter throughout this study. In my judgment, any structural similarities between Aristotle's ethical thought and that of Africans and African Americans should not be viewed as another instance of Western epistemological imperialism since the content of the content of the African and African American ethic is decidedly culturally specific.

9. I am indebted to my colleague William S. Simpson who introduced me to C.B. MacPherson's persuasive argument concerning the philosophical basis of the liberal tradition, which gave rise to the phenomenon he calls possessive individualism. See MacPherson's book, *The Political Theory of Possessive Individualism: Hobbes to Locke* (Oxford, Clarendon Press, 1962).

10. None has studied this phenomenon more carefully than the West Indian psychiatrist Franz Fanon. See his books, *The Wretched of the Earth* (New York: Grove, 1963) and *Black Skin, White Masks* (New York: Grove, 1967).

11. Nelson Mandela, "The ANC and the Government Must Meet to Negotiate an Effective Political Settlement: Letter from Prison to President P.W. Botha, July 1989," in Greg McCartan, ed., *Nelson Mandela: Speeches 1990: "Intensify the Struggle to Abolish Apartheid"* (New York: Pathfinder Press, 1990), 13.

12. Sylvanus Iniobong Udoidem, "The Epistemological Significance of Proverbs: An African Perspective," in *Presence Africaine,* New Bilingual Series 132 (1984): 134-35.

13. Nelson Mandela was an active participant and leader in the youth league of the African National Congress; Martin Luther King, Jr., was similarly an active member and leader of the Baptist Youth Peoples Union. Both constituted important training grounds for the two men.

14. Udoidem, "The Epistemological Significance," 133.

15. Mandela, "The ANC and the Government," 11:12.

16. David J. Garrow's book, *Bearing the Cross: Martin Luther King, Jr., and the Southern Christian Leadership Conference* (New York: Morrow, 1986), provides the most complete documentation in support of this argument. Another convincing argument in support of this type of syncretism is found in Gabriel Setiloane, "How the Traditional World-View Persists in the Christianity of the Sssotho-Tswana," in Edward Fashole-Luke, Richard Gray, Adrian Hastings, and Godwin Tasie, eds., *Christianity in Independent Africa* (Ibàdan, Nigeria: Ibadan University Press, 1978).

17. This position is supported by the work of J.N.K. Mugambi. See his *The African Heritage and Contemporary Christianity* (Kenya: Longman, 1989), 68-69.

18. I am indebted to Lamin O. Sanneh, who has provided a full demonstration of this argument in his important book, *Translating the Message: The Christian Impact on Culture* (Maryknoll, N.Y.: Orbis Books, 1989).

19. One of the most prominent African American scholars presently pursuing this type of scholarly endeavor is Cain Hope Felder. See his *Troubling Biblical Waters: Race, Class, and Family* (Maryknoll, N.Y.: Orbis Books, 1989) and also volume he edited, *Stony the Road We Trod: African American Biblical Interpretation* (Minneapolis, Fortrees Press, 1991).

20. For a summary description of the role of both of these prophets, see A. Adu Boahen, *African Perspectives on Colonialism* (Baltimore, Md.: Johns Hopkins University Press, 1990) 74-75; 88-89.

21. For one of the best studies of this movement, see Leonard E. Barrett, Sr., *The Rastafarians* (Boston: Beacon Press, 1978).

22. An enormous scholarly literature on these churches has been produced during the past quarter century. Two of the earliest studies of this phenomenon are B.G.M. Sundler, *Bantu Prophets in South Africa* (London: Oxford University Press, 1961), and H.W. Turner, *History of an African Independent Church: The Church of the Lord (Aladura),* vols. 1 and 2, (Oxford: Clarendon Press, 1967).

Postscript

1. My understanding of this method is rooted in my studies of Albert Schutz, *Collected Papers,* Vols 1–3 (The Hague: M. Nijhoff, 1962–66); and Gibson Winter, *Elements for a Social Ethic: Scientific and Ethical Perspectives on Social Process* (New York: Macmillan, 1966).

Index